Your
Voice Is Your
Calling Card

"Suzann Rye has designed a course which will absolutely inspire and empower you. In a step-by-step approach, she helps you discover and connect with your true voice—the real you, or the Dream Character, as she calls it. *Your Voice Is Your Calling Card* touches on the spiritual, the emotional, and the physical aspects of performance, allowing you to create an authentic, harmonious, and whole stage persona. Learn from Suzann's twenty years of stage experience, and let her help you find your Dream Character."

Roger N. Quevillon
Minister/Bachelor of Metaphysical Science (B.Msc.), University of Sedona
Coauthor of *Living in Clarity*, from the best-selling series, Wake Up . . . Live
The Life You Love
www.TheTruthBWiseCJourney.com

"I met Suzann Rye during a seminar on the power of the voice. I was amazed by her profound understanding of the mechanics of the vocal instrument, but perhaps even more importantly, I realized what a remarkable advocate of the holistic dimension of the voice she is. This book contains a wealth of practical knowledge. It is both helpful and inspiring. I invite you to let Suzann be your guide in this fascinating journey to discover your own inner voice and build it step by step to make it 'your calling card.'"

Nabil Doss
Speaker, Voice Specialist, and Narrator
President 2008–2009, Canadian Association of Professional Speakers,
Montreal Chapter

"What a fantastic book—simply packed with valuable lessons! There are many self-help books, programs, and systems that exist today. But this is really something fresh, exciting, and entertaining. Not only do I highly recommend this book for speakers and personal development teachers, but also for anyone prepared to take their life and their speaking skills to a new level. Reward yourself by bringing the messages of this book into your life."

Douglas Vermeeren
North America's Achievement Expert, Host of the television show *Success Factor*; Creator of *The Opus*
www.DouglasVermeeren.com

"The holistic approach to voice training offered in this book will benefit speakers looking to break free of formulaic approaches to overcoming speech fright that just don't work. A 'must add' for every speaker's library."

Susan Berkley
Author of *Speak to Influence: How to Unlock the Hidden Power of Your Voice*
www.GreatVoice.com

"In *Your Voice Is Your Calling Card*, Suzann Rye tackles your fears, expands your comfort zone, and emphasizes several breathing/projection exercises to improve your delivery. After she builds your confidence and your stage presence and you think there is nothing more, she digs down deeper to help you discover and remove what is holding you back. Suzann's book will definitely help you put your 'best voice' forward in all situations."

Mark Cravens
Author of *The Ten Commandments of Investing*™
www.TheTenCommandmentsOfInvesting.com

"Suzann Rye has produced a wonderful guidebook for anybody who relies on their voice. In particular, the section on vocal training provides an incredibly comprehensive explanation of the many aspects of voice quality and provides a full set of exercises allowing them to be developed. As a speaker and trainer, I have previously bought several self-help programs in this area, and this one is quite simply the best of them."

Michael Nicholas
Author of *Being the Effective Leader*
www.MichaelNicholas.com

"Take Suzann Rye's advice: learn how to make friends with your voice! This program is full coverage for your mind, body, and spirit. Benefit from all the practical examples, exercises, and wealth of information this unique package offers. Add power, sparkle, and an inner smile to your performance AND your life! Enjoy!"

Margaret Jankowsky
Advanced Communicator Gold, Professional Speaker, Intercultural Communication Trainer and Coach
www.WordsConnectWorlds.com

"Suzann Rye is the most amazing teacher I have ever come across, not just with speaking and vocals, but with the ability to build on people's confidence beyond anything you could possibly imagine. She literally helped me change my whole life around. *Your Voice Is Your Calling Card* is a perfect example of how Suzann works. She somehow manages to make you see the big picture and realize what you need to look at to grow and create great change and progress in your life, both professionally and personally. Suzann's work goes far beyond the boundaries of just teaching people how to use their voice.

"For the first time in my life, I experienced what it meant to really be heard. I discovered potential within myself that far exceeded any expectations I had when I first went for voice training! I am now a very successful vocal coach in my own right. Suzann made me explore endless possibilities, and gave me the confidence and self belief that I needed to grow. My gratitude will always be with her."

Sue Kemp
Voice Coach and Counselor

"*Your Voice Is Your Calling Card* goes beyond any conventional book on speaker training that I've come across so far. It is about communication—how to connect and communicate heart to heart. And it's about building confidence—the kind of confidence that allows you to speak in your own voice, both literally and metaphorically.

"As a child safety expert, I know the ideas presented by Suzann in this book need to be embraced and used by every parent on the planet! I say this because I know that confident kids are less of a target for childhood predators of any kind. Confidence is learned from and nurtured by parents. Mom and Dad need to be the best they can be before they have a prayer of teaching their child to be the best they can be—and this book will help them do just that."

Joyce Jackson
Child Safety Expert, #1 International Best-selling Author, Consultant, and Speaker
www.KeepingKidsSafeToday.com

"Suzann has an uncanny ability to inspire and enthuse people. Watching her draw the true voice out of nervous, timid students who truly feel they have none is an education in itself. As both a musician and university lecturer, I know the importance of truly communicating and connecting with your audience—and how important finding your own voice is to achieving your goals in any sphere of life. What I learnt from Suzann has stayed with me and proved just as useful from behind the lectern as it did onstage. Suzann is truly the teacher's teacher."

A.P. Langman, Ph.D.
University Lecturer, Author, and Journalist

"Suzann Rye really knows her stuff. Years of stage experience and goodwill to share freely shine through every single page of this amazing book. Rye takes you by the hand and leads you safely through the ins and outs of stage performance—adding to your confidence every step of the way. VERY comprehensive—and entertaining too! Brilliant—an absolute must-have for stage performers of all levels!"

Henrik Abel
Stand-Up Comedian, Entertainer, and Actor

"For a long time I suffered from low self-esteem and a fear of facing other people. I wanted to be a singer, but I had no belief in myself. The thought of performing on stage terrified me! Then I started working with Suzann. We were about 40 people in a group. I noticed that something extraordinary was happening. Suzann was gradually leading us to a totally new way of expressing ourselves. Instead of merely focusing on the technical stuff, she was showing us how to face our fears relating to our voices—the very thing that forces our voices to stay silent.

"For me, my worst fear was always people judging me and thinking ill of me. Suzann helped me face that fear. I now enjoy life as a performer. I am calm and comfortable on stage, and I no longer make myself 'small.' I recommend working with Suzann and most certainly reading her book. As with anything else she does, she has poured her heart and soul into it. Reading it is like having Suzann right there in the room with you. And if you ask me, that's a chance you don't want to miss!"

Gunnar Gunnerson
Performer and Healer

"I was always very nervous and insecure when performing in front of others. But working with the Dream Character gave me so much strength and confidence. Suzann helped me understand that you can become exactly what you dream about. And you CAN get everything that you really wish for. At first I didn't believe when she said to me, 'If you see yourself as you imagine yourself on stage—it becomes real.' But she was right.

"Now I feel one with my Dream Character. It no longer represents somebody that I would like to be—it simply IS me. This program is definitely something any performer should work with. Thank you so much, Suzann!"

Maja Hviid
Vocalist

"I was taught never to set my hopes too high and, perhaps as a result of that, I've always had quite a skeptical attitude toward life. I certainly never believed that I would have the courage to be a performer. Then I ran into Suzann. I was a student in one of her voice classes. She encouraged me to create a picture in my mind that represented me as the communicator and artist I wanted to be. At first I was very skeptical! But Suzann persuaded me to try anyway. You have to understand: Suzann is not like most people I've ever met—she's extraordinarily positive. It's simply impossible not be inspired by her.

"She told me that I could be anything I wanted to be, as long as I believed it. She inspired me to believe in the power of mind. It worked. It has helped me ever since to control my nerves before going on stage. I have enormous respect for Suzann and her work. She somehow manages to make you feel special. She makes you realize that you deserve to follow your dreams—that you *can* and *should* follow them."

Mia Louise Andresen
Voice and Performance Student

Your
Voice Is Your
Calling Card

How to Power-Charge Your Voice,
Boost Your Confidence, and Speak
with Joy, Ease, and Conviction

Suzann Rye

New York

Your Voice Is Your Calling Card

How to Power-Charge Your Voice, Boost Your Confidence,
and Speak with Joy, Ease, and Conviction

Copyright ©2009 Suzann Rye. All rights reserved.

ISBN 978-1-60037-567-5

Library of Congress Control Number: 2008943793

MORGAN · JAMES
THE ENTREPRENEURIAL PUBLISHER

Morgan James Publishing, LLC
1225 Franklin Ave., STE 325
Garden City, NY 11530-1693
Toll Free 800-485-4943
www.MorganJamesPublishing.com

In an effort to support local communities and to raise awareness and funds, Morgan James Publishing donates one percent of all book sales for the life of each book to Habitat for Humanity. Get involved today: visit **www.HelpHabitatForHumanity.org**.

This book is dedicated to you, the reader,
and to your continuous life journey and success.
I thank you for allowing me to be part of it.

Contents

Part 3 The Art of Performance

Part 4 Persuasive Speaking through Inner Power

Part 5 Simple Steps to Great Results

Foreword

We all have something special we remember from childhood that had a lasting impression on us and, in many cases, changed the course of our lives. In my case, as far as I can remember, I was always fascinated by the power of the human voice. I was immediately drawn to anyone whose voice stood out . . . whether it was soft and soothing or resonant and compelling.

I also remember, as a child, attending Mass on Sundays. My father was a trial lawyer and an eloquent speaker. He often volunteered to do one of the readings. His resonant voice, crisp diction, and powerful delivery, combined with his true belief in the Scriptures, would literally mesmerize the audience. People would gather around him after Mass to tell him how moved they were by his reading.

It all seemed so natural that only many years later did I begin to grasp the importance of the *connection of the voice with the inner self* to communicate with others on a higher (or deeper) level.

Studies show that 80 percent of the communication process is nonverbal. This means that only 20 percent of the impact can be attributed to the actual spoken word. How then do you explain the huge impact a voice can make on an audience? How do you explain the spellbinding effect of a skilled politician or other engaging speaker? Or, on the opposite end of the spectrum, how can a monotone and hesitant delivery have such sleep-inducing power over listeners? The answer is that without the 20 percent that the verbal dimension represents, the communication process simply breaks down.

Words and sounds, when truly connected to the soul (which manifests itself through nonverbal communications), are the essence of *communicating at a higher level.*

Sometimes your voice can even be the *only* connection you have with an audience. I have spent many years narrating Hollywood movie trailers and audiobooks, as well as performing presentations as the Voice of God, completely isolated in a darkened sound booth and speaking to millions of people who never see me. Body language, eye contact, and stage presence become totally useless. Here the voice is on its own and represents *100 percent* of the communication process. It is the vocal instrument that transports the audience to another

1

dimension through just the right balance of tone, pace, and articulation to carve out the words and light up the screens of their imaginations.

Imagine how powerful a message can be when both verbal and nonverbal communication are working together—when that message is delivered with both vocal strength and heartfelt sincerity!

Speakers who have cultivated both the courage and the skill to speak from their core in this way are in a position to inspire and to create great change. This ability is considered a tremendous gift—and it is! But it is also something that can be learned through the combination of inner and outer work.

These are the principles that are presented in this book. And these are the principles that seem to be the foundation of all of Suzann Rye's work.

I first met Suzann during a seminar on the power of the voice, and I must say she made quite an impression on me. Not only does she have the kind of engaging nature that one is immediately drawn to, but the moment she started to talk, I was won over by the smooth and melodic sound of her voice.

I soon realized that we shared a common passion. I discovered Suzann Rye the voice specialist, the consummate professional who has harnessed every aspect of the vocal instrument as a talented speaker, teacher, singer, and performer. I was amazed by her profound understanding of the mechanics of the vocal instrument, but perhaps even more importantly, I realized what a remarkable advocate of the holistic dimension of the voice she is.

This book contains a wealth of practical knowledge. It is both helpful *and* inspiring. I invite you to let Suzann be your guide in this fascinating journey to discover your own inner voice and build it step by step to make it "your calling card."

Nabil Doss
Speaker, Voice Specialist, and Narrator
President 2008-2009, Canadian Association of Professional Speakers—
Montreal Chapter

Acknowledgments

Many people have contributed to this book, directly or indirectly. I'm forever grateful to all of you.

Some need special mention:

Frank Stäudtner, my smuk Subba — Thank you for supporting me through this venture. I love you.

Mary Jo Tate — Need an editor? Call this woman! Thank you so much for your beautiful spirit, your eminent work, your dedication, your patience, and everything you've taught me. It has been such a pleasure working with you.

My fantastic consultant Tara Majumdar and her brilliant mind — You rock, girl!

Everybody at sonicVision europe GmbH, especially Alex Templin, Kerstin Schiessl, and André Harbig — Thank you for the hard work, long hours, endless dedication, patience, and mega-cool designs.

Sybille Schenker, my incredibly talented illustrator and creator of Clerk — Watch her space!

Natascha C. Bolden, my invaluable network guru — Keep spreading the love!

Nabil Doss — Thank you for your beautiful story about finding *your* voice.

Margaret Jankowsky — My love and gratitude to you always.

Sue Kemp — Leave it!!!

David Hancock, Ben Hancock, and everyone at Morgan James Publishing — Thank you for giving me this wonderful opportunity.

R.J. Jennings — You know why.

Mark Victor Hansen — Thank you for continuing to put on amazing Mega seminars. Great things happen there.

My students past and present — You've all contributed to my own learning process with your talent, curiosity, enthusiasm, love, and fun!

Anyone who is and has been part of my life — Thank you for the exchanges, great and small, that help make us who we are.

My love to all of you. I am grateful, blessed, fortunate, and happy.

My Little Voice,
Suzann

Introduction

Recently I met somebody who turned out to make a major difference in my life. It was one of those "chance" meetings that seem to appear just at the right time and place. You have a sudden flash of insight and inspiration, and you find yourself motivated to move forward in your life, to do things that have been put off for too long! I'm sure you can relate.

My newfound friend played a huge part in my creating this book. She urged me that this information—these insights and easy-to-apply techniques that I'm about to share with you—needed to be made available because "it represented a huge gap that needed to be filled." It didn't take me many seconds to realize that, of course, she was right.

As a coach, a teacher, and a speaker myself, I meet so many people who struggle with lack of confidence, stage fright, and voice problems. This is such a shame. It is also completely unnecessary.

You see, anyone can overcome fear. Anyone can learn to speak in a powerful, healthy, and unique voice. Anyone can learn how to develop a strong stage presence. In short, anyone can learn how to turn an average speech, presentation, or performance into an extraordinary one.

My friend reminded me of that. "You teach people these things every day," she said. "It makes a tremendous difference in their lives. You really need to write that book!"

Why didn't I think of that before? Well, if you're anything like me, you'll understand. Sometimes we don't realize potential until somebody points out to us that it's actually there, staring us in the face! Other times, we recognize that it's there—we just don't know how to unlock it.

Does this sound familiar to you? If so, allow me to offer you a *key*. Allow me to be *your* new friend. Let me assist you in making a difference in your life by developing a skill that will add new dimensions to both your professional and personal life—*communicating confidently, comfortably, and authentically in front of others*.

Let me show you how you can create major breakthroughs simply by using a few tools that are readily available to you 24/7—*your voice, your body, and your mind*. I hope that you will soon feel like I did when I was introduced to *my* new friend. You will ask yourself, "Why didn't I think of this before?" It will feel like pieces of a large puzzle falling into place.

There are two sides of learning how to use your voice properly and how to put on a great performance: one is technical—learning how to empower your physical voice so that you can avoid fatigue and wear. The other has to do with the psychology of speaking—the emotional aspects that affect us all, and consequently our voices, such as self-doubts, timidity, fear, and discomfort.

The emotional aspects play a huge role in creating real and lasting change. Because of this, my approach is clearly holistic in nature—working with the whole person, bringing out the true, unique and powerful voice that resides within each of us. It is in this voice that we find the gift of self-expression and fulfillment in the highest sense and in this voice that we are able to offer true value, service, and contribution to the lives of others.

I have run workshops and seminars for companies, schools, and small groups for over two decades now using the experience that I gained in my other field of work, which was, for many years, music. I was a professional singer. I worked all over the world, performing, recording, writing . . . and teaching.

Your Voice Is Your Calling Card is a result of all these years of working with people to help them find and nurture their own unique voice and to improve their physical voice and their performance skills. It includes a proven coaching system that I have used time and again to help my students and clients reduce stage fright, build confidence, and become outstanding communicators.

I have seen repeatedly what a huge difference just a few changes can make to someone's life—and career.

Are *you* ready to explore new potential, expand your skills, and move yourself to the next level? Is it time for you to tackle the art of authentic, joyful, powerful, and inspiring speaking and presentation?

If so, let's begin this journey together.

Part 1
You and Your Voice

CHAPTER 1

Make Friends with Your Voice

You've heard the expression that "the eyes are the windows to your soul"? Well, for a speaker—indeed anyone needing to present or express something to a crowd of people:

Your voice is your calling card.

Your voice is very personal. It is a direct expression of who you are. It is the most direct medium for communication—the immediate link between you and your audience. It is a powerful tool that you can use to communicate strong, poignant messages in a way that will grab the attention of your peers, colleagues, bosses, etc. You carry it with you at all times, honed and ready—so make the best of it!

If you haven't done so already, *make friends with your voice*. If you do, your voice will pay you back tenfold. It will open new doors for you and change how other people regard you.

You see, the way you present yourself and the way your voice carries your message across are crucial to how you are perceived, no matter what the actual content of your message is. Regardless of your expertise, you need to be convincing to be taken seriously. If you are not convincing, nobody will be interested in your presentation; it's that simple! Just like any other instrument, if you play it well, you can play any tune and people will listen. But play without conviction, and you will find yourself time and again playing even the most popular tune in the world to an empty room.

So what does it take to develop the necessary skills? How can you move from good to great; from bundle of nerves to comfortably, even astoundingly confident; and from your current skill level to inspiring, powerful, compelling, and convincing?

Since you're here, you've already taken the first and most important step: you have begun exploring the possibilities. The rest of the journey may be easier than you think.

However far along the road you may be, know this: there is *no* such thing as a *bad* voice. But there *are* such things as bad posture, shallow breathing, and tension which can influence your voice and prevent it from doing its job! Take a few simple steps and your voice will already be a lot happier. A seemingly little, weak, and breaky voice is rarely a chronic, physical problem, although it may seem that way. Voice problems arise mainly from insecurities leading to restrictions. Sure, they *manifest* physically, and they do seem very real—and *sometimes* they can be. But it is rarely as bad as it seems.

Much of basic voice training consists of teaching people not to be afraid of their own voice, not to be afraid of volume, and to *relax*—to set their voice free again. Your voice is a wonderful palette of colors that you can infuse in your language and use to captivate others. Use it. You have to allow your voice to work its magic.

Have you ever wondered why screaming kids and small babies never get hoarse or lose their voices for just five blissful minutes? Have you been amazed at how a tiny newborn can make *so* much noise for *so* long? Let me tell you why: because they don't hold back. They simply allow the body, including the voice, to do what it's supposed to do, without interfering. They just scream as if it were the most natural thing in the world. Well, guess what? *It is!*

Babies' breathing works perfectly, and they do not strain their voices, for they have not yet learned to hold themselves back. They have not yet learned that it is "bad" or inappropriate to be loud. Once they start learning "how to behave" and certainly once they're halfway through school, that all changes and they start getting the same voice problems as the rest of us because part of social conditioning, unfortunately, is learning how to hold yourself back—how *not to be too self-expressive!*

Illustration 1 - Baby Clerk

This may come as a surprise to you, but because of this conditioning, the older and more self-conscious we become, the more dysfunctional we tend to become as well. Is this a strong claim? Sure it is, but just think about it for a second. How often has somebody asked you or *told* you to be quiet at times of blissful self-expression? Maybe as a kid on the bus or train (perhaps listening to your favorite music wearing headphones) or somewhere else in public. Maybe at times you found yourself happily crooning away in the shower or perhaps while doing the dishes. Do comments like "Do you *mind*?" or "Don't give up your day job" sound familiar?

People often comment without even thinking. Maybe they mean what they say; maybe they don't. It doesn't matter. Comments like that may seem harmless at the time, but often they aren't. They frequently seem to haunt us much more than we are aware of—certainly much more than we'd care to admit. What a great shame that is!

Over the years, many people have come to me claiming that they had a bad, abnormal, or horrible-sounding voice. This is rarely the case, of course. Nevertheless, they seem convinced! Somebody told them, you see.

Do not listen! Refuse to be limited by other people's meaningless comments or mindless critiques. Express yourself freely and creatively, and pay no attention to other people's opinions unless they have some genuine, positive, constructive advice to offer—something that is useful to you. (Well, unless it's 4:00 in the morning and you're keeping your neighbor awake!)

I always encourage my singing students to work freely and unrestricted, to play with their voices and allow them to come out. You should do the same. Explore your voice. Be bold. Be loud if you want. It's all about expression.

Speaking—sharing your message with other people—can be a wonderfully empowering and fulfilling experience. Don't allow it to be a painfully awkward and terrifying struggle. It is a privilege to be able to express yourself, your views, your knowledge, and your wisdom—to have the opportunity to share information with other people. Enjoy that privilege.

Get familiar with your voice, overcome the first barriers, and open the floodgates! Allow yourself to speak with vitality, passion, excitement, and conviction!

It is all yours to have. It is a matter of small adjustments.

You can easily and quickly make friends with your voice. Everyone can.

CHAPTER 2

Your Voice Never Lies

Your voice is a sensitive little fellow, very susceptible to both physical and emotional influences. In order to establish a strong and long-lasting friendship with your voice and to get the best results, you simply *have to* be aware of both the voice technicalities *and* your emotional and psychological well-being.

Don't worry—I'm not going to put you on the couch here. I'm simply going to tell you how your voice, your mind, and your emotions work together and offer you a way of approaching your development. Then it's up to you to decide which information applies to you and which methods, techniques, and exercises are the most useful for your particular needs. This is always very individual. Some techniques you might already know, while some you might find to be strangely out of context. If so, please bear with me and rest assured that everything in this book is included because years of experience have proven it to be valuable, even crucial.

Most of the time the buck stops at one thing: your mind. Know this for certain: your voice *never* lies. It *will* reflect your psychological and emotional state of mind. It *will* support or undermine your verbal messages and reveal more than you might imagine about your personality and your thinking.

Being energetic creatures, we react subconsciously to energetic vibrations and to frequencies. And that is what sound is—a cluster of frequencies. Simply put, the sound and the energy of your voice send out frequencies and vibrations signaling emotional messages beyond your words.

And that's not all you've got working for you—or against you, as the case may be. Your body has a language all its own. Posture, gestures, and movements speak volumes. We will take a closer look at body language in chapter 13, where we talk about performance.

Body language, voice dynamics, and voice technique are all important factors for successful speaking. You can work on all of those and gain a certain degree of mastery from a purely practical perspective.

But what is it on a subconscious level that controls both body language and voice dynamics?

You do. You, the person behind the voice, add life and emotion to the sound and the message.

So using your voice properly really means two things. There is your *physical* voice, which is operated by your body and is clearly audible to everyone, and then there is *your* voice, as in who you are and what you project energetically. What kind of energy is behind your words? Do you speak with a balanced, clear, and strong energy—or do you sometimes communicate mixed messages when you speak? Is the message *behind* the message telling a different story than the one you wish to communicate?

Your voice, your mind, and your emotions are connected, and they always correspond. If you're feeling nervous or insecure—it will show. If you're feeling small, not worthy, not knowledgeable enough, or not successful enough—it will show. If you're impatient, anxious, needy, sad, or angry inside—it will show, and so on. People will be able to hear it in your physical voice— your sound, and they will pick it up energetically.

You are always transmitting something—so you are always communicating, even when you don't mean to and even when you are not aware of it.

If you send out mixed messages, people won't "get" you, or they will get parts of you that you did not intend or did not want for them to get. Your spoken message will not come across in the way that you wish for it to do if your energetic message counter-communicates. Your intended message will be tainted, diluted, or distorted. Often, when this happens, people subconsciously react with resistance or even distrust.

14

What does this all mean?

It means that it is not just *what* you say—it is *how* you say it. But perhaps even more importantly, it is *who* is saying it.

Who is the person behind the voice? What is the message behind the message? What are you transmitting beneath or beyond your words?

We obviously want people to realize how wonderful and amazing we are and how valuable our service is. This is why to be truly great communicators, we simply have to look the full picture. We need to work holistically. If we want to truly inspire and impact people, we cannot afford not to look at our own dissonance if it's there.

Technical skills will support and greatly improve how you come across. They will make your voice more powerful, more dynamic, and more resonant and so on. But nothing beats what I like to call "the resonance of authenticity." This resonance will extend *from* your heart *to* the hearts of others. When you listen to someone who clearly has a purpose and a vision that they are passionately compelled to share, you cannot help but feel their message resonate within you. And you cannot help feeling inspired by them.

When we are able to connect with that deep authentic part of ourselves that speaks our truth, our wisdom, and our passion—we don't need any gadgets or fancy stuff. We simply have all that we need inside of us.

We all have a natural resonance of authenticity—don't be afraid to use it. *Don't ever be afraid of being you.*

Listen to your heart and speak in your own voice. When you do, people will let you in and listen to you with open, receptive ears *and* hearts.

The more authentic and genuine you are, the more you will appeal to people and the more they will appreciate, trust, and respect you—even if they happen to disagree with your message.

During my years as a professional singer, the importance of both energetic transmission and body language was very obvious. What I learned back then has proven to be just as relevant for me as a speaker and teacher as it was for me as an artist. Music is a universal language, but not only in terms of technicalities, notes, and common terms. Music is about communication— heart-to-heart, person-to-person (or person*s*) communication, using emotional expression and signals which can be difficult to define but easy to read.

I have worked with many people. Some of them I could not *converse* with in the usual sense of the word, but we could certainly *communicate*. Although we were from opposite parts of the world, we did share a common language. Our shared passion—our *love* for music—opened our hearts and took us to a place where we managed to find that common language mainly by listening to and watching each other and allowing an exchange to take place. In other words, we managed to communicate clearly and strongly through emotions and by using nonverbal or *nonlinguistic* communication.

Nonverbal or nonlinguistic communication includes gestures, postures, facial expressions, and even the verbal inflections of the words that we use. The term *verbal inflection* refers to the musical qualities of the voice, such as the melody, tone, pitch, rhythm, volume, and pausing—basically the dynamics that we use when we speak. This adds an extra dimension to your performance—good or not. Again, one thing is certain: whatever is lurking underneath the surface is likely to pop out.

Just like energetic transmission, nonlinguistic communication can change the entire meaning of a given message. It supports, emphasizes, or contradicts what is being said. Multiple studies support this; some claim that between 60 and 80 percent of all communication is nonverbal or nonlinguistic! Salespeople, for instance, rely heavily on nonverbal communication.

If you were to make a presentation using no movement at all and speaking in a monotonous, undynamic voice, chances are that your audience wouldn't want to listen to you for very long. You would soon lose their attention. They would get bored, even annoyed. Worse still, they might not take you seriously and conclude that you are uninformed, ill-prepared, or just plain incompetent. Whatever the case, the overall feeling would be that something's not quite right about you. Like I said, if you send out mixed messages, people will subconsciously react with suspicion and resistance.

So there you are, with all your years of training and experience, your specialist knowledge, and the best of intentions . . . and nobody pays any attention to you. Being ignored, distrusted, and disrespected feels awful. When it happens in public, it's even worse. It's toe-cringing and dreadful— possibly the one time in your life where you wish the floor would open up and swallow you whole and bury you right there and then under the boards!

Perhaps you recognize this scenario. If you do, join the club! Trust me— you are not alone. For many people, just being able to live through this kind of ordeal without half fainting is a big step.

Sadly, many people are unaware that communication skills can be improved easily. As a result, they suffer years of stage fright and debilitating nervousness instead of simply taking the small steps necessary to conquer their fears. This is a great shame.

I'm certain you have something worthwhile to share. We all do. We all have some specialist knowledge to share, important messages to convey, or significant statements to make every once in a while. When we allow ourselves to do just that, we feel wonderful and excited and proud—no matter how scary the circumstances.

Nothing beats the high of being able to clearly speak your mind and your heart. Nothing beats the high of a good performance!

We are all performers. We're all trying to close the sale.

Whether we are professional stage performers and make our living expressing ourselves in public or we are business professionals confined to the company boardroom, we all have to get up there in front of bosses, colleagues, employees, etc., and perform.

When you teach, you perform. When you pitch a project, you perform. When you attend a job interview, you perform. When you go on a first date, you perform. Basically, any time you are speaking, entertaining, or presenting something, you are putting on a performance. You are presenting information, an opinion, an idea, a vision, or a creation to somebody else in order to produce a result, provoke a reaction, or even create an illusion, like an infomercial or a show of some sort. In any case, you have an agenda and you are looking for a particular response.

This is *always* the case. Whether you are looking to feed an emotional need (respect, recognition, love, etc.) or an outside results-oriented need (clinching a deal, pitching an idea or a project, etc.), you have a specific goal in mind. Perhaps you want to create change or to educate, motivate, help or inspire people in some way. Perhaps you want them to take some sort of action. Whatever it is, the agenda is there. You have something to "sell." And more often than not, the best performer comes out on top.

If you're smart, you accept the fact that this is how it works, you accept that this is part of everyday life, and you establish a way to integrate that fact into your own situation. You begin to nurture your performer gene. Think about how you would like to see yourself in the ultimate role—you as the very best that you can be.

Please don't get me wrong here. We've already established the importance of being authentic. So I'm not talking about just putting on a good show and *pretending* to be something that you're not. I'm certainly not talking about some psycho-technique to help you manipulate people, which, besides being unethical, I don't believe works in the long run anyway. I'm not saying that you should develop some fake personality to help you communicate better. I am, however, offering you a way to be practical and smart about improving your communication skills.

I'm proposing that you develop what's known as a *Stage Persona*. A Stage Persona is often seen as an alter ego. In this case, I want you to look at it as your very own performance identity that is *part of you,* as opposed to outside of you. I'll explain more about how to do this in chapter 14.

We are all performers because we all communicate. We all express ourselves to the world. Good performers spend time and energy establishing rapport. They interact with the audience, pick up signals, and respond to them. They make the audience feel part of what they do. Then when they have their attention, they strike, they deliver their message on a silver tray and they bring home the prize—the desired outcome of their presentation.

Your Stage Persona will be the part of you that does exactly that—and does it exceptionally well.

Remember I said that your voice never lies? When you are able to connect with that part of you that feels totally comfortable and confident in front of people, you won't have to worry about your voice telling tales because your voice will be your greatest ally. Your voice will help you put your message across so loudly and clearly that no one will doubt its legitimacy—and your authority.

EXERCISE: THE QUALITY CHECK

Think about speakers/presenters that you like.

- What are their qualities?
- What are your best qualities?
- How can you expand on those and make them work even better for you?

What do you hear in your own voice *physically?* Try to be completely objective here—simply listen to the sound.

- How do your perceive the actual sound of your voice?
- Is it deep or high-pitched, clear or raspy, maybe husky or even hoarse?
- Is it smooth and soft or sharp and shrill?
- Is it warm or cold?
- Do you have lots of resonance, or do you have a very flat sound quality?

What do you hear in your own voice *emotionally/energetically?*

- What could you be communicating energetically that is not resonating or not congruent with the message that you want to communicate?
- What are you transmitting as you speak?

A really great way to work on not just your physical sound but also your energetic transmission is to record yourself. Most people do not like this very much, but it really is great training. So record yourself and track your progress—you'll be surprised.

TO CREATE REAL IMPACT

Practice being totally present whenever you speak. This will project confidence and balance.

Practice total resonance between you and your message: say what you mean—mean what you say.

Look at the people in the crowd as your friends and speak to them accordingly—and they will regard you as their friend as well.

Show genuine interest in your listeners—and your listeners will show genuine interest in you.

Fuel your message with passion and real emotion—and you will move and inspire people beyond your words.

Celebrate what you are instead of regretting what you're not.

CHAPTER 3

The Number ONE Reason Why Your Voice Sometimes Fails and Your Performance Falls Short

I've been repeatedly alluding to one particular issue without really sinking my teeth into it. See, I was afraid that I would scare you. However, since it's a major factor throughout this entire book, I might as well dive straight into it. After all, it is a big and inescapable issue.

A speaker's worst enemy is *fear*.

Whether we are aware of it or not, we are all influenced by fears and restrictions imposed upon us by ourselves or other people or, more likely, a bit of both. And there you have the *number one* reason why your voice sometimes fails and your performance falls short.

The good news is that we've all been there. We've all been scared—and survived. When your world is collapsing around you and panic strikes, remind yourself that you are not alone. Others have gone before you and learned that even the most embarrassing moment ever eventually becomes just another brick in the wall, making it even stronger.

We humans can be afraid of all sorts of things. Apart from the obvious like two-headed monsters and little green men, we seem to have an ingrained tendency to invent lots of "dangers" and obstacles to prevent us from moving forward, pursuing our dreams, and generally doing what we want to do. Fear becomes a tool to protect ourselves from the disappointment we might experience if things shouldn't turn out the way we would like them to. In so-called obstacles, based in fear, we find excuses not to follow our hearts, live life fully, and journey courageously toward our goals. "Better safe than sorry," we think.

This is all very convenient—but not very productive and certainly not very fulfilling. If we would instead face our fears head-on, we would feel a lot happier and achieve much more.

Speaking in public is considered one of the scariest activities around. In fact, it's often said that more people are afraid of public speaking than of death! Why? I can certainly think of many more dangerous activities. It makes no sense . . . or maybe it does. We humans have an intrinsic fear of being exposed. The thought of being ridiculed or publicly shamed sends shudders down anyone's spine. As a speaker, you willingly expose yourself and ultimately run the risk of having your worst nightmares come true. Well, I guess you should congratulate yourself on your courage. You've already entered into territory that only a few people even dare to dream of. Good for you!

What is really behind our fear of being exposed? What can possibly be so wrong with us that it threatens to undermine our worth as human beings or experts in our respective fields when put under scrutiny?

Fear is hardly ever the result of logical thinking, and it is always rooted in some past experience or belief, resulting from conditioning, as we've already discussed. We all have different emotional baggage that manifests later on in life—often when and where we least expect it and often in disguise. We can be deeply affected by fear even when we don't see a direct connection to the real fear or the real issue behind it at the time.

So what kinds of fears are we talking about here?

Let's name just a few: fear of challenge; fear of change; fear of other people's opinions; fear of being thought less of; fear of being thought badly of; fear of not being loved, liked, appreciated, accepted, or respected; fear of ridicule; fear of missing out; fear of not being asked back again after a gig; fear of being asked back and dreading it; fear of not living up to your own expectations or other people's expectations; fear of not earning enough money; fear of poverty; fear of too much, too little, too in between; fear of fear itself.

Simple fear of life has prevented many great things from coming from many great people.

Public speaking in itself is obviously neither risky nor dangerous. Nobody *really* fears the speaking itself—they fear the possible outcome, the *repercussions that may occur* as a result of it.

OK, so what are the worst possible repercussions?

I guess we can boil it down to one word: *failure*. We fear not being good enough, not "making it."

What does failure actually mean?

Is it possible that failure is an illusive idea, merely a matter of perception, and that our experience of it is exactly that: a matter of perception?

I believe that part of our life purpose is to learn certain things. These things may very well disguise themselves in the shape of obstacles and failures. One of life's big challenges is learning to decode them, to turn poison into medicine, and to learn to perceive obstacles, problems, and so-called failures as exciting challenges and *opportunities for growth and evolvement* instead.

If we were simply able to say "I made an experience" instead of "I made a mistake" every time we experienced "failure" in our lives, wouldn't we then automatically look at ourselves and our "failures" in a completely different light?

Mistakes are good for us. They point out things that we need to look at. They are there to remind us not to fall asleep behind the wheel. They lead us further along the road to becoming even better at what we do so that we can go on to teach others, which is a great gift. Mistakes are there to *inspire* us and *encourage* us to keep moving and keep feeding our Soul and our mind—*to keep living!*

Nobody is perfect—whatever that means. Luckily, we all make mistakes every now and again, no matter how smart, how well trained, and how experienced we are. When we do, we feel terrible and stupid and think that we are all alone in making mistakes, so we have a tendency to put ourselves down. Well, this whole speaking business can be tough enough as it is. The last thing you want to do is start knocking yourself on the head.

Recognize the experience for what it is—a loud wake-up call! Consider what happened *and why*. Constructively evaluate yourself. Be disciplined and take responsibility; learn and then *move forward*. Remind yourself that learning and evolving is exciting. The day we don't do that anymore is going to be a sad and, most of all, very boring day. So be grateful that in this case you had a chance to learn something. Was it uncomfortable at the time? Sure. So cringe, if you must, then have a laugh and move on. *Don't be too hard on yourself.*

Look at it this way: each time you make a mistake, it is like making a deposit into your bank account. Your knowledge expands and grows, until one day you have so much in your account that you can afford to share freely with others. The more you give out, the more you will get back. So your wealth is automatically growing and expanding even more. And it all started with a few mistakes. Cool, right?

EXERCISE: LEARNING FROM MISTAKES

- Think of times in your life when a mistake or a major challenge turned out to be a blessing in disguise.
- What did you learn from these situations?
- How did they turn out to your advantage? How did you benefit in the end?

AWARENESS—FINDING THE PATH TO JOY AND EASE

By becoming more aware of ourselves and our fears—and not least where they are coming from and what caused them in the first place—we can avoid many unnecessary setbacks.

For example, speakers often get throat problems—especially just before an important event. Why? Simple: because of fear.

Fear creates physical reactions—in this case, a "sore" throat, which then gives the person a viable excuse to fail. In case they don't live up to their own expectations *and* the supposed expectations of others, they can say, "Oh, you know, I didn't feel too good; my throat was really hurting. I just wanted it over and done with, so I left out the best part" and so on.

Fear creates blockages in our system and prevents us from functioning properly. Nerves, suppressed emotion, and lack of honest expression are major causes of blockages, not least in the throat. (Ever tried suppressing something close to your heart that really should come out into the open and felt how it got stuck like a lump in your throat?)

Obviously, this is extremely inconvenient for a speaker. Not only do we sometimes have to deal with a raging storm on the inside, but if ignored for too long, what started as a nervous reaction on an emotional level will inevitably manifest itself in physical form. The usual pounding heart, trembling, and sweaty hands are only minor immediate reactions. The longer we leave the blockages unattended, the more stuck they get; they will eventually start spilling into other areas as well. This is probably why so many people get ill. Years of suppressing all sorts of things (including fear, instead of dealing with it once and for all) take their toll on the system. If our fears and issues are not dealt with, sooner or later they will resurface masked as something else. We *must* learn to recognize our fears and confront them so that we can prevent blockage from happening.

Emotional awareness helps us keep our channels unblocked so that positive, *constructive* energy can flow freely within our own little ecosystem. Clearing existing blockages will strengthen the functioning and the reliability of our entire system, including the voice.

If we can recognize the blockages and limitations caused by fear and understand what caused them in the first place, we can completely free ourselves from the old patterns and allow ourselves more joy, more freedom, and more creativity.

Joy is the key word here. We humans thrive on joy. Being good at what you do is a lot easier if you *enjoy* what you do. But if you are caught up in worrying about being "good enough" and living up to everybody else's expectations, your joy takes a back seat. All you will feel is constant pressure, and all you will see is your own perceived inadequacies compared to the advantages of the "competition."

Finding the path to true personal happiness and fulfillment has been the ultimate quest for humans throughout our entire existence. This is what being successful is really all about. Fame, fortune, admiration, and the recognition of your peers might bring you fleeting pleasure, but being true to yourself and fulfilling your life purpose will bring you lasting joy. When you are really following the road that you are supposed to—the one leading you toward your life purpose and your life work—things naturally tend to progress a lot more easily than if you are trying to achieve something that is not truly part of who you are.

Wherever you believe yourself to come from—whatever you believe to be the origin of the Soul—ultimately we are all left here with a set of tools. These tools are our passions, dreams, and talents guiding us toward our life's purpose and urging us to fulfill that purpose. We can choose to build something fantastic with those tools, or we can choose not to. We can choose to believe that someone or something inside or outside of ourselves will help us with the building or not. It really doesn't matter. The bottom line is that essentially *nothing happens if we just sit back and wait.* We must lay at least some stones ourselves.

If we assume that *we* are in control at *all* times—*we* create whatever is around us—*we completely and without exceptions create our own reality,* wouldn't it make sense, *with that amount of creative freedom,* to create something *truly, wonderfully glorious?*

Fear is what keeps most people from doing whatever it is that they want. It is what keeps people from pursuing their dreams. Fear makes people feel powerless and inadequate. It creates feelings of jealousy and resentment and tricks us into feeling less fortunate or ill treated. Fear is destructive and leads to no good at all.

Don't allow fear to stand in *your* way. Choose freedom. Choose courage.

Many great men and women have achieved great things because they chose courage instead of fear. When you hear or read about people like that, you might feel a sense of excitement and inspiration. That is your Soul reminding you that achieving great things is possible. Hold on to that feeling. Remain inspired and empowered by these wonderful tales from the realm of unlimited possibilities. Allow yourself to dream and think big, dare something worthy, make loads of mistakes along the way—and fill up your knowledge box to the brink!

Overcoming nerves and stage fright is something every speaker has to deal with. It is one of the most important factors in becoming a powerful and charismatic stage professional who can enjoy the lamplight as opposed to merely enduring it.

Enjoy what you do. *It's a privilege.*

EXERCISE: FIRST STEPS TO LETTING GO OF FEAR

Ask yourself these questions and try to come up with as honest answers as you possibly can:

- If you are feeling overly nervous and fearful, from where and what do you think those feelings stem?
- Are they (the feelings and ultimately the fear) serving you in positive and constructive ways?
- If so, how?
- Do you need them?
- Could you let them go?
- *Would* you let them go?
- What would happen if you did?

CHAPTER 4

Expand Your Comfort Zone

It's five minutes to curtain call, you've put on the funny hat and are about to face the music, and dread sets in! "How did I get to be in this situation—*what was I thinking?!*"

Legs shaking, palms sweaty, face purple, heart pounding double speed—sheer terror.

Enter public (speaker) enemy number one, the fear factor, again.

Yes, we've all tried it. We have all been terrified and on the verge of blacking out from pure dread just before walking on stage. Really. Anyone who says they haven't is either the most self-assured person in the entire Universe—or there's something seriously wrong with them! Or they might just be lying to you.

As performers—and I will use that term broadly from now on to include speakers, presenters, entertainers, etc.—we all deal with the same issues and the same emotions, and we all tend to make the same mistakes.

So what do we do?

Well, clearly, *we first make sure that we are well prepared and know our stuff.*

If we don't, we cannot possibly be 100 percent comfortable. We'll be at much greater risk of having those horrible underlying feelings of inadequacy and fear—the fear of failure, of being exposed or found out.

"I'm a fake. If only they knew the real me, how I really feel inside right now, they probably wouldn't like me, respect me, or admire me so much."

Maybe you recognize these feelings. I know I do, and I've worked with so many other people who did too—even people who were highly competent and already very successful in their respective fields.

Being well prepared and knowledgeable is not always enough. Being competent does not necessarily equal *feeling* competent and being able to put your point across in the most effective way. We have established that nerves can cripple anyone and fill them with horrible feelings of inadequacy and incapability. We've also established that these kinds of feelings are not rational. They are not based on facts. They are based on fears that we might not even be aware that we have. And these fears prevent us from doing what we want to do, being who we want to be, and *becoming* who we want to become. They prevent us from showing our true colors in their entire splendor, and they prevent us from evolving and moving forward. They make us feel insecure and inadequate even if we *do* know our stuff inside out and we *are* well prepared!

But *why?*

Because we tend to believe that we are being judged all the time. And maybe we are. But we will always be our own worst critics—it's simply human nature.

The curious thing is that other people spend a lot less time thinking about us and forming opinions than we imagine. They are far too busy thinking about themselves and their own performance—and worrying about what other people might think of *them*, just as most people find it hard to listen, mainly because they are more concerned with what their own next response should be.

If you feel uncomfortable, daunted even, by the very thought of public speaking—if you're somehow unable to express yourself in the way that you would like, if what comes out of your mouth and what you overtly portray don't quite match the picture you had in mind—you need to look at what may be holding you back and find a way to deal with it.

You need to *expand your comfort zone.*

If you are crippled by nerves in such a bad way that you cannot function, you *have to* do something about it. You must take an honest look at how you think and change any minuses to plusses.

Here are some suggestions of things to look at for now:

EXERCISE: ADDING UP VALUE

- Do you ever feel that anything is holding you back, preventing you from being the best that you can be? If so, what?
- Are you keeping yourself from exploring the brilliance and the insight that you truly have to offer? If so, *why*?!
- Are you worried about how you are perceived by others? If so, why?
- Does worrying about others sometimes prevent you from being who you really are and offering what you are truly capable of offering?
- Do you see yourself as sharing your knowledge, wisdom, information, etc., bringing value to people and serving them—or do you feel that you are imposing it on people, stealing their time, and annoying them?
- What do you see as the real value in what you are offering?
- Do you need to offer more, or do you already offer plenty?
- Do you perhaps need to reevaluate your own perception of what you are offering?
- Do you feel adequate? Do you feel that you know your stuff well enough—or not?
- Do you enjoy what you do for a living? If not, why not?
- What would it take for you to enjoy it?
- Change your perception from minus to plus and see what it does for your comfort zone!

THE PROCESS

As I said earlier, you may not understand why you feel the way you do, but it is crucial for you to consider what might be causing these feelings in order for you to deal with them better. We all have our different backgrounds and reasons for being who we are. We are all influenced by things deeply rooted in our past or within our character. When we find ourselves in uncharted waters that challenge who we are, how we see ourselves, *and how we wish to be seen by the outside world,* we react to that—sometimes in ways we wish we hadn't.

Worrying about other people's opinion or perception of us is an absolute killer for a performer. It is a major underlying cause of stage fright and nervousness, which undermine our performance levels and take the joy out of what we do.

This is why we have to approach this process from both angles—the practical and the psychological. One complements the other. Getting rid of fears and increasing confidence makes it a lot easier for you to relax on stage and allow your voice and your body to work properly. At the same time, learning all the practical and technical stuff—knowing that you can rely on your voice and your body to support and give power to your message and knowing that you can trust in your own abilities—adds to your confidence. It's a win-win situation.

Are you allowing fears and limiting beliefs to get in the way of progress, success, and ultimately joy in what you do? If so, now you know that this is not unusual and you're not alone. You also know that you do not have to continue to feel that way. By the end of this program, you will have the tools to change.

I rest my case—for now. This either resonates with you or it doesn't. If it doesn't, stick around anyway. There's loads of practical and technical stuff coming up next.

Our overall plan looks like this:

- We will work on voice technique—the physical and technical aspects, like body posture, breath control, voice projection, etc., and we will look at other tools that you can use to enhance your vocal performance.
- Next we'll explore the art of performance—tips on relating to the audience, body language, do's and don'ts, etc.
- Then we will look at you, the person. What would you like to achieve? Where and how do you see yourself? What kind of speaker or performer are you? What kind of performer would you like to be? How can you get there? How can you deal with fear and nerves?

- We will finally collect all the information we've learned so far and put it together in a way that suits your needs. We will then find the best way for you to practice and take action.

To make it easy for you, the rest of the book is divided into four sections—one for each theme and in the same order as above. It is important to remember, though, that they should all work together.

For the best result, approach this more like a virtual coaching program than a book that you just simply read and then put away. Do the exercises as described. I will help you bring it all together at the end, where we will construct your personal training program and your Vision Board that you can continue to develop in the future.

Besides using this book and some of the exercises here, consider joining your local Toastmasters club. You don't need to have any experience before you join, and it is a fantastic and very comfortable forum in which to develop your speaking skills even more. You'll receive advice on how to construct powerful, engaging speeches and how to speak convincingly in front of others. You'll get encouraging, constructive feedback and learn to evaluate others as well. It's all done in a friendly, relaxed, but professional atmosphere, and membership is very reasonably priced.

There are Toastmasters clubs worldwide. They are a nonprofit organization that has helped develop public speaking and leadership skills through practice and feedback in local clubs since 1924. You can find a local club by visiting www.toastmasters.org/find/.

If you prefer to work one on one, consider consulting with a communications coach. You can find one by simply typing "communication coaching" or "communication coaches" plus your city and state into Google, and you will get plenty of results.

If you are interested in online classes, you could visit the Learning Annex at www.LearningAnnex.com. They offer many different types of classes. Last time I checked, I didn't find anything under "communication" per se, but in the Business/Career section, I found many great options for improving communication skills. The Learning Annex also does local classes in some cities like Los Angeles, New York, Minneapolis, San Francisco, San Diego, and Toronto.

Part 2
Voice Training, Facts, and Practical Strategies for Speakers and Other Voice Professionals

CHAPTER 5

Voice Technique: How Does It Work? What Are the Benefits?

Voice technique and *vocal technique* are terms used to describe the workings or mechanics of the human voice. When a voice is allowed to function properly and is supported in the right way, it stays healthy and strong. However, if a voice is suppressed and squeezed and not supported as it should be, it may get damaged. Unfortunately, many people speak incorrectly and as a result have very limited use of their voice. Because they are not aware of their voice's true natural potential, they settle for what they have and decide that great voices belong to the select few. They remain unaware that they could easily enjoy a much broader range of vocal expression.

As speakers, we cannot afford to remain oblivious to this great tool that we have at our hands. We cannot afford to damage it either. Correct use of the voice is crucial.

There are three main reasons why people speak incorrectly. One is fear of letting go, leading to suppression. Another is laziness. Simply out of habit, we do not breathe and we do not support and project the voice properly, so we utilize only part of the power available to us. Finally, conditions such as stress or anxiety also affect our breathing and therefore our voice. We tend to take shallow rather than full breaths, producing even more stress, until shallow breathing eventually becomes the norm. We simply forget what a full breath feels like, so we forget what proper voice functioning feels like too.

Many people speak incorrectly their whole lives and never notice because their voice is not a focal point and they don't rely on it to do their work. But when you do rely on your voice for your work on a daily basis, there is no getting around learning how to use it properly. Straining your voice will impair your performance levels and cause discomfort. In the worst case, unhealthy speaking habits can impair the voice permanently. Severe or persistent dysfunctions can cause physical damage. Getting rid of physical damage to the vocal cords can be a grueling procedure. Some cases even require surgery. When a voice gets this badly damaged, full recovery is needed before training can commence. This means *no* speaking *at all* for up to two weeks! Then very gradual rehabilitation and eventually work can begin to correct the fault that led to the damage in the first place. Finally, additional training can follow.

Don't abuse your voice—it's not worth it.

Perhaps you're still wondering, "Is voice training really necessary? I mean, how hard can it be? Breathing and speaking are natural, instinctive functions, right?" Absolutely, but you'd be surprised how many people seem somehow to have forgotten their instincts. Remember the example with the noisy children in chapter 1? I can honestly say that voice training mostly consists of correcting or deconditioning and reconditioning incorrect speaking habits.

Maybe your voice works fine and you've never had problems. If so, that's great—congratulations! Maybe you still want to add some more power and sparkle, though. In any case, there is no doubt that taking the time to learn basic voice technique will benefit you and actually save you time and effort in the end. Good technique and a healthy voice make speaking much more enjoyable. So why not get the training? It's simple to learn, and it doesn't take long.

I will tell you everything you need to know about the voice—how it works and how to keep it happy, healthy, and strong. We will work with verbal inflections and voice dynamics. In chapter 12, "The Voice Doctor," you will learn about the kinds of problems you could run into and how to deal with them, such as what to do in the unlikely event that you lose your voice.

Then I will continue where I left off explaining about the psychology of speaking—the emotional aspects that affect the voice, such as timidity, fear, and discomfort. We will identify the common problems that typically occur, understand the thought processes behind them, and learn how to change them gradually. In other words, you will learn how to create a safe and comfortable space—a state of mind where you are calm and confident. It's time for you to enjoy the attention and the recognition that you deserve.

CHAPTER 6

The Basics

Before we get into all the theoretical, technical, rule stuff, remember this—it is possibly the most important piece of advice that I'm ever going to give you:

Don't be afraid of being you.

Keep it real. To express emotion, follow your emotion! *Speak in your own voice.* I mean that both literally and metaphorically.

That said, it's time to look at how you can easily and quickly improve your voice performance skills.

First, golden rule number one—and there are *no* exceptions to this rule:

Using your voice is supposed to be comfortable and easy.

If it's not, you're doing something wrong and you need to correct it. If you don't, you *will* eventually have problems. It's as simple as that. So you need to become familiar with your own natural sound and master the Basics.

The Basics are the cornerstones of voice technique. We will go through each of them separately and in detail. In chapter 11, "Basic Voice Exercises," you will find a huge choice of relevant exercises. These will help you learn, understand, and build voice power and control.

OVERVIEW

Basic 1

You've already been introduced to the most important basic, which is *to relax, not to strain, and not to hold back, which will squash the voice.*

Straining comes mainly from not thinking right. Once you learn where to direct your attention—your energy and your sound—and you keep doing it, your body will begin to recognize it and then remember it from one time to the next. This is called conditioning. Some refer to it as muscular memory. What it means is that after a while you don't need to think about your technique any more; your body (including your voice) will simply know exactly what to do and when to do it. It is like learning most things, such as driving a car. At first you have to concentrate on every detail, but eventually you just automatically take the correct actions—you no longer have to think about them every single time.

Basic 2

Next up is your *breathing.*

Your voice needs air to function. And it needs the right amount of air. The air carries the sound as you exhale in a controlled manner.

Basic 3

Controlled exhalation is called *the support.*

Your body supports your voice. It lifts or carries it up, forward, and out. Without the support of the body, the voice cannot work properly. Controlled breathing out means that you are holding the air off as though working against resistance. Together breathing and support are referred to as *breath control.* I divide breathing and support into two basic functions because I've found that it makes the whole process easier to comprehend. You see, for many people, this whole idea of controlling their breath is unfamiliar. It also makes sense because although the two go hand in hand and are part of the same overall function, they are also exact opposites.

Basic 4

How you *initiate or attack* your tone has an important effect on how it is going to continue its journey. If you start right, you're more likely to continue right and have good sound and strong tone. As a speaker, initiation is not something you'd normally focus on much. However, as a singer you'd normally work with your initiation to perfect your tone.

I'm including it here so that you can get a more comprehensive understanding of how voice technique works.

Basic 5

After initiating the tone, you need to *project* it right.

Projection is how you focus and project the sound of your voice. Your projection generally needs to be condensed, or tight, as I always call it, not spread out as if you were talking through a sieve (unfocused, with excess air fizzzzzzling out). An unfocused voice has an airy, thin sound and is very annoying to listen to—if you can hear it properly at all. It is also unhealthy to speak like this.

You *can* speak with a breathy, husky sound, but it needs to be controlled and on purpose, not by accident.

Generally you want to condense your sound, to concentrate it as if you were talking through a funnel or a reversed megaphone. Focus your sound and project it forward using inner imagery; basically you *think* your sound forward. This will give you a strong, convincing, and pleasing sound.

I always tell my clients, "You wouldn't want to wear a skimpy suit. Why would you want a skimpy voice?"

Speak with conviction; speak with authority; speak with passion! Remember: *Your voice is your calling card.*

We will now go through each Basic in detail. Enjoy.

BASIC 1: HANG LOOSE—RELAX AND ALLOW YOUR VOICE TO WORK FREELY

Golden rule number one: relax—hang loose—*never, ever* strain!

If you feel yourself tightening up, especially in and around the larynx (voice box, encasing the vocal cords) or in the soft spot underneath your chin (behind your jaw), *stop!* Straining inhibits your voice and affects your performance in a bad way. Long term, it can cause voice damage.

The most common mistake that people make is stretching their neck upward and forward, protruding the jaw. Do not do that—ever! Do not tighten your jaw. It immediately cuts off the airflow, like bending a garden hose and stopping the water. This will create constriction. A good trick is to look at yourself in the mirror to make sure that you never protrude your jaw.

Also, make sure not to tighten your lips. And don't pull your tongue back in your throat, which will make you sound like Kermit the Frog (from *The Muppet Show*) and make you choke on your own sound.

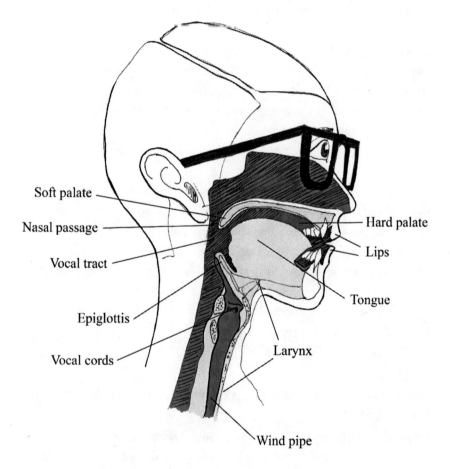

Soft palate

Nasal passage

Vocal tract

Epiglottis

Vocal cords

Hard palate

Lips

Tongue

Larynx

Wind pipe

Illustration 2 - The Vocal Instrument

Be careful not to lift your shoulders or chest. Keep your head and upper body in a normal, relaxed but well-postured position (don't slouch).

Pay attention to what you *think* if you find yourself doing any of the above no-no's. You will probably find that you are feeling insecure in some way at that moment and, subconsciously, you are starting to hold back while at the same time trying to push your sound and your message forward. This simply won't work. You cannot push forward and pull back at the same time without causing a conflict. You will clash in the middle! The result is blockage and strain.

I cannot stress this enough: if you restrict yourself and hold your sound back, you work against the natural voice function, which is to allow sound to flow freely and openly without being squashed in the throat.

A tense throat blocks air from traveling up onto the pathway (see Basic 5, "Projecting Your Voice").

The more tension in the throat (and anywhere else, such as jaw, tongue, and shoulders), the more access to the pathway is cut off. This is uncomfortable and damaging, and it impairs the quality of your voice and your performance. Your voice will sound thin and strained.

So don't hold back; don't restrict yourself. Choose power and freedom of expression and avoid constrictions!

Remember what I told you earlier: the vast majority of basic vocal problems arise from tension leading to constrictions. Other problems can be traced back to lack of breath control (correct breathing and support), unfocused projection, and incorrect use of the Modes (different settings or gears used for different sounds and volumes, which we'll discuss in chapter 7).

Whatever the problem is, it usually starts with some sort of tension. Working *against* the voice as opposed to working *with* the voice is what causes *all* problems.

What do constrictions feel like? A constriction will normally annoy you straight away. Mostly you will feel an urge to clear your throat again and again because the nuisance forces your mucous membranes to produce more mucus. After a while your throat will start to hurt, and you might gradually find yourself trying to avoid speaking because it feels more and more strenuous. You will probably be able to hear the constriction as well. There will be a tiny scratchy noise as if you are breathing with something stuck in your throat, and the overall sound will be strained.

Remember—as I mentioned earlier, tensions are not *always* directly linked to restrictions imposed *in the present*. They may come from other areas of our lives that we may be unaware of. If, for instance, you "carry a lot of weight on your shoulders," it is very likely to create tension in your back and shoulders. This tension would not be directly voice-related but would, however, affect your voice. Muscular tension can develop over time, and it can be difficult to determine what initially caused it. Once tension is muscular, meaning it sits in the muscles as opposed to being created purely in the mind at that very moment, it takes time for the muscles to regain a normal relaxed state before real progress can be made. So you see, hanging loose and allowing yourself to relax both physically and mentally is very important! A healthy, relaxed position should feel completely comfortable.

I use five different images to describe the sensation of the basic open, relaxed position: the posh opera singer, the inner smile, the yawn, drawing a deep breath through your nose but with your mouth open, and the hot potato.

All these images (explained below) should help you find the basic setting and should leave you feeling open and relaxed. Working in this position has the advantage of being an easy vantage point for learning. It is almost impossible to get it wrong, it is very easy to feel if something *does* go wrong, and it has an immediate soothing and relaxing effect on the voice. Always start here when you practice voice exercises.

As you progress, you will learn about other settings as well. But for now we will concentrate on the basic setting. From there we will gradually add more sounds and settings. You will learn how you can play around with different settings to change your sound. The whole idea of this book is to give you choices and to teach you how you can use your voice in many ways to become a more dynamic, exciting, and compelling speaker. When you want to add extra volume, for instance, your settings will have to change slightly. The reason why many people get problems when they try to up the volume is that they do not change their voice settings accordingly. More about that later—for now, let's concentrate on the basic stuff. OK, so let's get into it then, shall we?

Imagine that you are a veeeery posh and important *opera singer*. In fact, you are so full of yourself that you maintain a constant *inner smile* of pure self-contentment! Note that this is an *inner* smile only; it should be imagined and felt but not seen. This image should help you to raise the soft palate (roof of your mouth), giving a full and rounded sensation in your mouth and throat, just like at the beginning of a *yawn* or *when drawing a deep breath of air through your nose* only, but with your mouth open.

Notice how the inside of your mouth and your throat feel when you do any of those. It's a very open, big, and roomy feeling, right?

Remain in this position while you breathe in. Notice how much space you have inside and how relaxed it feels. Now exhale on *aahhhhh*, keeping your mouth, tongue, and jaw in the same open, relaxed position. This should feel good and add warmth to your sound. If it does, you're on the right track. As a bonus, the inner smile actually makes you sound friendlier and automatically more sympathetic; it literally adds a smile to your tone when you speak.

OK, great! Now try another image: imagine trying to keep a big bite of *hot potato* in your mouth. A natural reaction would be to lift your palate to make more room inside your mouth and for cool air to enter to relieve the burning sensation inside your mouth. Does this image produce the same kind of feeling for you? If so, you're beginning to get the idea.

You could also have a feeling of *lifting* the voice into place while at the same time allowing the larynx to *fall* into a relaxed and slightly lower position to create a bit more space. This is called the floating, natural, or resting position and is not to be mistaken for a forcibly pressed-down larynx, which will create tension. We also want to avoid the opposite, namely forcibly pulling the larynx up (as opposed to gently *lifting* the larynx—more about that later). This is a very common mistake when people try to raise their volume or pitch. They somehow think that high volume and high notes mean pulling the larynx way up high and also stretching their neck upward and forward. Not so! In fact, you might want to tilt your head slightly down, as stretching upward is exactly what will *prevent* volume and high notes. You should feel like you have a huge opening extending all the way from your larynx to your front teeth—like an open channel through which your sound can flow.

Somebody once said, "You should feel your voice as little when you sing (or speak) as you feel your eyes when you see!" This is a good rule to keep in mind.

Although you will always feel a sense of vibration around your larynx (because sound *is* vibration), you should never actually feel your voice work! Do you understand the difference between the two?

To understand what's really happening when you use your voice, you need to understand about the vocal cords. Your vocal cords sit in your voice box (larynx—see illustration 3). When you speak or shout or sing or use your voice in any way, the cords vibrate, producing sound.

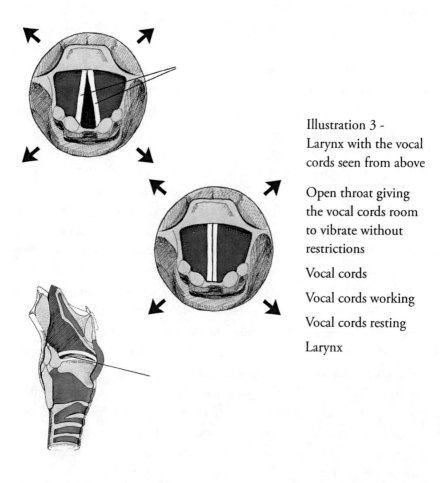

Illustration 3 -
Larynx with the vocal cords seen from above

Open throat giving the vocal cords room to vibrate without restrictions

Vocal cords

Vocal cords working

Vocal cords resting

Larynx

The cords stretch and retract (back to resting position), depending on the pitch of the tone you are using. This is the cords' natural function; when it is in any way disrupted or thwarted, you get problems. The cords are elastic, kind of like rubber bands, and so, like rubber bands, when you stretch them they thin out. You *stretch* them when using high notes, and you *retract* them or allow them to go back to work in their relaxed, short, fat, and wide position when you are using the lower part of your voice, which mainly resonates in your chest (and throat).

This is the part of the voice where you would normally speak in conversation, with low to medium volume. It is also where the voice rests, which is why we refer to this as the natural position. However, there is nothing unnatural about the stretching of the cords. In fact, it is when we *prevent* the cords from stretching by restricting and holding back that we get problems. If you try not to allow the cords to stretch out when reaching for higher notes, you will be working against the grain—like pushing and pulling at the same time or trying to speak while keeping a lid on.

If you attempt to maintain a certain sound or volume by trying to force the cords to remain in either condition—thin/narrow or fat/wide—while traveling up or down the range, you are in effect preventing your cords from performing their natural function. By doing this, you produce a clash—a friction between muscles trying to stretch and muscles trying to retract or to maintain their short, fat state. You are creating severe tension and constricting your voice, preventing it from working naturally.

Of course, you're not doing any of this on purpose. You probably don't even realize that you're doing it—most people don't. Nevertheless, this is what leads to problems. It is very unhealthy, sounds terrible, and strains the voice. Ultimately the voice will rebel and stop working altogether. "Sod this; I'm going on vacation," said the grumpy little voice, tired of all the abuse!

Don't upset your voice; it's not worth it!

In chapter 11, "Basic Voice Exercises," you will have plenty of opportunity to understand and practice your Basic relaxed settings.

BASIC 2: BREATHING—HOW TO FIRE UP YOUR ENGINE AND GAIN EXTRA POWER

Breathing is a natural function—we all know how to do that. To put it differently, our brain and our lungs know how and when to breathe.

Unfortunately, over time, most of us tend to develop what is known as shallow breathing. As I pointed out earlier, there are several reasons why we develop shallow breathing, including stress, anxiety, and indeed any emotional or physical tension. But it could also be simply because we forget to use the full capacity of our lungs on a regular basis and so we condition ourselves not to do so—we become lazy. Perhaps we have nurtured our lazy habit for so long that we have forgotten what a really deep and satisfying (diaphragmatic) breath feels like. We mistakenly associate it with filling up the chest, which means using only a small part of our full lung capacity. You will easily notice when people do this because their chest will lift when they inhale. This does *not* work. You will run out of air before you've even started, and you will create immediate tension in the throat.

Let me point that out to you one more time, for it is very important and one of the most common misconceptions: proper deep breathing means *filling your lungs all the way down*. Shallow breathing means breathing into your chest (lifting it) using only the top part of your lung capacity as opposed to drawing the breath all the way down into the lower part of your lungs. Shallow breathing is like driving on an almost empty tank of gas—it won't get you very far. You need to breathe deeply and fill up the tank, or your engine will start to sputter. Breath is the fuel that powers your voice.

Unless they are accustomed to working with their breathing, most people don't actually know the difference and will, when asked to breathe deeply, automatically fill their chest up to the point of bursting! This acts as an immediate tension trigger. When you cut off half your breathing capacity but at the same time try to fill up, you are creating a conflict of interest which will feel like a lock has been put in place. It immediately puts strain on the vocal cords.

So maybe by now you're thinking, "OK, got it—but *what* is a proper breath then, and won't it take forever?!"

No, not necessarily—it's only a matter of how you do it.

A proper breath means letting your lungs do their job as they were built to do; it is not supposed to be an exhausting exercise but rather a relaxing one. You do not need a controlled deep breath every time you speak. Your brain will soon learn to recognize how much is needed

A proper breath means taking the exactly right amount of air—no less and no more—leaving you feeling comfortably "full" and satisfied.

A proper breath need take no longer than a split second.

When, for instance, you meditate or do yoga, you work with deep breathing—only here you tend to purposely draw your breath out, inhaling very slowly. Take a deep breath yourself right now. If you find this difficult, join your thumb and your middle finger (long, third finger) and press them lightly together. This will help your deep breathing.

Breathe in slowly, preferably through your nose or, if you must, use your mouth or a mix between nose and mouth. Feel how your lungs are filling all the way down. Breathe out naturally through your mouth, pressing your lips ever so slightly together, not closing your mouth completely. Repeat.

When you speak in front of an audience, you obviously won't have time to breathe in and out slowly like this unless you want people to fall asleep within the first sentence. So you aim for your proper breaths to be quick, rather like short but very full sips of air. This can be easily learned. In fact, once you remember how to relax properly, you are almost there.

Remember earlier when I told you about kids and babies? Well, you need only observe a baby's breathing to understand what I mean. Notice how when a baby sleeps or cries, it seems the entire body breathes. A baby's bodily functions are completely natural and harmonious. Babies don't think much about what they do and how—they just exist. Well, when you work with the basics, most of what you do actually consists of remembering or *relearning* how to allow your body to function naturally without restrictions!

Often we are not aware of the restrictions that we impose upon ourselves. Only when they are pointed out to us do we recognize them. They might be small and fairly insignificant habits that could easily be changed. Making those changes would allow us to perform better and be much more comfortable.

So, to sum it up: correct breath control habits for powerful and healthy speaking often call for us first to unlearn bad habits, then to remember what deep breathing is, how it *feels*, and how it naturally functions—and then to *learn to consciously control the process of exhaling.* This is basically what breath control means. Once we have reprogrammed the body to work properly, the process becomes automatic again, only this time it is *automatically correct.*

I can't point this out to you enough: your voice and your whole body should always feel *completely comfortable* and energized but *relaxed* at the same time, *or something is not working right!* You *must* feel comfortable! If you don't, find out what the problem is, find out what causes *or caused* it, and deal with it.

Again, it could be something really stupid and simple like sucking in your tummy on stage in order to look good. Well, you might look fabulous, but your performance will suffer, for pulling your tummy in does not exactly aid natural breathing!

Correct breathing is more easily done through the nose. But you can of course breathe through your mouth or both at the same time, if you prefer. It is really a matter of personal preference. Both methods have some advantages and disadvantages.

Concentrating on your nose can sometimes help lift up your voice or tone, condensing it more and making it stronger. But at the same time, your nose could cause you to produce a more nasal sound, which resembles the sound of a wind instrument, such as a saxophone. Breathing through your mouth is more likely to cause shallow breathing.

<u>Recap</u>

When speaking in front of an audience:

Always take quiet, low, quick breaths. (A proper breath need only take a split second.)

Allow your lungs to take in the amount of oxygen they see fit.

Your glorious brain will tell them how much air is needed, and it will all work perfectly as soon as you have reconditioned your body to function properly (naturally) again.

Do not cut off the flow, and do not deep-breathe to the point of suffocating!

Too much air is no good either. A proper breath means taking the appropriate amount of air for the occasion—no less, no more.

Do not lift your chest and shoulders when breathing in.

As you inhale, expand! As you inhale, your stomach (particularly the lower abdomen) should move outward, and you should feel an expansion of your lower back and ribs.

Feel your breath all the way down and all the way around your body—not just in front but around the sides and your back as well. (See the discussion of "the belt of power" in Basic 3, "Supporting Your Voice," for more info about this.)

When you have enough air, your body will tell you—you will automatically feel the urge to exhale. (Breath/exhalation with sound = speaking.)

As you exhale, keep your posture straight and try to keep your ribcage expanded as opposed to sinking in and down.

Dispose of excess air before releasing support (see Basic 3, "Supporting Your Voice") and taking a new breath.

If you really want to keep your voice healthy and if you want to be able to utilize all the power available to you—if you want more authority and control, you must first master breath control.

BASIC 3: SUPPORTING YOUR VOICE

OK, so we know about breathing in the right way.

Now we need to exercise breath control, which is the combination of breathing and support.

Support is holding and lifting your energy and your breath—basically, breathing out (exhaling) in a controlled, economical manner. You are holding off the air, resisting the diaphragm's natural urge to release the air that has been inhaled and return to its normal resting position.

The strength of your support is shown by how much air you can hold off and for how long. Notice that your ribcage should expand as well and remain expanded till support is released.

The support has to happen in a slow, gradual, sustained, and continuous manner. The movement must be smooth, yet powerful.

There must be good balance between the air pressure from below (carried by lower support muscles) and the resistance to that airflow by the diaphragm and the lower ribs (see illustration 4).

The stronger and fitter you are, the more powerful your support. As a speaker, of course, there are limits to how much power you need compared to actors or singers, who need a lot. Some need more than others, depending on vocal style. But one thing is true for all: when your body is neglected or tired and hasn't got enough energy to support properly and according to your needs, your voice and your performance will suffer the consequences.

Look at the support system as your engine. Your engine needs upkeep and fuel to run smoothly. It consists of three muscle groups: the abdominal, back, and loin. Imagine a "belt of power" extending 360 degrees around your lower abdomen. When the engine works properly, you should be able to both feel it and see it very clearly! If you do not feel it working in the way that I am about to describe, using a simple exercise, you are probably doing something wrong. If this is the case, stop and start again.

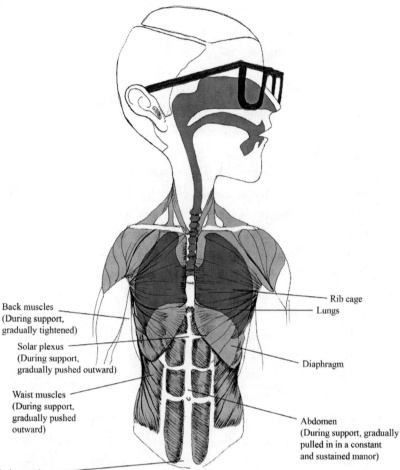

Rib cage

Lungs

Back muscles
(During support,
gradually tightened)

Solar plexus
(During support,
gradually pushed outward)

Waist muscles
(During support,
gradually pushed
outward)

Diaphragm

Abdomen
(During support, gradually
pulled in in a constant
and sustained manor)

Loin muscles
(During support, loin muscles
are trying to push the pelvis backwards,
while the abdominal muscles are
trying to pull the pelvis up under the body.
This resistance battle created between
the abdominal muscles and the loin muscles
is an important part of the support.)

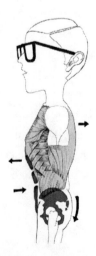

Never practice something you are not sure of or something that seems or feels wrong! Not only is it a complete waste of time, but it could also be damaging. Moreover, as I said earlier, if you build bad habits, you will first need to get rid of those again before you can build new, better ones. This means double work and double time!

So make sure it feels good, right from the beginning.

Notice if you have a straining or locking sensation around the abdominal area and the solar plexus, which could indicate false support. False support is *not* support; *it is tension*. It has no other purpose than to trick you into believing that you are indeed supporting when, in fact, you are not—you are locking your engine.

How do you know the difference between real support and no support? You need to feel yourself lifting and working in a smooth, sustained, gradual manner. You should never feel locked. Support takes physical strength, *but it does not require you to strain*. Remember, if your engine is struggling, so is your voice! The more natural and comfortable it feels, the more right it is.

Use the following exercise to establish how breath control and support should work and feel.

Exercise: Identify Support

Take a deep breath through your nose or mouth, making sure that it fills your lungs all the way down as described earlier. Remember not to lift your shoulders and not to move your chest up. As you inhale, your stomach (particularly the lower abdomen) should move outward, and you should feel an expansion of your lower back and ribs.

When you have enough air, your body will tell you—you will automatically feel the urge to exhale. When you feel this, hold your breath for a few seconds, then exhale through your mouth using the sound *tzssss* (sounding like a hissing snake or a leaky bike tire).

The tip of your tongue should sit behind your lower front teeth, with the middle of your tongue touching the roof of your mouth, and you should feel a slight air pressure on the roof of your mouth and your front teeth.

Keep pressing out air in a smooth gradual movement till you feel that your lungs are completely empty and you need to breathe again.

Then give it a last little squeeze, all the time keeping the same upright strong posture, without slouching, as the last bit of air is squeezed out.

Then stop your *tzssss* sound, hold your breath again for a second, and then *instantly and completely let go of your support* (still holding your posture!), causing a natural deep breath to take place automatically in a split second!

It is important always to keep holding the support till just after the ending of any sentence or phrase instead of releasing it too early. If you don't carry your sound all the way through to the end, you will lose power and control, and your sentence or phrasing will fizzle out toward the end, sounding weak, too breathy, loose, and unconvincing.

When you exhale on *tzssss,* you should feel your engine working intensely but smoothly—gradually *expanding at the sides,* moving your *lower* abdominal area *gradually inward.* The movement *must be gradual.* If you push all your strength out at once in one or two staccato movements, you will lock your support and it won't work. There will be nothing to give—no support and no power.

Again, watch out for tension. It undermines the function of the diaphragm and support muscles. Be careful not to mistake tension with support. Speaking with correct support, you should feel *no strain* or tension whatsoever anywhere. You should feel yourself working, but it should be a *completely comfortable* sensation.

Support takes physical strength; however, it doesn't require you to strain!

If your tone seems weak or shaky and you're lacking in power and volume, chances are that your support is too weak.

In order to have even, smooth, and pleasant sound, cords must be left to vibrate smoothly. If your tone sounds forced or too shouty and harsh, you might be forcing or pushing your air too much. Too much air hitting the cords all at once will blow them open like floodgates and then slam them into motion really hard. This is not healthy.

I will give you plenty more easy exercises in chapter 11. Play around with them and find the right balance for you. As long as it feels good and comfortable with no strain or tension, you are safe and on the way to improving your skills.

BASIC 4: INITIATING THE TONE

OK, let us now assume that your first three Basics are working, your body and your vocal apparatus (mouth, jaw, tongue, throat, and larynx) are relaxed, and your air is lifted and ready to go.

You now have to *initiate* the tone. The initiation is the very beginning of a tone. Some teachers refer to this as the *attack*. You might find this reference misguiding because it has a somewhat violent ring to it as if you slam, bang, or smack your tone into action! This is not what is meant. There are different kinds of initiations/attacks depending on what kind of sound you are initiating; none of them, though, is supposed to violate your voice.

The way your air is lifted, then the sound/tone *initiated*, then also *lifted and carried forward*, will determine the quality, the strength, the power, and the sustainability of the tone. It literally sets the tone and determines how much control you'll have. For your tone to be completely healthy and fully controlled from start to finish, the initiation/attack needs to be *fully supported* (breath control). It also has to be tight—not tight as in strained but tight as in fitting perfectly. This is a bit hard to describe, but I shall do my best.

First, immediately prior to the initiation, the lift (support) needs to be in place.

Then the amount of air that is produced during the initiation needs to be just the right amount for the vocal cords to vibrate smoothly and evenly. This will create the perfect *tight fit* opening and a healthy tight (concentrated) tone. You can actually feel this working. It feels like the cords are gliding into action in a smooth flowing movement, coming together around the tone, almost like a soft caress, but all in a split second.

If you use too much air pressure, you will overblow the cords. This is like having the gates blow open by force. The opening will be too wide, and air will simply burst out. You will waste air and energy and annoy your cords.

You don't want to be sloppy either. You do need power. If you hold your power back and only somewhat initiate the tone—kind of support it, but not quite—it doesn't work either. Your cords will react in kind. They will be loose and sloppy like a pair of old worn-out rubber bands that have lost their elasticity. They won't close (come together) around your tone properly. This will cause excess air to spread or fizzle out, stealing power and energy and not least annoying or even straining the cords.

In other words, the opening (called the glottis) through which your tone has to be projected must always be made to fit the tone like a hand in a glove. It has to be just right according to the tone and the sound. For the best and healthiest tone, you'll have a perfectly condensed flow of air with no accidental leaks, meaning no excess air fizzling out along with the sound.

Strong, loud sounds sometimes call for strong attacks. (Here I do use the term *attack* because in this case it actually fits quite nicely.) With strong, loud sounds you might not get the sense of the tone *gliding* into action—it kind of *springs* into action instead.

That's OK as long as it doesn't give you the feeling that your cords are being *knocked* into action with a bang (like a door slamming). This would indicate overblow and could cause bruising in the long run. You can feel when this happens because you immediately have less control over your voice and phrasing and you also tend to run out of air faster because you spend too much too fast in the beginning of the phrase. Even if you manage to gradually steer your tone into the right direction, the damage will already have been done and the overall result will never be as good as if you had initiated correctly in the first place. A healthy tone is clear, focused, and whole without spills.

Pheeew! Did you get all of that? If you didn't quite understand, don't worry. You'll get it once you start practicing it along with your projection.

BASIC 5: PROJECTING YOUR VOICE—HITTING RIGHT ON TARGET WITH STRENGTH AND AUTHORITY

Projection quite literally refers to how you project or *send out* your sound when you speak, sing, etc. Some people refer to this as *focus*. I prefer the term *projection* because I think *focus* is what you *need to do* first in order for your projection to work. Saying that you need to focus *and* project makes much more sense to me.

For you to control your projection, the other three Basics have to work first. Without them, there will be no healthy sound to project. All the Basics need to work together; they are linked. There can be no one healthy function without the others (unless you're doing breathing exercises without sound).

Once your tone has been initiated correctly, you have to focus and project it forward *and sustain* it till you choose to end it. This means *holding* your support till *after* you have ended your tone. Then *and only then* do you release your support and allow your lungs to instantly and automatically fill up again, ready for the next tone initiation and following phrase. *Sound production must always start with the lift and end with the release of the support.*

A smooth and fully controlled process of first initiating and then projecting and sustaining the tone requires focus. How you focus first your thought, then your sound determines the sound quality, power, and control.

Although the process of sound production is physical, much of it is hidden—we cannot see it. In order for us to understand what is supposed to go on inside of us, we have to rely on abstract, inner imagery to describe it. We have to find ways of describing how to *think it into action* and how it *feels* (or how it is supposed to feel) when done correctly. Not all images work equally well for everybody, but the following exercise tends to do the job for most people.

Exercise: Focus, Attention, Shoot!

Create a reference point—a point of focus.

Ideally, this should be a small circle within a greater circle—much like the inner and outer circles of a dartboard.

Your focus point should be straight in front of your face, extending directly from the tip of your nose.

Place it at a distance of between four and seven feet away from you at first. If you need to shout very loudly, you might find it helpful to extend the distance between you and your focus point. You can practice longer distances as your confidence and your voice grow stronger.

Focus your attention on the small circle. This is where your sound should be directed, much like a bullet or, better still, a laser beam.

Now, imagine your energy traveling *up through your body, up into the back of your head, and around your skull into your mouth* ready for takeoff!

This principle of *up, behind, around, and forward* seems to work pretty well (with one exception, which I will tell you about later).

Intend the initial tone in your mind and then imagine the journey of the tone *from onset to its final destination* as if you were *carrying* it all the way to the exit point (the front of your mouth) from which you shoot it out and *forward* toward your focus point!

Now, using the previous Basics, say the sound *ahhhh* in a comfortable tone/ pitch that comes naturally to you. For now, we assume that this is your natural pitch, though for most people, their natural pitch often turns out to be tonally higher than they initially thought before they started training their voice.

Feel how it gradually becomes easier to control your sound when you are using all the Basics to produce sound and aim it at your focus point.

Keep doing it, changing between different sounds. Remember to lift first, then initiate, almost like gliding the tone into action. Emphasize the vowels.

First initiate on H:

- *Heeeeeeh*—as in "h<u>e</u>" or "f<u>ee</u>ling"
- *Heeeeeyyyh*—as in "h<u>ey</u>"
- *Haaaaaaaah*—as in "(h)<u>a</u>venue"
- *Heeeeeeeh*—as in "(h)<u>e</u>nough"

Now try initiating straight on the vowel:

- *Eeeeeeeh*—as in "h<u>e</u>" or "f<u>ee</u>ling"
- *Eeeeeyyyh*—as in "h<u>ey</u>"
- *Aaaaaaaaah*—as in "<u>a</u>venue"
- *Eeeeeeeeh*—as in "<u>e</u>nough"

Also, try to vary your volume a bit. But stay within your comfortable zone. If anything starts to feel uncomfortable, *stop!* Go back to where it was comfortable.

Don't overdo it. If your voice is not used to working out like this, it might get tired—much like your body would if you were to exercise excessively hard after a long break.

You will learn more about working with volume in chapter 9.

When working with speech dynamics, it is helpful to work on your pitch/ range between your lowest and highest notes/tones. This is the next step.

Start moving your tones up and down, beginning with your basic tone and then sliding a few notes first up and then down. As you do this, slightly move your focus along with the tones. Always stay within the bounds of the outer circle, though. When moving toward *low tones, aim slightly upward.* Simply visualize your tone moving slightly *up*ward. When moving toward *higher tones, aim slightly lower/downward.* Basically think and focus *opposite.*

This may seem weird to you at first, but trust me—it works. Thinking like this will help even out the feeling or idea of a huge distance or gap between the low and high notes in your range and also help smooth out the tonal transitions and the sound in general. This "pull" in the opposite direction makes it easier for you to reach the tone. It helps create evenness and a feeling of oneness in the voice. Also, by focusing the sound/tone in this way, we condense/concentrate it into one strong force of beaming, direct energy. No excess air fizzling out—no wasted energy!

This will give you a strong, authoritative, and confident-sounding voice.

Imagine a solid concentrated laser beam projecting precisely toward and through its target. In this case, the target is your chosen point of focus.

Recap and a Few Extra Pointers

Focus/aim forward and slightly up or down, depending on your pitch. Remember to think *opposite!* It is a common mistake to think that high notes require thinking high and reaching for the notes. It does *not*.

Do not lift or stretch your jaw upward, protruding it, as this will immediately create tension and disrupt the air passage.

A good idea is to have your focus point on a mirror in front of you—preferably full size. It's even better if you make it the center of your DC Vision Board (see part 5, chapter 20). Or maybe somehow combine the two.

Using a mirror as a focus point has certain advantages. It can help you keep an eye on any visual tension as well as holding the focus. If you are very used to being tense, you might not even recognize tension, and in that case, it helps to be able to actually see it. (Tension in the jaw, neck, and throat area is very visible, for instance.)

No matter where you are, you can always find a focus point. Say you are backstage just about to go on and you want to make sure that your voice is clear and ready. Look for a spot on the wall.

Failing that, you can always use the finger trick. Simply make a circle using your first and second fingers, stretch your arm out in front of you, and focus your voice through the circle. Voilà!

It might also be helpful for you to imagine your sound traveling through a reversed megaphone (see illustration 5). This is a good image because of the triangular shape. Imagine the rim of a megaphone springing from inside your mouth toward the back of your throat, capturing your tone as it travels along the pathway through your mouth and out the mouthpiece in the end.

Illustration 5 - Perfect Projection Clerk

Some people find it very hard to lift their pitch. Concentrating and placing a certain amount of attention *on the nose and upper front head* can help make this easier. That does *not* mean that you should place your sound solely in your nose, though. Aim for a sensation of creating sound *through, around, above, and behind your nose* as well as from your mouth. Lifting your focus *up and forward* takes attention away from the throat area, which is very helpful.

The throat needs to be left free to resonate without strain. Too much attention on the throat is the root of all evil . . . and exactly what we want to avoid because it is likely to be the one thing that will prevent us from having the power and reaching the tones that we are aiming for.

In general, air will exit through both the nose and mouth at the same time—mostly through the mouth, but probably about 10 percent through the nose, depending on which range you are working in. As a rule, the higher up on the scale you go, the more air exits through the nose.

Oh, and by the way, *don't think that speakers don't need range.* I recently saw a very well known speaker who blew my socks off! He was yelling and screaming and Lord knows what just to prove a point—and he did! He had the whole lecture hall in a trance, all eyes firmly fixed on the stage, all ears and hearts open. Yep, he surely knew how to catch people's attention and keep it. What he gave was not just a speech; it was a truly magnificent performance. He didn't just tell us a story; he acted it out for maximum effect. Did his message come across? It sure did! It took a lot of guts to do what he did—and a lot of voice power. He had both. He was not just a good speaker; he was an excellent one.

To be able to put on a performance like that, your voice really has to be on autopilot. You have to be able to just lean back and settle into your story. If you have to worry about how to get through the performance without harming your voice, it will clearly dampen the experience, not just for you but certainly for the audience as well.

It's a shame if your degree of technical proficiency has to determine or even limit how you present your material. If you want to make a strong, dramatic, or even theatrical point because it really suits the topic, it's frustrating if you can't do it just because your voice won't let you.

Your voice should be working with you, not against you. You are a team, working together to communicate important messages and create maximum impact.

When you reach a point where your tone is flowing smoothly, you feel the vibration, but other than that it almost feels like your sound comes from somewhere else and is kind of disconnected from your body; then you know that you are getting somewhere.

You will note that in this state, speaking/performing/singing feels and sounds easy, like play. You are physically working but relaxed at the same time and seem to be able to produce maximum sound with (a feeling of) least effort!

Congratulations! You are beginning to master the Basics of voice technique. Are you still enjoying yourself? I hope you are.

Now, move on to the next chapter to learn about vocal modes—how you can work with high volume, for instance, without getting worn out. Then you will learn about resonance and how you can color your sound to your liking. Then we'll talk about verbal inflections and other voice tools before rounding out this section with basic voice exercises in chapter 11. These will help put it all together for you so you can develop your skills even further. Enjoy.

CHAPTER 7

Vocal Modes—Different Gears for Different Sounds and Volumes

In recent years, much new research has gone into pinpointing the actual technical and mechanical functions of the voice and what are now mostly referred to as vocal modes. *Mode* means function or method. The term *vocal modes* was first introduced in the late eighties by one of the world's leading voice specialists and researchers, Cathrine Sadolin.

Knowledge about the modes has developed, and they have become an integral part of modern-day voice training. It has now become commonly accepted that beyond the Basics, there are not just one or two ways to produce or add to or enhance sound correctly, but actually quite a few.

Cathrine Sadolin now runs vocal academies internationally and has made it her life's work to further study and develop the voice and to educate singers, vocal coaches, and other voice professionals all over the world. She probably wasn't the first—or at least she wasn't alone in viewing technique in this new and revolutionary way—but she certainly was the first that I know of to thoroughly investigate and expand on her findings, to clearly define them and name them, and to put them into literature.

The modes are used according to taste and style. For performers including singers, actors, teachers, and speakers, the correct use of modes is crucial. Many vocal problems occur as a result of incorrect use of the modes.

Each mode has its own distinct marks as well as advantages and limitations. The easiest way to describe modes is as gears. These gears are controlled via adjustments in the mouth, jaw, and tongue settings and by changes in the epiglottis funnel. (See illustrations 2 and 3 in chapter 6.)

OVERVIEW

There are four modes: Neutral, Curbing, Overdrive, and Belting. (In her most recent work, Cathrine Sadolin refers to Belting as "Edge." We will stick with the original term, Belting, here.)

These are divided into categories of nonmetallic, half-metallic, and metallic (or full metallic) Nonmetallic is soft; metallic is harder, rougher, edgier, and more direct; half-metallic is in between. I'll start with a very basic, general description of the modes, then provide more detailed facts about each mode.

Neutral

The Neutral mode is the most common speaking and singing voice for the average, not overly loud person. If you sing a lullaby to your child, a birthday song, or a psalm in church, it is very likely that you use the Neutral mode. In the West, neutral is the most commonly taught mode in singing tuition (for women) and is often used in church and school choirs.

Neutral can range from very breathy (with air, like speaking in a breathy voice or whispering) to very compressed without air. Neutral without air is characterized by a nonbreathy but soft, clear, rounded sound. Neutral is described as nonmetallic, meaning it doesn't have an edge or metallic sound.

The Neutral (soft) approach, including the classical/operatic sound, is easily learned; most people are very comfortable working with this one immediately or after just a few sessions.

But Neutral has a natural volume ceiling (except in classical/operatic singing, in the high part of the voice). If you try to push the volume beyond that ceiling, your voice will feel and sound strained. You will have the feeling that you are somehow trying to break an invisible sound barrier, like your mouth is covered with a piece of cling film and you need to burst a hole in it to break through.

Do you recognize this feeling? If you do, it means that you are trying to push the Neutral mode beyond its volume limit. You are possibly holding back as well, keeping the lid on, forcing your voice to stay in the same mode. This won't work. It is like pushing and pulling at the same time or trying to speed your car up in the first gear. No good—you need to change gears.

Like I said, modes are exactly that—gears. You use different gears for different volumes.

If you need to add volume or a bit more edge to you sound, you need to change gears.

Curbing

Between the soft and the hard modes we have Curbing.

Curbing is described as half-metallic, meaning that there's a slight edge to the sound. It is characterized by a complaining, agitated, whiney, plaintive, or restrained sound—like crying or moaning. The volume is medium.

I tend to stay away from Curbing when I speak, unless I'm making a theatrical point, where it kind of hits the mark. Otherwise, in speech, it can be quite tedious to listen to, so you probably won't be using it much in your presentations.

Nonetheless, my guess is that you curb a lot already. I'll explain about that in a minute.

Belting and Overdrive

If you need loads of volume—say you need to reach right to the back of the room, you're speaking in a large room without a microphone, you need to really grab attention, or you're just really fired up and feel like adding a bit of drama and dynamics to your speech—you need the third or even the fourth gear. This is where the so-called hard or metallic modes, Belting and Overdrive, come in handy.

If you've ever tried screaming or shouting really loud without feeling sore in your throat afterward, then you've tried either Belting or Overdrive.

Belting and Overdrive are voice modes used by voice professionals of all styles—and by everybody else who has ever dared to let out their voice in all its glory. The two modes are similar in nature—they are both classed as metallic and both have high volume. But they are different modes with distinct differences in sounds and settings.

Each favors certain vowel sounds in the top range. Belting has a very condensed, pointy, light, sometimes sharp and screamy sound to it. Overdrive has thicker, darker, more voluptuous, and more shouty qualities.

From a voice health perspective, there's absolutely nothing wrong with screaming, shouting, talking several hours a day, talking loud, talking low, talking very dynamically, being very dramatic, making funny voices, using different sound colors, effects, whatever—as long as you do it correctly by applying the Basics and the correct settings for the respective modes. More about sound colors and effects later.

The challenge is that you first need to know and recognize what *correctly* means. And most people simply don't. (This includes many medical doctors and throat, not voice, specialists.) So when they get a problem with their voice, they are not sure why, they often draw the wrong conclusions, and, worst of all, they don't know what to do about the problem.

Do you really need all this information? Do you actually need to know?

No, you don't necessarily need to know—but you will clearly have an advantage if you do know! You will have a much greater understanding of the voice; you will be more confident, daring, and able to express yourself more freely. And when you do run into problems or limitations, you will know why and what to do about them.

That little bit of extra knowledge will give you more power and control and much more creative and expressive freedom when you speak.

SETTINGS AND SOUNDS WHEN USING THE DIFFERENT MODES

In the past, many voice trainers favored working only with the Neutral mode, preferably leaning toward a classical sound that has the tongue lying flat, pressed down in the mouth, and a loose-hanging jaw. Many, including me, grew up to learn that the Neutral mode was the only right mode. As a result of this, I ended up having problems when I first converted from classical to contemporary singing.

However, as I pointed out earlier, knowledge in this field is forever evolving, and we now know that while this setting works perfectly well for the softer sounds, it does not work so well with the louder and harder sounds—and will lead to problems if applied to those. This is probably why many voice trainers used to think that rock singing, for instance, was technically wrong and damaging to the voice per se.

But studying rock singers and other singers indulging in a harder sound and not seeming to harm their voices in the process made it obvious that they had to be doing something right. It turned out that they simply used different settings for the harder, rougher, and louder sounds—the settings we now refer to as Belting and Overdrive. So we now know that that there are better ways to approach certain sounds. We also have accepted that all sounds are OK and possible to produce without straining and damaging the voice.

Following is a more in-depth description of the use and settings of the four different modes. It includes tongue and jaw settings and advice on which vowels and sounds work best with each mode. You can apply the modes and the different settings to all the voiced exercises (like slides, etc.) in chapter 11, "Basic Voice Exercises."

When practicing without supervision, be careful—make sure that it feels right. If in doubt, go back and read the appropriate chapter again. Then practice slowly from there, one step at a time.

NEUTRAL MODE

Neutral always has the jaw hanging loose and typically has the tongue resting, lying flat in the mouth, like when you are speaking normally and calmly in conversation.

When doing exercises in the Neutral mode, press down the tip of your tongue behind your lower front teeth. Be sure not to pull your tongue back. If you find that you have a habit of doing this (as many do), hold your tongue with a napkin while exercising till you learn how to relax your tongue properly.

Your mouth and lips should be loose, like when speaking normally, to oval-shaped (like a church choirboy). It can be lightly smiley, depending on the pitch and color of the sound (dark or light—see chapter 8, "Resonance, Sound Colors, and Voice Registers").

The soft palate (front roof of the mouth; see illustration 2) can either be neutral (again, meaning "normal," like during normal calm conversation) or lowered, making the vocal tract smaller, overall resonance smaller, and voice color lighter. Or it can be lifted, making the vocal tract and the overall resonance bigger (think operatic) and voice color darker.

How do you recognize the Neutral sound? Neutral is generally a softer (nonmetallic), more rounded sound. It can range from breathy to voluminous with lots of resonance.

All vowel sounds work well with this mode.

Remember that Neutral has a natural volume ceiling that should never forcefully be extended, as this will strain the voice. The loft is where it starts to feel uncomfortable and restrained. You may have the feeling as if you were talking with a piece of cling film over your mouth, spending too much energy with too little gain. For higher volume, change into a harder mode.

CURBING MODE

I doubt that you will use Curbing as your preferred mode of speaking, as the sound tends to be a complaining, kind of agitated sound, which could be off-putting (think female soul singer who's just been left by her lover and is crying her way through the song while at the same time trying to sound sexy). Great for singing, but for speaking . . . hmmmmm . . . not so great.

As I said, I stay away from Curbing when I speak unless I'm making a theatrical point. I also suggest staying away from Curbing when doing exercises until you're feeling very secure, as it is easy to mistake the hold that establishes the Curb setting with speaking in the throat and straining, which is what you don't want to do! It is easy to get it wrong and cause strain. However, I'll tell you how to find the setting. If it works for you, great!

When Curbing, the mouth and lips should be loose to tight, like when you are speaking calmly to being a bit more, shall we say, "engaged." When doing exercises, you should have a neutral (here meaning "normal" like when speaking normally) to smiley mouth. The tongue and jaw should be the same as with Neutral; perhaps your jaw won't feel quite as loose—more like a tight or fake kind of smile.

Curbing has more edge and a higher volume loft than Neutral without being fully metallic like Overdrive and Belting

Curbing can be found by establishing a hold. It feels a bit as if you are holding your voice in a grip as you speak or as if you are holding the sound back a bit, like keeping it in the mouth (not the throat), putting on the brakes just before releasing it. A good way to make this work is to simply back off the feeling of focusing and projecting your sound forward. But again, be careful—don't mistake this for speaking in your throat and straining.

Imagine complaining or moaning, just on the verge of crying: *Eeeehhhhhh . . . heeh*, like the cry of a baby, or maybe the evil laughter of an old witch: *heh, heh, heh.* Try also *o* as in "w<u>oooo</u>man" and *uh* as in "h<u>uuuuu</u>ngry"!

With regard to the voice coloring—the size of the vocal tract—you have the same options here as with Neutral. But the mode on its own will change the sound from soft, round, and perhaps breathy to flatter, less roomy, and more edgy without the full metallic blast of the next two modes.

All vowels work well in the lower area of the chest and in the midrange (middle register). However, if doing exercises in the high range of your voice (head voice), direct all vowels toward the following vowel sounds:

- Moaning/complaining: *Eeeeeeehh-huh,* like you are about to cry
- Moaning/complaining: *Ooooooooohhhhhhhh-huh,* like "<u>Oh</u>, my tummy hurts so bad" or *o*, as in "w<u>o</u>man" or *uh*, as in h<u>u</u>ngry

BELTING MODE

I'm sure you've heard the expression that someone was "really belting it out."

You use Belting if you need to be very loud and literally point something out in no uncertain terms! This sound can be very pointy indeed. It is a strong, aggressive, and occasionally sharp sound.

You cannot do half a belt. Either you go all out and give it all you've got or you don't. Belting is loud; it's supposed to be loud. If loud is not what you want, do not Belt! But if it is, feel how that wonderful outburst of energy sends the little freedom fighter endorphins rushing through your system—ahhhh!

In Belting, the forward-focused projection described in "Projecting Your Voice" in chapter 6 is extra important.

Belting lends itself to higher pitched sounds and features lighter, sharper, screamier qualities versus the fuller, darker, shoutier qualities of Overdrive. Belting is described as (full) metallic, meaning that there's a distinct metallic edge on the sound.

71

If belting is not supported and projected correctly, it can sound shrill, harsh, piercing, and tedious. Not only that, but it is also harmful to the voice. So be careful with this one.

For Belting to work properly, you need to change your mouth, jaw, and tongue settings. Chances are that you are already making these adjustments without even noticing.

The mouth shape is more "triangular" as opposed to oval, like the shape of a smile (think the Joker, but do not force a very wide smile, as this is counterproductive and can create tension). Follow your mouth's urge to open and widen—the higher the note, the wider the smile. I will explain more about the importance of the smile in just a moment.

As opposed to hanging loose, the jaw is held in position (but not tightened). It sits in what is mostly referred to as the *bite* position (see illustration 6). The best way to establish the bite is to imagine that you are just about to bite into a big apple. Notice how your jaw opens downward and slightly inward, drawing back as it drops fully open, creating a slight overbite. If you point your finger as if to scold somebody, then place the fingertip behind your upper front teeth, holding it there in a straight up-and-down position, you should have the bite.

Illustration 6 - Bite Position Clerk

Belting also requires you to twang your epiglottis funnel. If you don't twang, this mode will not work properly and you will strain. I know this may sound complicated, but it's not. To twang your epiglottis funnel, you simply twang your tongue. Twanging the tongue will automatically cause the epiglottis funnel to twang as well. The twang has the body of your tongue arching (like a bow), sides pressing against the upper back teeth. The tongue feels wider, and the tip of the tongue remains behind the lower front teeth. This setting condenses or sharpens the sound and adds volume but also has a tendency to make it a bit more nasal sounding. (It isn't, really, but it can sound like it.)

You probably are very familiar with twanging already. To identify this setting, simply say the word *twang* and notice what happens in your mouth. If you don't notice anything, try making your accent more southern U.S. You can also try to imitate the sound of a baby crying or a duck. It changes the space inside your mouth, which causes the sound to change. Be sure not to pull your tongue back, as this will cause strain.

The smile literally flattens out the sound, much like the blade in a wind instrument, such as a saxophone. It works together with the raised tongue of the twang and the neutral to lowered positioning of the soft palate (causing the larynx to automatically rise as well) to make the vocal tract very condensed (small), resulting in the very concentrated, strong, pointy (less rounded), powerful, high-volume sound even in the top range of the voice.

Right here it's time for a classic myth bust. Many people wrongly associate the strong sound of Belting only with the chest voice. (You will learn about *voice registers* later.)

They think that when somebody is fully voicing by using a tone that is full (clean, condensed tone, not breathy) in their head voice range, for instance, they've somehow managed to "lift their chest voice higher into their head." This is not the case. Over a certain tonal point on the musical scale, they will inevitably enter into their head voice. They are merely using the Belting mode to condense the sound, maintaining the same strong sound qualities normally associated with the chest voice.

Belting works in all registers and is used to add or maintain full power and volume. Belting is always fully voiced; there's absolutely no breathiness associated with this mode, ever! If your projection is loose in this mode—if you allow excess air to escape one time too many—you will cause damage to your voice. Period! This is why people think that being loud—shouting and screaming—is damaging to your voice. But those are not in themselves damaging. It is easy, however, to get Belting wrong, mainly because most people tend to hold back and push forward at the same time, creating friction by doing "half a Belt"; then it's damaging.

Belting is a full-speed-ahead, perfect-technique-only mode. Hanging loose, proper breathing, full support, perfect initiation, strong focus, and super-tight projection are musts!

If in doubt, don't do it. Go back and check up on your Basics before you continue.

All vowel sounds work well in the lower range of the chest voice. However, as progress to your midrange (middle register), direct all vowel sounds (and diphthongs) toward the following vowel sounds:

- *E* as in "h<u>e</u>" or "f<u>ee</u>ling"
- *EY* as in "h<u>ey</u>"
- *A(y)* as in "<u>a</u>pe"
- *A* as in "<u>a</u>venue" or "<u>a</u>nd"

- *IE* as in "t*ie* or *I*"
- *OE* as in "w<u>o</u>rd" or "h<u>e</u>rb"
- *UI* as in screaming loudly at a concert: woo-eeeeh!

In your top range (head voice), which you will use when you do voice exercises, use only the above vowel sounds.

OVERDRIVE MODE

If you have ever shouted at your partner, your kids, your best friend, your boss, or your ex, chances are that you are very familiar with the Overdrive mode. Overdrive is like shouting, only in a controlled, technically healthy way. You often hear Overdrive in rock singing.

Illustration 7 -
Rock Star Clerk

Overdrive has full, dark, shouty qualities versus the lighter, sharper, screamier qualities of Belting. Both are very powerful modes that work only with fairly high volume to very high volume.

As a dynamic speaker, you will use Overdrive. Some speakers use it all the time. It's mainly a matter of taste, style, and personality. Circumstances can make it a matter of necessity as well. If, for instance, you are addressing a large crowd without a microphone, chances are they won't hear you unless you pump up the volume.

Tonally, women can only go so far with the Overdrive mode. At some point, they will need to change their mode to Belting, which allows a strong and very powerful sound even on high notes.

The mouth is fully open, oval shaped with a slight tendency toward the more triangular shape of a smile on the higher notes just before transitioning into the more pronounced smile of Belting. (Follow your mouth's natural urge to open and widen.) The jaw is held or dropped into the bite position. The tongue will be arching, with the tip positioned behind the lower front teeth. A strong sound in Overdrive will feel like it is sitting or hitting against your soft palate just behind your upper front teeth.

Start medium loud and progress to shouting as loudly as you possibly can, using the focus point to send the sound forward. In Overdrive as in Belting, the forward-focused projection described in "Projecting Your Voice" in chapter 6 is *very* important.

If it feels good, you've got it. If it feels strained or uncomfortable, you're straining, either because you are disconcerted by the high volume or because you haven't quite gotten the gist of the technical part yet.

All vowels work well in the lower range of the chest voice. However, as you progress to your midrange (middle register), direct all vowel sounds toward the following vowel sounds:

- Try shouting *Hey!!!!!!!!!!!* (*Haa-yyyy-eeh!!!!*) or as in "sta<u>y</u>"
- Then *Woh!!!!!!!!* as in "I w<u>o</u>n't do it!!!!"
- Or *Home!!!!* with emphasis on "<u>O</u>(h)"
- Or *Soh!!!* as in "s<u>o</u>"

In your top range (head voice), which you will use when you do voice exercises, use only the above vowel sounds.

Now you know why you may sometimes have found it hard to be loud and powerful without feeling the strain on your voice afterward. You may simply have had the wrong setting. From now on, apply what you've learned about the modes, and you will never have this problem again.

CHAPTER 8

Resonance, Sound Colors, and Voice Registers

The terms *resonance, sound colors,* and *voice registers* tend to create a lot of confusion and misunderstanding. This is not surprising, because they are all *part* of the same thing. They are connected and they are dependent on each other—but they are *not* identical.

RESONANCE—YOUR OWN BUILT-IN SPEAKER SYSTEM

The voice has its own natural three-way speaker system, referred to as the resonators. This system consists of the bones and cavities of the throat, the larynx (voice box containing the vocal cords), mouth, head, and chest.

The front/upper resonators or the *mask* are terms used to describe the resonating cavities above, behind, and around the nose, the forehead, and the cheekbones. The lower and middle resonators are the resonators in your chest and throat area.

Perhaps this makes more sense if we use our three-way speaker system metaphor from before. Imagine your lower and middle resonators as the subwoofers, woofers, and midrange speakers and your front/upper resonators as the tweeters and the super-tweeters, even, for very high frequencies. Got it? Great—you have your own built-in speaker system!

Illustration 8 - HiFi Clerk

Your physical build and bone structure determine the specific sound quality of these resonators, which is part of the reason why we all sound different. The size of your resonators or cavities determines your own personal resonance and therefore your particular sound. Another influence on your sound is the size of your vocal cords, which vary in length and thickness.

Different body build equals different size cords. Also, men's vocal cords are thicker than women's—therefore they have darker voices.

However, you can learn to color your sound. More about that in a minute.

Lifting our tone forward into the mask gives it clarity and brilliance; the tones are *resonating* in the mask and in the mouth. Your head voice resonates in the mask. (Head voice is a *voice register*. More about registers coming up later in this chapter.)

Place your hand on or slightly above your chest and in a very deep voice say *ahhhhh*. Feel something? What you should feel is a slight vibration sitting in your chest. This is your *lower chest resonance*. The lower chest resonance is the lower chest voice speaker—your *subwoofer*.

Now, place your hand on/slightly above your chest again and in a normal speaking voice say *ahhhhh*. Feel something? What you should feel is a *strong* vibration sitting in your chest. This is your *chest resonance*. The chest resonance is the chest voice speaker—your *woofer*.

When you lift your tone through to your middle voice (throat, *midrange speaker*) and further into your *head voice*, this vibration will gradually move higher till it has finally disappeared from your chest and been replaced by the head resonance, your *tweeter*, or if you have the ability to enter into your whistle voice, your *super-tweeter*. (You won't do this, though, as a speaker, unless you want to be arrested for setting off the fire alarm! The whistle voice has a very high-pitched, sharp piercing sound, almost like an alarm bell.)

Your middle voice has the vibration sitting somewhere between your chest and your head (surprise!), gradually moving either way. Your head voice vibration can feel like your sound is literally sitting inside your head or in your forehead, a bit like a pressure sensation or even a pinging.

As a simple rule, the resonance qualities are:

- Chest voice—naturally dark, warm resonance qualities
- Middle voice—naturally medium dark to medium light resonance qualities
- Head voice—naturally light, bright resonance qualities

I doubt you will ever need to use these:

- Lower chest voice—naturally very dark, boomy resonance qualities

- Whistle voice, which sounds like a flute or a bell—naturally very light/sharp/pinging resonance qualities

SOUND COLORS

You can add sound color to the natural resonance qualities. If the resonators are our own built-in three-way speaker system, sound colors are kind of the equalizers. We use the equalizers or the sound colors to add on the one hand lightness, brightness, and clarity, and on the other hand darkness, thickness, warmth, and depth to our sound.

Sounds can be either neutral—meaning natural or basic—or they can be colored lighter or darker. When a sound is neutral, it has the natural, unprocessed sound of the register it sits in. Remember that dark, warm qualities are naturally features of the lower resonators (throat and chest cavities), and light, bright qualities are naturally features of the upper resonators (head cavities). We can, however, add color to the natural sound, thus making it more pleasing, if you like, to the ear.

Now, just as beauty is said to be in the eye of the beholder, so a pleasing sound is ultimately a matter of preference. However, just as certain features tend to be commonly perceived as beautiful, so certain voice features are commonly perceived as "good" or pleasing. It is generally felt that the most desirable sound is a rich, smooth, calm, and balanced one, perhaps leaning toward the darker end of the scale.

A balanced and full sound is achieved by mixing dark and light/bright colors. Again, dark in this case means depth, and warmth and light mean lightness and brilliance.

Metaphorically speaking, you mix or "blend" colors and natural resonance in order to achieve the sound that you want. You add depth, warmth, and richness/fullness to high-pitched tones and brightness/brilliance to low-pitched tones. The mix takes place in the mouth before the finished tone leaves the mouth cavity and is carried along the outer pathway to its final destination, your point of focus.

OK, I hear you: "How the heck do I do that then?! Sounds like a *lot* of work!" Well, no, not really. Look, I know, it all sounds a bit complicated and technical, but it really isn't. You already do this all the time when you speak dynamically. But you are probably not aware of it, and therefore, on a conscious level, you wouldn't know what to do and how, should you want to enhance your sound in any particular way.

To add sound color, you alter the "settings"—the shape and size of the vocal tract.

The vocal tract is the throat from your vocal cords up through to the nasal passageway and your mouth and lips. Like I said, your physical build, the shape and size of your vocal tract, your bone structure, and the size (length and thickness) of your vocal cords determine your natural sound. These are the physical factors that make us all sound different.

To alter the vocal tract and adjust your sound balance, you expand or retract the tract by either raising the roof of your mouth and lowering your larynx (voice box) or lowering the roof of your mouth and raising your larynx. Basically, you make the tract bigger or smaller.

The smaller the vocal tract, the lighter-colored the sound.

You make your vocal tract smaller by lowering the soft palate (the roof of your mouth), which will automatically cause your larynx to rise, making less room.

Then you can add your tongue into the equation: the higher the arch of the tongue, the smaller the space between the surface of your tongue and the soft palate, making the vocal tract even smaller (space flattened).

Add to that the shape of the mouth, which can go from oval to the shape of a slight smile (be careful not to force it and create tension though). The smile literally flattens out the sound, making it less rounded.

To make your vocal tract smaller, speak normally in a calm voice, then retract your vocal tract using this image: being tired or lazy and sighing because you have to do something that you don't feel like doing. When you breathe out your sigh, purse your lips slightly as in "phhuhhhh, I really can't be bothered." Notice anything happening in your mouth? If you don't feel anything yet, don't despair. You will get it eventually.

The bigger the vocal tract, the darker-colored the sound

You make your vocal tract bigger by lifting the soft palate, automatically causing your larynx to lower, making more room.

Then you can add your tongue into the equation. When your tongue lies flat in the mouth, the flatter, more pressed down the tongue is, the bigger the space between the surface of your tongue and the soft palate, making the vocal tract even bigger (space rounded).

Add to that the shape of the mouth. An oval, round opening leaves the sound more rounded.

To make vocal tract bigger, speak normally in a calm voice, then expand your vocal tract using these images, which were explained in chapter 6, "The Basics: Hang Loose":

- Yawning or breathing in, just about to yawn
- Having a hot potato in your mouth
- Being a posh opera singer

Finally, to help you work with your vocal tract settings, try the following as well.

Try imagining or thinking your sound darker or lighter, and the correct adjustments are likely to take place automatically. When you want a lighter sound, simply think light and airy and maybe high, if it helps you. When you want a darker sound, think dark and boomy and maybe low, if it helps you.

Does anything automatically happen in your vocal tract? Do you feel a natural urge to change settings? When you can not only hear the sound change but you also feel either lighter or darker, then you know that you're really getting somewhere.

Try to record yourself as you try out different sound qualities and ways of talking. If you are not used to hearing yourself played back, you will probably sound different than you expect. This is natural.

Working with Sound Colors

You can change the shape of the vocal tract by changing:
- The shape of the epiglottis funnel (twanged or not twanged)
- The position of the larynx (raised, lowered, or floating [neutral])
- The shape of the tongue (flat, arched, or twanged)
- The shape of the mouth (round, oval, or triangular [smiley])
- The position of the soft palate (raised, neutral, or lowered)
- The opening or closing of the nasal passages

Remember, as I explained in chapter 6 in the section about "Projecting Your Voice," if you are trying to reach a note at the edge of your range, either top or bottom, you need to think the opposite way when you are focusing your tone—as opposed to when you are attempting to color your sound. When coloring light, for instance, you think light, which may feel high. Do not confuse it with focusing your tone and your pitch—these are two different things! Changing your sound color and changing your pitch are *not* the same.

There are limitations though to how much you can change the color away from its natural habitat, which *is* associated with pitch. A very low-pitched tone cannot have a very light color and vice versa because dark to medium dark qualities are naturally features of the lower resonators (throat and chest cavities), and light qualities are naturally features of the upper resonators (head cavities). You can only color the sound quality to a certain extent.

Also, each mode has its distinct basic sound qualities. You can add to them by coloring, but again, you cannot change your setting so much in order to change color that the setting is no longer the right one for the mode.

For instance, if you are Belting out on a high pitch and you want a darker, warmer sound, you cannot just apply the Neutral classical setting (jaw hanging loose, tongue lying flat, pressed down as opposed to twanged), as in that case you would simply be changing your mode, not the color of your Belt.

Now, in principle, there would be nothing wrong with changing the mode, but if a strong, loud Belted sound is what you want, then Neutral is not the answer.

Are you beginning to understand the difference between modes, natural resonance, and sound coloring?

If not, don't despair. It really is a lot simpler than it sounds. Maybe the final piece of the puzzle will help put things into perspective for you. Let me explain to you a little bit more about the voice registers.

VOICE REGISTERS

I've mentioned the terms *head voice* and *chest voice* a couple of times.

These terms refer to voice *registers*. The difference between resonance and register is that resonance can be mixed and altered by adding color, as you've just learned. *Register* is simply a term used to specify a certain tonal area within the vocal range (on the musical scale). It does not, as commonly believed (old school), refer to a particular vocal mode or a certain sound—nor does it necessarily have to cause a substantial change of sound or even a voice break. (See chapter 15, "Frequently Asked Questions: Sudden Voice Breaks.")

For any voice professional, it is convenient to know about the registers and their positions on the musical scale. It gives you a greater understanding of overall technique and can also help you when working on pitch problems.

Apart from that, it is not helpful to restrict your thinking and set up vocal boundaries by concentrating on registers. Rather, work with the idea of blending modes and qualities of resonance and colors to achieve the required sounds. Separating the voice into two, three, or sometimes more different boxes—breaking it up into parts and emphasizing the distinction of registers, as opposed to working with the idea of *one whole voice*—tends to confuse rather than enlighten. Moreover, focusing on registers instead of transitioning between modes is often what *causes* the experience of unwanted and uncontrolled breaks in the voice.

The voice is naturally whole, without breaks. I guess the confusion partly is in the names of the registers (head *voice* or chest *voice*) which do make it sound like they are two different voices. It would be much more appropriate, I think, to say head *register* and chest *register.*

However, the terms *head voice,* etc. are most often used instead of *head register*, so these are the terms we will use here as well.

Chest Voice (Register)

Some people prefer to use the term *full voice* rather than *chest voice.* This is misguiding because it can easily be mistaken (and often is) for the term *fully voicing,* which merely indicates a condensed tone without breathiness. *Full* as in *full voice* merely refers to the state of the vocal cords in this register.

Others refer to this voice as the *speaking voice,* probably because most people tend to speak mainly in this voice (register).

Where does this register sit on the musical scale?

- Female: Tone below c1 on the scale
- Male: Tone below c0

Resonance can be felt in the chest, hence the name.

Middle Voice (Register)

The middle voice (register) is the area of your range between the chest and head voice. It is often considered the difficult area where most people tend to experience a break. There is obviously no physical break in the voice; however, a break in the sound can be experienced because of insufficient support when transitioning form one register to another, like from chest to middle, and form middle to head voice.

Where does this register sit on the musical scale?

- Female: c1–c2
- Male: c0–c1

Resonance can be felt in the upper chest and throat (hence, some coaches refer to this as the upper chest voice or the throat register).

Head Voice (Register)

The male head voice is also referred to as *falsetto*.

Where does this register sit on the musical scale?

- Female: c2–3
- Male: above c1

Resonance can be felt in your head (in the mask), like a pinging or a slight pressure.

Whistle Voice (Whistle or Flute Register)

The male whistle voice (flute register) is also called *falsetto*.

Where does this register sit on the musical scale?

- Female: above c3
- Male: above c2

Resonance can be but may not be felt in the head.

A voice operating in this range has a very high and either very airy or very sharp flute-like sound.

This register can be compared to the flageolet tones on a string instrument. Not everybody has the natural capacity to use this voice (register). As a speaker, you'd probably get barred for using it; it might get you some serious attention though.

Lower Register

The lower register lies beneath the chest register and is very rarely used. In fact, it is rare to have access to it. In some cultures this register is considered very precious and is cultivated when discovered. The male voice in this register sounds similar to the Australian Didgeridoo. Some women can have use of this register as well.

That was a lot of information, I know. But you should, by now, have a pretty good idea about how your voice works and how you can make it work even better for you.

Of course, you have to play around with it all to really get the hang of it. When you do, you will soon discover what feels right and what doesn't. Normally when you speak, you mainly use your chest and throat resonances and perhaps your head resonance if you are very dynamic.

You'll have plenty of opportunity to practice what you have learned so far in chapter 11, "Basic Voice Exercises."

CHAPTER 9

Verbal Inflections and Other Voice Facts and Tools

Remember earlier, in Part 1, when I was talking about the verbal inflections, the voice dynamics that we use to enhance our performance and strengthen our message when we speak? It's time to take a closer look at the tools we use to achieve those inflections. (Note: both the dynamics and the tools are often referred to as verbal inflections.)

In this chapter we will look at what I like to refer to as the tools. If your body is the engine, the Basics are the cornerstones or the building blocks, and the tools are the little bits that are chiseling away, helping to knock it all into shape to create the perfect powerhouse! There's only one thing missing after this—the ultimate power tool. Wonder what that might be? Read on and you'll soon find out.

The tools help us build a strong vocal impression. They add the extra spice and sparkle that take us to the next level. They will transform an average-to-good speaker into a brilliant force of nature!

Your toolbox contains the following tools, each with its own little manual:

- Voice Quality
- Pitch
- Volume
- Rate
- Pauses
- Articulation, Pronunciation, and Accent
- Vowels
- Placement
- The Pathway
- Voice Categories and Range
- Special Effects

VOICE QUALITY

Your voice quality is not set in stone.

Your voice has a natural base sound that is neither good nor bad—it just *is*. If anyone ever told you differently—said that your voice was "bad"—they were wrong. We all have different voices determined by our physical build. If you haven't already, learn to appreciate and love the sound of your own natural voice because it is going to be with you for a very long time.

Over time you may have developed constrictions which affect your voice quality. This can be solved by unlearning bad habits and using the right technique. Also, as you become more and more comfortable speaking, some tension will automatically start to ease off, which will make a difference on its own.

As a speaker, you want your voice to sound pleasant and friendly. You want to sound natural and confident and to exude vitality and strength. You also want to speak in a way that reflects your true personality.

So how do you do that?

As I said earlier, first of all be *you*. Be *inspired* by other speakers, but don't try to *be* them—*speak in your own voice*. This will automatically affect the way that your voice quality is perceived. I've said this before and I'll say it again and again: your voice is affected by your personality and your state of mind. You are expressing *your* opinions, *your* knowledge, and *your* emotions—do it in *your* voice. Be authentic and genuine, and people will appreciate, trust, and respect you even if they happen to disagree with your message.

You can then use the tools and techniques that you learn in this program to *enhance* your performance. Following are some tips on how to do that.

Tips for Working with Voice Quality

Record yourself speaking and *force* yourself to listen to it. (Most people *hate* this!) Do it anyway—even if you hate it. See, it is good for three reasons:

First, the more you do it, the more you get used to the sound of your own voice (and yes, you *do* sound like that).

Second, you can pick out the things that continue to bother you, decide what you would like to do differently, and work on them using recordings as reference points.

Third, you are able to hear if there are any telltale signs of tension such as sounding very breathy, very harsh, overly hoarse, very nasal, or shrill.

Also, notice how you *feel* in your throat when listening to your recorded voice. Do you have a reaction? If you *feel* physically tense when listening, it could indicate that you *are* physically tense when you speak. (I always know when someone has a problem because I immediately *feel* it physically when listening to them.)

But try to be objective here. Don't mistake not *liking* the sound of your own voice for something being wrong with it.

PITCH

The pitch of a tone describes where it is on the musical scale—how high or how low.

Aim to speak naturally in the range that suits your voice best (where your speaking voice naturally sits, defined by voice category). From there you can vary your pitch, moving it up and down as you speak. This will add dynamics, convey emotion, and make your speech more interesting and exciting to listen to, whereas speaking in a monotonous, droning voice will hypnotize people to fall asleep—probably not what you're after!

Generally, a high pitch conveys excitement and enthusiasm—or perhaps frustration. Low pitch indicates calmness, seriousness, thoughtfulness—or perhaps sadness.

Again, follow your emotion and adapt your pitch to the material you are presenting, but do not force your voice to work with a certain pitch that doesn't come naturally. This will only sound, well, unnatural.

Maybe you are not yet sure where your natural range actually is. Some people (mostly women) have a tendency to lift their pitch too high and constantly speak in their head voice (register), perhaps thinking that this is their natural speaking voice and pitch. While it is not necessarily *unnatural* to speak in your head voice, it is normally preferable to speak mainly in your chest voice, which has a fuller and warmer sound. From a psychological standpoint, an unusually high pitch often indicates a subconscious need for distance from something or somebody. It *could* also indicate excitement or frustration.

Most people misjudge their own range simply because they've never really used their voice properly and to its full potential. It is not uncommon that when they finally do, they find that their voice sounds different (clearer, stronger, and less breathy) and their pitch "changes" slightly. This is a good sign. Obviously, their natural pitch hasn't *really* changed—the way they use their voice has.

Some people feel that that a high-pitched voice is less desirable than a lower-pitched voice. They claim that a high-pitched voice lacks authority. While in some cases this may be true, in my opinion, most normal voices *in a relaxed state* have a naturally pleasant sound, and any voice can have as much authority as the next one regardless of pitch.

The key word here is *relaxed*. A very high, thin, harsh, or squeaky-sounding voice is most likely a *strained* voice, and a strained voice is always tedious to listen to regardless of the pitch. Listen to a very deep, unclear, and mumbling voice and tell me if that's any better.

If your pitch is working against you, find out *why*—look at the full picture.

Has your voice always sounded like that? Is this really your natural sound, or are you somehow straining? Do you actually *like* speaking in public? *Do you feel like <u>you</u> have and deserve the authority that your voice apparently lacks?*

People's overall perception of you is shaped by *you—all of you*—not by the pitch of your voice alone. I guess what I'm trying to say here is to dig a bit deeper. Find out what is causing your voice to be small, squeaky, or whatever.

Your sound is linked to your person—it is part of your personality. *If you have authority, so does your voice.*

A distressed, tedious-sounding voice is likely to reflect emotional stress—some condition or issue within you. If that is the case, you should be putting your energy toward resolving whatever issue is causing your voice to react. What does it *reflect?*

Making the best of you automatically means making the best of your voice.

We will look into this in more detail in part 4, "Persuasive Speaking through Inner Power."

Finally, a "pitch problem" can turn out to be something else entirely.

If your tone is being squashed in your throat and mouth by closing up and straining, you are making the room for resonance very small. This will make your *sound* very thin and small—and easily mistaken for a high pitch.

Ever done karaoke? Ever noticed how many songs suddenly seem to have a higher pitch and be more difficult to sing than you thought? Well, if the original singer's voice has a thick, warm sound or color, it will make the *pitch* sound darker than it is. You too can learn to color your sound, as we discussed in chapter 8. Let me make this very clear, and I apologize for repeating myself, but this is one of the major misunderstandings: Changing the pitch is *not* the same as changing the sound color. Coloring your tone will make your voice *sound* higher or lower pitched; but in reality, you've just added some bright or dark sound color to your voice, creating the *illusion* of a different "pitch." If you want to add warmth, depth, and a fuller resonance to your voice, work with color—do not focus so much on your base pitch.

As far as I'm concerned, all voices are initially good and have a potentially pleasing and not least *personal* sound. What you should be concerning yourself with is learning how to relax and how to use the voice—*your voice*—correctly. Cultivate a healthy, *natural* voice (in a healthy, natural *you*).

Once you know how to do this, your voice will automatically sound good, relaxed, and pleasing, no matter your pitch. And this is what you should aim for with your voice.

Take what has naturally been given to you and make the best of it.

Now I would like to tell you a story.

Years ago I had a student who was very emotionally troubled. She clearly had schizophrenic tendencies, and for months, I tried to persuade her to seek professional help. I urged her, pleaded with her, even offered to help her find the right therapist and accompany her there. I spent many extra hours talking to her and trying to guide her. But nothing seemed to work. In fact, things went from bad to worse. I was frustrated and blamed myself for being unable to help. As time went on, she pushed everybody away. Every day was different—we never knew which personality would walk through the door.

All the other teachers and students grew afraid of her. She was disrupting classes and terrorizing the entire college with her behavior. I was the only one she would at least talk to.

Determined to help, I failed to recognize that all I was doing was feeding an obsession. I had become her "guru," and her fate was in my hands. When finally I tried to stop it, all hell broke loose. She blamed me for all of her misfortune, called me all sorts of awful names, and even threatened to kill me. (Yet another interesting story for the memoirs . . .)

My point here is that every day she would come into the college and her voice would sound different, depending on which of her two personalities she would "be" that day. The sound of her voice and her pitch would change! She sounded like two different people.

When she was in her "good way," her voice would sound reasonably calm and had a warm, midrange sound. When, on the other hand, she was suffering, her voice sounded terrible! The pitch was very high, and there was no resonance to her voice at all. It sounded paper-thin and razor-sharp like it would cut through metal (and it wasn't because she was screaming and shouting—she was speaking "normally").

Part of the reason for this is that when you are distressed, your breathing is affected and sits in your chest like you are constantly short of breath. This locks the voice, giving the impression that the air passage is extremely restricted, almost like you are going to choke on your own breath. This raises the pitch in an unnatural way and thins out the voice, leaving no resonance whatsoever. This can also happen if you are extremely nervous. Again, strained person equals strained voice.

Anyway, after a while, my student was expelled from college and I never spoke to her again. But I heard her. A few years later, I was walking in a London subway station when all of a sudden I froze. . . . There was that razor-sharp voice again!

I instantly knew it was her. I also knew for certain that she was a lot worse off than when I had last seen her in college a few years earlier. The hairs on my neck stood up as I lowered my face and rushed by. For a second I found myself considering offering my help yet again, but I knew that I wouldn't accomplish anything. If I couldn't help her then, I certainly couldn't help her now. I simply had to let it go this time. The steely, cutting sound of her voice was telling me all I needed to know.

This story is just another example of how closely connected the voice is to the psyche and how important it is to look at both when working to improve our sound and our overall speaking and communication skills.

VOLUME

Volume is one of your most important dynamic tools.

Different rooms and settings require different output. More importantly, people's attention span is said to be very short and divided into sections. That means that if you are giving a long presentation, it is very likely that occasionally people will momentarily drift off even if they are very interested and engaged in what you have to say. A volume change is a great attention jolter!

Volume changes are necessary. If you stay on the same level during your entire speech, you will probably bore people to death.

If you are constantly *too loud,* it'll be annoying, and if your volume is *too low*, your audience will have to struggle to hear your words, and eventually they'll give up. You want a good balance between a loud and a soft but always audible volume.

Many speakers, especially women, struggle with volume. They have problems being loud enough. This is often rooted in fear and can be easily solved. Volume is controlled by breath control, voice projection, using the right mode—and courage.

We will practice volume control in chapter 11, "Basic Voice Exercises."

RATE

Rate simply refers to your speed—the number of words you speak per minute.

If you speak too fast and shoot off like a machine gun, your audience will not be able to keep up with you and will lose interest.

From a psychological standpoint, people tend to speak too fast either because they are nervous and overly keen to please—or because they are very self-important bordering on arrogant. Phew, I hear you say, that was a strong claim! Perhaps, but I believe it's true.

Very fast talkers tend to come across as *self-serving*. They seem to care less, even forget about the audience that they are there *to serve* and be more concerned with themselves and their motormouth presentation. This is off-putting. You and your message are never more important than your audience.

Without your audience, you wouldn't have an outlet for your message. Without you, however unique you are . . . well, the world is full of brilliant speakers who would be happy to take your place. I'm not trying to put anyone down here; I'm merely trying to make a point.

An audience likes *to be communicated* <u>with</u>, not *spoken* <u>at</u> as if they were back in second grade. So slow down a bit if you're on the fast side. Not too much though. Speak *too slowly*, and the audience will lose interest or fall asleep.

So . . . speak fast enough to keep their attention but slowly enough for them to digest your words and feel like an *exchange* is taking place. The most effective rate is said to be 125–160 words per minute on average. Vary your rate, though, as you go along to emphasize certain points or to explain detailed information.

PAUSES

Take time for pauses!

Pauses give you an opportunity to take a deep breath, clear your head, and refresh your focus. But not only that; pauses are also powerful speaking tools. A well-timed pause will add impact to your speech. Use pauses to emphasize main points and underline important statements.

A pause *before* a statement creates anticipation and screams attention. A statement *followed* by a pause will bring the point home and engage the audience, inviting their thought on the matter.

Generally people will pay as much or more attention to a pause as they will a sudden increase in volume. But if your pause is tooooooo long, people will begin to feel uncomfortable. Ah, the trials and tribulations of the speaker!

ARTICULATION, PRONUNCIATION, AND ACCENT

It goes without saying that as a speaker you should aim to be as articulate and speak as clearly as possible. If you have difficulties pronouncing certain words, try dividing the words into small bites and practice slowly till you get them right.

Nervousness can sometimes cause poor articulation and slurred, mumbling, too-fast, or otherwise unclear speech. Also, the expression "being tongue-tied" is literally not far from the truth. Tension of the tongue, jaw, and lips can cause articulation problems. Relax, slow down, and make sure that your Basics are working correctly—breath control, support, etc.

Use the lip, tongue, and jaw exercises in chapter 11 to relax as well as to improve articulation.

Practice any difficult words and phrases. If you continue to have difficulties, consider working with a speech therapist or a voice coach specializing in this area. Actors, for instance, work with coaches all the time to perfect a dialect or accent. It's really just a matter of training.

If you are speaking in a language other than your mother tongue, perhaps you need to train your ear as well. Listen to the language you wish to speak and get used to and copy the correct sounds. Practice till your speech is clear and easily understandable. Nobody expects you to sound like a native speaker in a foreign language—but they do expect to be able to understand what you're saying. Actually, if you ask me, I'd say that having a slight accent is not necessarily a bad thing. As long as you are well spoken and can make yourself perfectly understood, it can be quite a charming asset. But obviously, if your accent is so strong that it throws people off, then you need to get to work on it.

I am aware that some people might disagree with me on this one. There are those who claim that somebody with an accent might be taken less seriously, perhaps even be presumed to be less educated. While this might have been the case ten or fifteen years ago, I really believe that these days with the global market and the world opening up and the influx of multicultural societies, this presumption no longer holds true.

I have an accent myself, and I have certainly not run into any problems because of it for a very long time. If anything, people tend to find it interesting and an obvious opportunity for striking up a conversation. I even get compliments from people who find it appealing!

At this point I have lived abroad for so many years that I could easily speak without an accent should I choose to do so. But I don't. My accent represents part of me and where I come from—and I like that.

If you have something to say and you are able to express yourself clearly, people will hear you no matter your accent.

VOWELS

You can help change your voice color by changing the sound of your vowels. This basically means modifying your vowels slightly so that they get a lighter or darker feel. Notice, for instance, the difference when you say the vowel *a* in different ways. Just think English versus American accent: *tomahtoes, tomaytoes*. Now say the word *ant* (*ahnt, ant*)—again, a different *a* sound produced by an alteration of your vocal tract. Play around with vowels and see how they automatically alter the settings in your vocal tract.

Vowel modification also happens naturally as your pitch ascends or descends. If you work within a great range, your vowel sounds will need to change slightly as you move up or down the scale. This is not cheating but simply a natural process. If you fight against it—if you try to maintain exactly the same vowel sounds throughout your entire range—you will eventually run into trouble.

If you do not allow for the vowel modification to take place, you will basically prevent your vocal cords from working naturally and you will block the passageway and create strain.

When, for instance, your pitch ascends, the natural thing is for your cords to stretch out and thin the sound slightly. When you are working in the lower range, your cords retract, become shorter and fuller (resting position), and naturally maintain the fuller, warmer quality of the chest voice.

This is one reason why many speakers prefer to stay in the lower (chest) range. They simply find their sound to be warmer and more pleasant, perhaps also more authoritative. Another reason could be unfamiliarity and insecurity with the higher range and the added volume that can come with it.

If you ever find yourself having difficulties with a certain word, you can work with vowel modification to ease the problem. Simply pick a similar vowel sound from the examples in chapter 11, "Basic Voice Exercises," that fits the particular sound you need. Then pick a mode, depending on the volume you need. If the sound you need doesn't fit with the mode that you've chosen, find the sound that comes closest. For example, if you need to use the word *you* but you want to *shout* it very loud, as in "*you* can do it!" you would bend the *ou* sound toward *yow* (Overdrive). If you would want to *scream* it out loud, you would use Belting and bend it toward *yew* (*ui* as in screaming loudly at a concert: woo-eeeeh!)

Now you can use the appropriate exercise to solve the problem by transferring the vocal setting from the exercise to the word that is causing you problems. Gradually direct the sound even closer to what you need while keeping the right setting.

PLACEMENT

Placement is really a figure of speech. It is a term used to describe the imagined positioning of tones and tone qualities. It is, of course, not literal, as you cannot physically grab a tone or a tone quality and place it somewhere, but you can *think* it there and work with the *sensation* of it sitting in a particular place.

THE PATHWAY

Pathway is a term used by many to describe the journey or the route of the air from the cords to outside the mouth. I find it more helpful to extend the image by explaining it as the pathway along or through which the tone is carried from the cords up behind and around the inner pathway (the higher the tone, the further up and behind), twirled around in the mouth cavity (anchored), and then carried forward through the mouth and along the outer pathway all the way to its final destination—the focus point.

I find that working with this image of the traveling tone strengthens the idea of focus and normally helps achieve perfect, clear projection.

VOICE CATEGORIES AND RANGE

Category tells us about the nature of your voice and directs us to its natural habitat—that area of the range where the voice is most comfortable working and where it shines at its best. You may not be clear about what type of voice you have. Don't worry about that—your voice knows and in due time will reveal its true colors to you. As your voice is allowed to unfold naturally through proper and healthy practice, it will automatically unfold and find its rightful place. Besides, for a speaker, category is not important.

There is no one category that is better than another. Your voice is your voice; it's unique and beautiful in its own right, no matter what kind of voice it may be.

Range is technically defined by your category. A singer is expected to have a certain range within a certain category. However, for everybody else, range simply refers to the notes available as you travel from your lowest to your highest note. Everything in between, theoretically, is your range. Use a piano or a guitar to determine your range if you want to know.

These are the voice categories for the female voice: soprano, mezzo-soprano, alto, and the very high lyrical soprano. And for the male voice: tenor, baritone, bass, and the very high countertenor.

SPECIAL EFFECTS

Special effects can be added to the voice for extra dramatic effect. Singers, actors, comedians, and voiceover artists use special effects all the time to alter their sound, copy somebody else, or perhaps portray a certain type or character.

As a speaker you can use effects too—for instance, to make a humorous point. This is not at all harmful to the voice, as long as you do it right. It is possible, with the right technique, to create any sound you like without ever being in danger of compromising the condition of your voice. This used to be taboo, as did the use of the hard modes described above. Most respectable teachers once strongly opposed such blasphemy! "If you're going to continue to submit your voice to that kind of vile abuse, you're asking for it. Don't come running to me when your voice is wrecked and perhaps lost forever," said my singing teacher when I joined my first rock band! Well, as it happens, I did wreck my voice for a while, but only because back then I didn't know about the modes. I didn't recognize the difference between singing in church, singing classically, and belting out loud rock tunes. My teacher obviously couldn't help me—according to her, rock was harmful, full stop!

Well . . . not quite true. As I pointed out earlier, today we know much more about the voice and its many functions, and we have learned how to distinguish between healthily and unhealthily produced sound effects and hard sounds. The difference basically is that healthy effects are produced away from the vocal cords (i.e., in the vocal tract) and do not involve any wrongful contact or misuse of the vocal cords.

You can alter your sound by adding, for instance, hoarseness, growling, rattle, vocal breaks, creaks, breathiness, and distortion. You can even make loud screams.

Many rock singers, especially hard and heavy rock singers, use rough effects all the time. For someone like that to stay on top and stay in business, doing many tours and concerts over a long period of time, the importance of correct technique is second to none! They cannot survive without it, or at least, their voice can't. This is why hard rock singers, if they are any good, tend to have impeccable vocal technique. Your grandmother might not believe you if you tell her, but nevertheless it is a fact.

If you are interested in knowing more about special effects, go to www.CompleteVocalInstitute.com and purchase the book *Complete Vocal Technique* by Cathrine Sadolin. She also offers lessons online. When it comes to advanced voice training and technique, few are as qualified and absolutely phenomenal as Cathrine.

OK, so these are your most important tools to be aware of as a speaker. Combined with the right technique, you are set to be a speaking powerhouse!

I hope these last three chapters have left you more enlightened than confused. And I hope you are still keen to learn and not getting bored with all the technical stuff.

It is time for you to learn how to put all of this into practice.

CHAPTER 10

How to Practice

First of all, based on what you've learned so far, identify what your actual needs are and focus on the most important things first. Remember, though, that if your Basics don't work, nothing else will either in the long run.

Relate your practice to things that are immediately relevant, like a speech you have coming up or a speech that you have already given, so you can compare. If you have audio recordings or, better still, video recordings of some of your speeches/presentations, use these as references. If you haven't already done so, start out by recording something right now and then work with that for a while. Have fun with it and track your progress. It is important to track progress; otherwise you might not notice any changes. If you don't see yourself improving, you will lose interest in the practice. It's like a diet—if you don't see any results, then you're likely to give up.

Be aware of how you *feel* as well. Often you will *feel* a difference before you can actually hear or see it. Does part of you feel relaxed and comfortable now, whereas before you felt tense, tired, and uncomfortable? Also know that sometimes as you improve, your voice could get worse before it gets better, especially if it is currently in a poor state. You could feel all tickly and have an urge to cough and clear your throat more than usual. For advice on how to cope with this, refer to chapter 12, "The Voice Doctor."

Take your practice and your own progress seriously. Take the time and commit to doing it. Whether you commit to practicing five minutes a day or a week—or five hours—make those minutes or hours productive. Make them *your* time, your investment in *your* future. Do it properly. Doing half a job is worse than not doing any job at all because that is what you will be teaching your body—to do half a job.

If you practice while being all tensed up, that is what you will teach your body to do in the future. We do not want this; we want the exact opposite.

Remember, as a speaker, your voice is one of your biggest assets. It would be a shame not to get the absolute best out of it.

Choose exercises that suit your needs. Write them down (or copy from this book or go to www.SuzannRye.com and download an exercise sheet there).

Make your exercises visible and easy to follow without having to think about what to do next. Many people spend more time thinking about what to do next and how than they spend just doing it. Having an organized plan in front of you gets rid of this pitfall.

Ideally, you should *always* conclude your daily exercises by working on a speech of your choice. This is the most logical, productive, and encouraging way to implement the techniques that you are learning and have already learned. It puts everything into perspective, speeds up the learning process, and strengthens your relationship with and understanding of your voice. Again, record yourself and track your progress.

In chapter 19, "The Personalized DC Training Program," I will suggest a practice routine that will turbocharge your learning process.

PRACTICE UNDISTURBED

Explain to your family and other people around you what you're doing and ask that they respect your commitment. Ignore any silly comments that might come your way as your exercises progress in volume. Commenting is human nature, I'm afraid. To be fair, voice exercises can sound a bit strange. Don't be put off—just get used to it. Once you've come through the first few barriers that most people have about using voice volume, you'll be hooked. Allowing your voice to work freely is very liberating. For many, breaking through the sound barrier for the first time is almost like a revelation.

HOW WILL YOU KNOW IF YOU'RE ON THE RIGHT TRACK?

You should be able to feel the difference between right and wrong pretty soon. But as I said, if you are used to straining your voice, you might not notice so easily at first. In any case, it is a great help to actually be able to watch yourself in action—especially in the beginning. So use a mirror (preferably a full-size one) and add your focus point. It's great for working on body language too.

Once your technique is working reasonably well under these ideal conditions, start transferring what you've learned into real-life situations. On stage you will obviously want to perform in whatever way suits you and your style best, so there's no way you'll be standing there like a dead puppet in the grounding position all the time doing slow, deep breathing! (You will learn about the grounding position and practice more deep breathing in the next chapter.)

When you feel comfortable and reasonably secure in your technique, start playing around. Try walking, sitting, moving fast, moving slowly, etc. Work on different expressions. Add drama and dynamics to your words. Pay attention to both technique and performance. Soon you will find yourself being much more confident. You will relax more while at the same time naturally adding more life and sparkle to your speeches.

HOW MUCH WILL YOU NEED TO PRACTICE?

If all you need is a bit of adjusting, then a one-time overhaul with regular follow-ups or checkups may be enough to put your voice straight.

If, however, like most people, you have restricted your voice for years and you are accustomed to using wrong or insufficient technique, you need to de-learn to re-learn—get rid of bad habits and gradually build up your new, healthy ones. You will need to recondition yourself so that you can go back to using your voice naturally without constrictions. In any case, you can benefit from the tools in chapter 6.

Depending on the urgency of your needs, I'd say go through your choice of basic exercises every other day or at least once a week. The more you do it, the better the results. But even just ten to fifteen minutes two or three times a week will do wonders. Ten minutes done properly and with enthusiasm is better than hours done half-heartedly.

REMEMBER TO HAVE A POINT OF FOCUS

Focus on a point in front of you, extending from the tip of your nose (see chapter 6, "The Basics: Projecting your Voice"). Perhaps draw a circle on your mirror and use that as your focus point; that way you can keep an eye on any tension as well. Again, if you are very used to being tense, you might not even feel it or recognize it as tension; in that case, it helps to be able to actually see it.

Choose a point between four and seven feet away from you. If you need to shout very loudly, extend the distance between you and your focus point.

A quick tip: no matter where you are, you can always find a focus point. Say you are backstage just about to go on and you want to make sure that your voice is clear and ready. Look for a spot on the wall. Failing that, you can always use the finger trick: simply make a circle using your first and second fingers, stretch your arm out in front of you, and focus your voice through the circle.

PRACTICE—GOLDEN RULES

Always make sure that you are *completely comfortable and relaxed, with no straining or tightening—no tension anywhere!*

Keep your grounding position/correct posture—no collapsing, no Hunchback imitations.

Keep your chest and shoulders down—no lifting up.

Keep your knees subtly and slightly bent—no locking, which will restrict the flow of energy and disrupt your sense of grounding.

If you find yourself stretching your neck, throat, and jaw upward and forward, you might subconsciously be trying to reach for the tone. *Stop!* Dynamic speaking is great, but this is not the way. Go over your Basics once again.

Your tongue can be a major culprit. The back of your tongue is directly connected to the muscles around your larynx. If your tongue is tense, so is your voice. As a general rule, your tongue should rest comfortably on the bottom of your mouth, with the tip just behind your lower front teeth. Sometimes you need to bend your tongue up or down in a bow to change sound/mode (we will go through that later), but always aim to keep the tip of the tongue just behind your lower front teeth.

Don't pull your tongue back in your throat, as this will block and strain your voice (and make you sound like Kermit the Frog).

Keep your jaw loose and relaxed.

Allow your jaw to drop naturally. If you are using any of the hard modes, follow the instructions on jaw and tongue placement in chapter 7. Do not tighten the joints or the area underneath and between your jawbones. If you find yourself doing this, *stop!* Relax and start again.

Make sure to relax your lips and to *open your mouth properly* when you speak! This may sound fairly logical, but you'd be surprised how many people have a habit of subconsciously holding back by restricting the natural opening of their mouth. This doesn't work. "You cannot sing (or speak) with your mouth closed," I once famously said in a singing class at college. My students were rolling over laughing so hard! They were like, "Really?! Doh!" Well, I said it because half the class in fact did *not* open their mouths properly, and it was causing them problems. You cannot speak or express yourself properly if you try to hold back at the same time. Not only does it affect your output, but it also makes you appear strict and unapproachable.

Allow your mouth to open properly. Don't force it wide open in a contrived kind of way (which will strain as well)—just open your mouth naturally so the sound can flow.

Make sure to *relax your lips.* Because they are nervous or perhaps in an effort to look serious, many people tighten their lips when they speak. When you tighten your lips, you automatically tighten your jaw and the soft area underneath your jaw. This will affect your voice. Relax your lips and allow them to move naturally when you speak. Besides being healthier for your voice, it makes you sound better and brings life to your face and your personality.

In the next chapter, I will give you very thorough instructions on how to relax all your face muscles and your voice properly. The exercises are all meticulously explained and easy to follow.

TELLTALE SIGNS OF TENSION
How can you identify tension? These are some sure signs:

- Larynx pulled up in a choking position (can feel like you have a tightening string around your neck)
- Eminently visible veins and muscles on neck and throat
- Feeling choky, with an irritated throat, needing to cough, constantly needing to clear throat (and not because you have just steamed or are using your voice for the first time after a long rest), frogs in the throat (see chapter 12, "The Voice Doctor")
- Soft area under jaw tight and perhaps slightly protruded like a double chin
- Overly red face
- Basically *any* discomfort or straining feeling

You might also feel dizzy. Dizziness can be caused by strain and tightness of neck, throat, and/or jaw and the area under the jaw or by locked support that blocks the air and energy flow. *But dizziness can also be caused by the unfamiliar use of deep breathing and of unfamiliar mask resonance and pinging in the head* (see chapters 5 and 6). So we cannot automatically assume that dizziness indicates strain.

LAST REMINDER—PREPARING FOR EXERCISES
Practicing the wrong way is worse than not practicing at all.

Make sure that you are relaxed and loose. No tension! If you practice while being all tensed up, that is what you will teach your body to do in the future.

- Loosen your body. Ground yourself. Stand with feet slightly apart, well weighted on both feet. Straighten your back.
- Lower and relax your chest and shoulders.
- Hold your head up.
- Relax your jaw and your tongue.
- Breathe deeply.
- Have a point of focus.

OK—now you know *how* to do it. Let's get into *what* to do! Next up: Basic Voice Exercises. Have fun!

CHAPTER 11

Basic Voice Exercises

Use these exercises to practice the things you've learned, train your voice, and get amazing results fast.

Please don't be put off by the number of exercises. You don't need to do all the exercises every time you practice. They are there to guide you and to give you a choice. You will soon find your favorite exercises and discover what works for you, and you will soon develop a sense of what is right and what is wrong technically. Once you know how, it is easy to feel the difference.

As a rule, go with your feeling. If it feels good, easy, comfortable, and right, chances are that it is. If it doesn't—go back and find out *why*. What are you doing wrong?

However, *always* start your voice training with relaxation and breathing exercises.

Deep breathing clears your mind and calms you. It sends oxygen to your brain and revitalizes your body and gets it going. It prepares your voice.

You speak on breath. Breath is the fuel that powers your voice. No matter what else you do, make sure to do deep breathing exercises every day, and you'll soon notice a difference.

Again, if an exercise feels uncomfortable, it probably is wrong, so stop and start again. When it feels good and comfortable, you are doing it right. Always hold on to that feeling because it is the feeling that is ultimately going to alert you when it is right and when it is not. *Repeat the good feelings as often as possible to condition your voice, your body, and your brain to* <u>automatically</u> *do it right.*

Note: I have made an effort to explain everything very thoroughly to you. In so doing, it is possible that I have made you feel that it is all very complicated and that you have to think about a thousand things just to be able to speak well! If that's the case, I apologize. Please know that technique is merely a tool. It is there to *help* you and to give you choices. The settings are there for you to know, to be aware of, and to make things *easier* for you. They are not there to confuse you.

Using your voice correctly is not rocket science! It is just that often, due to a variety of reasons that we've discussed, the voice is being compromised *and needs a little extra TLC.* It needs reconditioning. But first do what comes naturally to you. If that works, congratulations—you're a natural! You've managed to work freely without restricting your voice function at all.

If it doesn't work, you'll know that at some point something has interfered with your natural voice function and taught your voice and other parts of your body to restrict themselves. In that case, it's time to reapply the Basics and make use of the settings/functions/modes to set your voice free again and optimize its use.

RELAXATION AND PREPARATION EXERCISES

Exercise 1: Loosen Your Body
Move around—do a few jumps, stretches, shakes, and neck rolls. If you are into yoga or prefer any additional relaxation methods, feel free to use those.

Exercise 2: Grounding Position
Good posture is very important for your voice to work well. For air to flow freely through your lungs and vocal cords, you must remain unblocked. Bad posture, slouching, hunched shoulders, head held down, etc. will block the energy and reduce the flow of air.

- Ground yourself. Stand straight, feet slightly apart, well weighted on both feet, knees slightly bent.
- Straighten your back, but don't curve it. To avoid curving, pull in your bum slightly (as opposed to sticking it out).
- Lower and relax your chest and shoulders, holding shoulders slightly back.
- Now, hold your head up straight as if someone were pulling at the top of your head with a tiny string—but *do not stretch* or bend your neck!

This is the grounding position. Feel how it adds power to your body. At least in the beginning when you start training your voice, you should always assume the grounding position and use a focus point as described, as it gives you the best base to work from and makes it a lot easier to discover if you're doing something wrong. Moreover, it will make you feel strong, and you will have the ultimate opening of your channel. Your energy, your breathing, and your sound can move freely within you.

Exercise 3: Face and Throat Massage

- Place your three middle fingers just underneath your cheekbones and start massaging your chin and face.
- Gradually move downward to your throat.
- Place your hands on your throat and knead your throat muscles ever so lightly for about 30 seconds to a minute.

Exercise 4: Yawn and Wiggle

- Yawn. On closing your mouth, wiggle your jaw and churn your entire face. Suck your cheeks in and let go.
- Imagine that your face is an elastic rubber mask.
- Repeat twice.

Exercise 5: Hum

- On a comfortable tone (in a comfortable range), hum very quietly like this: *Hmmmmmm.*

- If you can, try to slide up and down a few tones, still on *hmmmmmmm.*
- Repeat at least 10 times.

Exercise 6: Relaxing Your Lips

Relax your lips and open your mouth properly when you speak. Many people tighten their lips when they speak. When you tighten your lips, you automatically tighten your jaw and the soft area underneath your jaw. This will affect your voice. Relax your lips and allow them to move naturally when you speak. Besides being healthier for your voice, it makes you sound better and brings life to your face and your personality.

- Pucker your lips as tightly as you can, hold for a few seconds—then widen them as much as you can. Do this 5–10 times. Repeat, only this time, do it rapidly.
- Now, repeat the following syllables first slowly, then gradually increase your speed. Exaggerate your lip movements, following your lips' natural urge so you can really feel the difference between each syllable.
  1. *Po-po-po-po-po-po-pooooh* . . . (*po* as in p<u>o</u>le)
  2. *Pe-pe-pe-pe-pe-pe-peeeeh* . . . (*e* as in w<u>e</u>)
  3. *Be-be-be-be-be-be-beeeeh* . . . (*e* as in b<u>ee</u>)
  4. *Bo-bo-bo-bo-bo-bo-booooh* . . . (*o* as in "show")
  5. *Blee-blee-blee-blee-blee-blee-bleeeeh* . . . (as in "bl<u>ee</u>p")
  6. *Flee-fee-flee-flee-flee-flee-fleeeeh* . . . (as in "flee")
  7. *Wa-wa-wa-wa-wa-wa-waaaah* . . . (as in "w<u>a</u>ll" then as in "w<u>ah</u> w<u>ah</u> pedal")
  8. *Wai-wai-wai-wai-wai-waihhh* . . . (as in "w<u>ai</u>t")
  9. *Mla-mla-mla-mla-mla-mla-mlaaaaaaah* . . . (as in the name "Miller" spoken really fast)
  10. *Mi-mi-mi-mi-miiiih* . . . (as in "T<u>i</u>na")
  11. *Muh-muh-muh-muh-muuuuuuh* . . . (as in . . . well, "m<u>uh</u>"!)

Exercise 7: Relaxing Your Tongue

Many people have a habit of pulling their tongue or the root of their tongue backward as they speak. This blocks and strains the voice.

- Stick your tongue out and *down*ward, stretching it all the way as far as you can. Hold for 5 seconds.
- Pull it back in and wiggle it around in your mouth. Open and close your mouth and wiggle or churn your face around.
- Repeat 2–3 times.
- Stick your tongue out and upward, stretching it all the way as far as you can.
- Hold for 5 seconds.
- Pull it back in and wiggle it around in your mouth. Open and close your mouth and wiggle or churn your face around.
- Repeat 2–3 times.

Exercise 8: Relaxing Your Jaw

Keep your jaw loose and relaxed.

Allow it to drop naturally when opening your mouth to speak. Do not tighten the joints or the area underneath and between your jawbones. If you find yourself doing this, stop! Relax and start again, making *sure* that the soft area underneath your jaw is relaxed.

Do not protrude your neck and jaw!

- Wiggle your jaw from side to side and up and down.
- Say the following syllables, exaggerating your jaw movements:
  1. *Mah-mah-mah-mah-mah-mah-maaaaaah* . . .
  2. *Fah-fah-fah-fah-fah-fah-faaaaaah* . . .
  3. *Wah-wah-wah-wah-wah-wah-waaaaaah* . . .
  4. *Pah-pah-pah-pah-pah-pah-paaaaaah* . . .
  5. *Bah-bah-bah-bah-bah-bah-baaaaaah* . . .
  6. *Bee-bee-bee-bee-bee-bee-beeeeeeh* . . .
  7. *Kee-poh-kee-poh-kee-poh-keeeeeeh* . . .

- Say the following sounds. Exaggerate your jaw movement and prolong the vowels every time.
  1. *Wah-ah-ah-ah-ah-ah-aaaah* . . .
  2. *Why-y-y-y-y-y-yyyyh* . . .
  3. *Wee-ee-ee-ee-ee-ee-eeeeh* . . .

- Say the following, exaggerating tongue and jaw movement:
  1. *Dah-dah-dah-dah-dah-dah-daaaah* . . .
  2. *Jah-jah-jah-jah-jah-jah-jaaaah* . . .
  3. *Lah-lah-lah-lah-lah-lah-laaaah* . . .
  4. *Thah-thah-thah-thah-thah-thah-thaaaah* . . .
  5. *Sah-sah-sah-sah-sah-sah-saaaah* . . .
  6. *Kwah-kwah-kwah-kwah-kwah-kwah-kwaaaah* . . .
  7. *Gah-gah-gah-gah-gah-gah-gaaaah* . . .
  8. *Kah-kah-kah-kah-kah-kah-kaaaah* . . .
  9. *Nah-nah-nah-nah-nah-nah-naaaah* . . .

- Now, still completely relaxed, tongue resting in the bottom of your mouth, say the following syllables. Again exaggerate. Allow for natural movement; follow the natural urges of your tongue. Notice what happens. You should feel your tongue naturally pressing down (tip forward pressing against lower front teeth) for clearer articulation and then returning to its relaxed position afterward:
  1. *Sah-say-see-so-soo*
  2. *Zah-zay-zee-zo-zoo*
  3. *Kah-kay-kee-ko-koo*
  4. *Gah-gay-gee-go-goo*

BREATH CONTROL EXERCISES

<u>Exercise 9: Deep Breathing</u>

If you are still not sure that you are breathing properly, go back and read chapter 6, "The Basics: Breathing," again.

Rule number one is not to lift your chest and shoulders when you breathe in, as this indicates shallow breathing. You want proper, deep breathing filling your lungs all the way down.

- Stand in grounding position. Relax your body. If you like, join your thumb and your middle finger (long, third finger) and press them lightly together. This will help your deep breathing.

114

- Breathe in slowly, preferably through your nose, or if you must, use your mouth or a mix of nose and mouth.
- Feel how your lungs are filling all the way down. When you are full, your body will tell you—you will automatically feel the urge to exhale.
- Exhale naturally through your mouth, pressing your lips ever so slightly together, not closing your mouth completely.
- Repeat.

How many times you repeat each exercise is, of course, up to you. I would advise you to do the breathing exercise at least 5–10 times per day to really get the hang of it.

Besides, it's really good for you. The extra flow of oxygen does wonders for your system. Not only your voice but also your brain, your entire body, and your emotional state benefit from deep breathing.

As you inhale, you should expand. Your stomach (particularly lower abdomen) should move outward, and you should feel an expansion of your lower back and ribs.

Feel your breath all the way down and all the way around your body— not just in front but around the sides and your back as well. (If in doubt, see chapter 6, "The Basics: Supporting Your Voice.")

As you exhale, do not slouch! Keep your posture straight and try to keep your ribcage expanded as opposed to sinking in and down.

Exercise 10: Hungry Lungs

- Exhale all air from your lungs. Simply push out till you feel like there is absolutely no air left—then give it a last squeeze!
- Hold for a few seconds.
- Let go. Notice how your lungs crave the air and therefore air will automatically rush in, producing a natural deep breath. Notice also how satisfying a deep filling of breath like this feels. This is candy for your body and for your brain.
- Repeat.

Exercise 11: Bend and Exhale

- Stand in grounding position.
- Bend over forward with your body as if to touch your toes. This will expel your air.
- Hang limply. Remain like this for 30 seconds.
- Straighten up, breathing in as you go.
- Repeat.

Exercise 12: Hissing Snake with Slow Release

One of my students once dubbed this group of exercises "Hisssssssing Snakes."

It comes in many variations divided into two categories: one uses the h*ssss* sound, the other the t*ssss* sound. They all work to improve breath control and support and to expand lung capacity.

Depending on which sound you use, you will sense the pressure points of your support move slightly as well as the amount of pressure you experience.

Illustration 9 -

Hissing Snake Clerk

Hssss . . .

- Stand in grounding position.
- Take a deep breath (as described in the previous exercise), filling your lungs all the way down. Allow your abdomen to expand.
- Again, be careful not to lift your chest or shoulders. Keep the same posture as before as you allow your lungs and your diaphragm to work.
- Now, slowly exhale on the sound h*ssss*. This feels like you're breathing out through your teeth, almost using your teeth as a filter.
- You should have a sensation of your breath coming from your lower abdomen.
- Keep gently pushing or lifting your air out till you feel that there is no more.
- Hold for a second.
- Then, in one go, *completely* let go. You should *immediately* feel the same expansion as you did before when you took a real deep breath—only stronger! This is a proper natural deep breath.
- Repeat—only this time continue the exercise again and again, each time using the natural deep breath for the next round of *hssss*. You will soon realize that your lungs have far greater capacity than you thought.
- Repeat 10 times without a break so you get a feel for a natural circle of deep breathing. It may feel extreme to you, and you may get a bit dizzy. If you do, take a break. It is not an unusual reaction.

Tssss . . .

- Take a deep breath, filling your lungs all the way down.
- Allow your abdomen to expand.
- Do not lift your chest or shoulders. Keep the same posture as before as you allow your lungs and your diaphragm to work.
- Now slowly exhale, this time using the sound t*ssss*.

You will notice that this sound feels more aggressive, more pressurized than the previous one. This is because it is a closed sound as opposed to an open one. *H* is open; *T* is closed.

Say the two sounds and feel the difference. When you push your air upward and out on the sound t̠ssss, depending on how hard you push, you might feel pressure in your head, almost as if your head is a balloon being pumped with air. You should also notice that the air is more concentrated on the hard palate, the front roof of your mouth, as opposed to filling your mouth and spreading out like hsss does. This time your front-teeth filter is more closed than before. It feels like the sound seeps out from between your upper front teeth. With this sound, it feels like more power is concentrated on the higher abdomen and on the lower back and sides in particular. To check that your support is working properly, stand with your hands on your waist, your thumbs pressing slightly backward. Feel your waist and back muscles working, moving in and out in a strong movement. If you don't feel any movement, you are not supporting properly.

- Again take a deep breath, filling your lungs all the way as far down as you can. Allow your abdomen to expand.
- Keep gently pushing or lifting your air out till you feel that there is no more.
- Then in one go, *completely* let go; you should immediately feel the same expansion as you did before when you did the *hsss* exercise—only stronger! This is a real lung-power booster!
- Now, repeat—only this time continue the exercise again and again, each time using the natural deep breath for the next round of t̠ssss. Again, feel how your lungs have enormous capacity.
- Repeat 10 times without a break, continuing the exercise again and again, each time using the natural deep breath for the next breathing out on t̠ssss. Your lung capacity now feels even greater than before. Exercising on *tsss* is even more powerful than on *hsss*.

Again, if you are not used to deep breathing, it may feel extreme to you at first, and you may get a bit dizzy. If you do, take a break. It is not an unusual reaction.

Exercise 13: Hissing Snake with Fast Release—Pumping the Bike

- *Without* breathing in first, say t̲sssssssss . . .
- Then let go (release your support) and immediately allow a natural breath in; this time it *must* be through your nose.
- Keep breathing in through your nose and push out on *tssss* in a steady rhythm like you are pumping a bike.
- Start slow, say 3 seconds in, 3 seconds out—then gradually increase the tempo till you go as fast as you can, approximately 2 rounds (one in, one out) per second/5 rounds per 10 seconds.

Exercise 14: Hissing Snake on 4 with Sips and Counted Release

- Breathe in through your mouth in small sips, counting to 4 in your head.
- Exhale on h̲ssss, counting to 4 as well: *hssss, hssss, hssss, hssss.*
- Repeat, only this time continue the exercise again and again, each time using the natural deep breath for next the round of *hssss, hssss, hssss, hssss.*
- Take a short break when necessary. Then repeat the exercise. Continue till it feels easy.
- Then add two more repetitions (6 x *hssss*).
- Continue adding till you can comfortably handle a count of 12.
- Repeat the exercise, this time on t̲ssss.
- Repeat both exercises, this time *inhaling through your nose.*

Exercise 15: Hissing Snake on One Breath with Counted Release

- Take a deep breath (as before).
- Now, *without* breathing in between, push the air out in short bursts of t̲ssss.
- Start with 10 bursts. On the 11th burst, push out the last remaining air, emptying your lungs completely, *tssssssssssssssssssssss* . . . as if you were leaking.
- Then release your support and allow a natural deep breath in as in exercise 10, Hungry Lungs.
- Repeat. Play with the tempo—slower, faster, etc.

- Now, add 10 more bursts and after that gradually add 10 more, then 10 more, etc., till you reach 50 bursts in one go with no breath in between.
- Repeat.

Remember—the more you work with your breathing and support, the better and faster the results.

Also, always remember to keep your posture. Do not slouch or collapse when running out of air. Keep yourself in a strong posture, and you'll find that you have more power than you thought.

Exercise 16: The Panting Dog

- Open your mouth like in a surprised look.
- Breathe in through your mouth on *haaaah*.
- Exhale on *haaaah* (without sound, other than the natural sound of the breath).
- Again breathe in through your mouth, counting 4 seconds, and breathe out counting 4 seconds.
- Repeat the exercise again and again in a regular rhythm like heavy breathing: *haaaah* in—*haaaahhh* out.
- Gradually change the tempo till it is real fast—counting approximately half a second each way. You now find yourself panting like a dog, breathing very fast in and out: *hah* (in)—*hah* (out), *hah* (in)—*hah* (out).

Exercise 17: The Running Car

This exercise is known to cause some difficulty, particularly in the beginning. It simply is not possible to conduct it without the proper support—which is why it's so great! I should add that occasionally some people find it hard to do it even with the right support.

- Breathe naturally through your nose; make no effort to consciously take a breath.
- Purse your lips, then gently and slowly push out using the sound *brrrrr*—sort of like a running car engine.
- Continue till you run out of fuel.
- Repeat 5 times.

Exercise 18: The Stalling Car

- Now without breathing in between, push the air out in short bursts of *brr, brr, brr* . . .
- Start with 5 bursts, using the last burst to empty your lungs completely. When you've finished your last round, release support and allow your lungs to naturally take in all the air they need to continue on the next round.
- Gradually add 5 more till you reach a total of 20 bursts in one go with no breath in between.

Later we will add sound to this exercise and combine it with the slide.

In the beginning when you do these breathing and support exercises, you might feel slightly dizzy or lightheaded. That's OK—just take a short break and then continue when you feel normal again. Generally breathing exercises will leave you feeling great, refreshed, and empowered—and they really help your voice and your overall performance ability.

There are, of course, numerous different exercises available, but I find these to be the simplest ones. They really are efficient and cover all the basic areas.

VOICED EXERCISES: HUMMING

Exercise 19: Humming

In a very easy and relaxed manner, hum on the following sounds:

- *Hmmmm* . . . (mouth closed)
- *Ngggg* . . . (mouth open)
- *Ngggaaa* . . . (mouth open, sound lifted upward and forward into the nose)

Feel how the resonance moves slightly.

Now slide the sound resonance backward and forward between the roof of your mouth behind your upper front teeth and your nose and forehead like an ambulance siren.

It should feel completely comfortable and relaxed, with no tension. The sound should be big inside your head and small outside (output).

Humming is very good for your voice. It works like a massage. If you have any mucus, the humming will gently rattle it loose and clear your vocal cords. It is always good to include in a warm-up. It's a safe and comfortable exercise for the voice.

VOICED EXERCISES: INITIATION

You have already learned about the terms *initiation or attack.* They are used to describe exactly that—the attack or initiation of a tone.

How you initiate your tone will have a great effect on how it continues and ends. If, for instance, you forget to support your voice during initiation of a tone, you will run out of air too fast, and your tone/sound, especially the end of your phrase/sentence, is likely to fizzle out with no impact whatsoever. You will simply lose volume and control.

Singers are taught to perfect their initiation in order to always have the perfect tight tone. But that's not all. Voice problems can arise from not supporting and initiating right. Loose (un-tight) initiation and following loose (un-tight) projection will tire your voice and in the long run lead to damage.

Following are some exercises to show you how to support, initiate, and close or *condense* your sound/tone and avoid any fizzling out of excess air.

Exercise 20: Initiate Directly on Vowel

- Take a medium breath.
- Initiate each sound separately, starting with low volume and then gradually increasing the volume for as long as it feels comfortable.
  1. *Aaahh . . .*
  2. *Eeehh . . .*
  3. *Iiihh . . .*
  4. *Ooohh . . .*
  5. *Yyyhh . . . .*
  6. *Uuuhh . . .*
  7. *Eyyyh . . .* (like "hey" without the *h*)

Feel how you are carrying or "lifting" the air up, initiating the tone and sending it out. Notice how different volumes require different measures.

- Keep the tone till you have run out of air, then softly stop the tone. Then, and only then, release your support, keeping your posture all the time.
- Repeat a couple of times.
- Take a medium breath and initiate your support.
- Now, initiate the same sound as before. This time vary between low and high volume several times till you run out of air, making sure that your tone does not fizzle out underway but stays tight all the way through the exercise. Feel how your body (support) has to work very intensely to do this.
- Go through each sound in the same way as before.
- When you've done all the sounds separately, do them together as one long exercise on low, then medium, then high volume like this: *Aaahh-eeehh-iiihh-ooohh-yyyhh-uuuhh-eyyyh* . . . (like "hey" without the *h*), holding the last tone till you run out of air.

Exercise 21: Initiate on H Followed by a Vowel

- Repeat the above exercise using the following sounds:
  1. *Haahh* . . .
  2. *Heehh* . . .
  3. *Hiiihh* . . .
  4. *Hoohh* . . .
  5. *Hyyhh* . . .
  6. *Huuhh* . . .
  7. *Haeyyyh* . . .

Notice how your initiation on *H* feels softer and more airy than the initiation directly on a vowel.

- When you've done all the sounds separately, do them together as one long exercise on low, then medium, then high volume like this: *Haaahh-eehhh-iiihh-ooohh-yyyhh-uuhh-aeyhhhh* . . . holding the last tone till you run out of air.

Aim to hold a full, pure, condensed tone all the way through the exercises, with no excess air fizzling out; you are fully voicing. This is a strong, healthy, and authoritative sound.

You'll probably find that you like some vowel sounds better than others. That's not unusual. Most people have their favorite sounds. Play around and see what suits you best. Start working on your favorite sounds and then gradually equalize into other sounds, keeping your focus in the same place as when you did the first sound that you liked—all the time keeping the lift, your support. Imagine that you are carrying your breath and your sound along up and forward, mixing it all in your mouth before you carry it further forward on a silver tray and present it to someone. It is very important that you envision your sound as being carried forward as opposed to straight up or down.

Remember that it must feel comfortable! If it doesn't, you are doing something wrong and wasting your time. Stop, identify the problem, and try again.

When you feel comfortable working with varying volumes, it is time to start playing with varying the pitch as well. Enter the slides, my favorite exercises!

VOICED EXERCISES: SLIDES

The slide is an all-purpose exercise. It can be used to train all the Basic functions, as well as modes, registers, resonance, color, pitch, volume, etc.

A slide is simply *sliding from one tone up or down the scale to another—and then back down or up.* This is also called a *glissade* or *glissando.*

The difference between a slide and a scale is that when you do scales, you cut your slide into single notes or steps, whereas a slide is one long, continuous movement.

You can do slides in all sorts of different ways using different vocal modes (see chapter 7) and different intervals. It is an advantage to have a piano or perhaps a guitar at hand—but it's not vital. If you don't have an instrument and you know nothing about tone intervals, stick with free sliding (explained below) or ask somebody to help you. You will also find a link to audio samples at the end of this chapter.

As with any of the exercises, you usually start where your voice feels most comfortable and then gradually work your way up and down the scale, stretching your voice and your range further and further *without straining.*

As you slide through the different registers, you'll gradually get a sense of wholeness in your voice, along with a greater sense of control. Once you get the hang of it, you'll find that slides are ridiculously simple yet extremely powerful. They'll work wonders for your voice in no time.

As with any exercise, always remember to keep your support working and hold your posture till the slide is *completely* finished—no more sound needing to come out. Then *and only then*, release support.

Notice how different notes, tones, pitches, ranges, and functions require different measures.

Personally, for a quick voice fix or warm-up, or for days where I have limited time for practice, I prefer free sliding—doing slides with no set tones or intervals, not using any particular scale. Simply start on any one note of your choice and slide up and down in one smooth movement—kind of like a siren!

Hold the top note for a second and then slide back down to the same note you started on or perhaps even a deeper note. When the slide is *completely* finished (no more sound intended), release support.

As you get more and more comfortable sliding, gradually work your way up and down the scale, stretching your voice and your range further and further without straining.

Listen to your voice (metaphorically)—when it tells you to stop, *stop!*

Then check that you are still *loose and relaxed everywhere* (double check tongue, jaw, and larynx), that you are still *breathing and supporting right*, and that you are *thinking* right.

Normally I approach slides in two ways:

1. The soft approach, including classical/operatic (referred to by the Cathrine Sadolin Method as *Neutral*)
2. The semi-hard to hard or shouty approaches (referred to by the Cathrine Sadolin Method as *Curbing, Belting*, and *Overdrive*)

The soft approach (soft mode) allows you to practice safely in a comfortable and familiar mode and gives you an instant feel for resonance and sound placement.

The harder sounds (hard modes) really help open up the full power of the voice and are great when you need to add more dynamics, drama, volume, and authority.

Beware, though, that when doing slides without supervision, you need to pay extra attention to the hard functions because when done incorrectly, they can damage your voice and in the worst case create permanent problems.

When you get to Exercise 25, "Free Sliding," there will be specific sound examples for you to use. You will use these examples for the maintaining exercises.

If you need a recap, go back to chapter 7, "Vocal Modes: Different Gears for Different Sounds and Volumes."

When working with slides, you need to play around a bit:

- Vary the *volume, pitch, range, and length* of your slides and see how your voice behaves. I bet you'll surprise yourself. (Remember, though, that certain sounds have certain volume requirements that you need to consider.)
- *Pay attention to your body.* How are your *breathing* and your *support* working?
- Do you remember to *focus and project* your voice *forward* like you've learned?
- Gradually expand your range, going as *deep* and *high* tonally as you can *while still feeling completely comfortable.*
- Always start with a *soft* setting and then gradually go harder.

For your first slide, imagine the sound that you intend to do and just throw yourself into the exercises without thinking about how to do them at all. Do what comes naturally to you. Allow your voice to do what it already knows how to do. If it works straight away, great! Continue to work like this, gradually expanding pitch and volume.

Then, if this starts not to work for you—*if it feels the least bit uncomfortable* or it feels like you are hurting your voice—begin to consciously work on your settings. You might have to do this straight away; you might not. It doesn't matter—we're all different.

Do what feels right for you. You need to learn to listen to your voice from the beginning, work with it and follow its natural urges instead of working against it. Working against the voice, as you now know, is what causes problems.

Before you do your first slides, here are a few final reminders:

- *Practicing the wrong way is worse than not practicing at all.*
- *Make sure that you are relaxed and loose the whole time.* That means no tension anywhere! If you practice while being all tensed up, that is what you will teach your body to do in the future. I repeat this because it is so very important!
- Loosen your body. Ground yourself. Stand with feet slightly apart, well weighted on both feet. Straighten your back. Lower and relax your chest and shoulders. Hold your head up.
- Relax your jaw and your tongue.
- Breathe deeply. Make yourself comfortable.
- *Use a focus point* as described earlier to focus/project your sound correctly. If you lack focus, you could run into difficulties, particularly in the top and lower ranges of your voice.
- Continue to work with your breathing and your support the way you've learned so far. You'll easily know if you are off track: you'll run out of air, lose tone control, and find the exercise difficult and uncomfortable.
- *It should never feel uncomfortable*—if it does, something's not right. Go back to the Basics and start again.

Now you're ready. Have fun.

Exercise 22: Brrrr . . . Slide/Car Slide

Remember the "Stalling Car" exercise? We are now going to expand on that exercise by adding some sound!

- First, to remind yourself, repeat the original exercise.
- Then imagine that you have to *brrrrrrrrrrreathe* sound out of your nose.
- Lift normally (support) and focus upward and forward at a small point 1½–2 meters in front of you. Purse your lips into *brrrrr* position, lift, and carry the air up and

forward through your pursed lips and your nose at the same time.

- Start on any tone within your immediate range and slide up and down the scale on the sound *brrrr* as far as is comfortable for you.
- Work with 3–5 tones within each slide. It will be a thinnish sound. Make sure that you don't tighten or strain anywhere.

There are several good things about this exercise. It is not possible to conduct it without the proper support, and it tends to take all attention away from the throat area and lift it up into the mask. Moreover, it is very good for stretching the top end of your range.

Some people (especially if they have small, thin lips) find this exercise really difficult. If this applies to you, don't worry. Give it your best shot for now and then leave it for next time.

Exercise 23: Up Your Nose Slide

- Place the tip of your tongue behind your upper front teeth, with the front part of your tongue pressing softly up against your palate.
- Now, mainly through your nose but with your mouth open, produce the sound *nnnnng*. It is a nasal sound. You should feel a slight vibration in and around your nose and perhaps the entire mask area.
- When you've got it right, start sliding like you would with any other slide, only this exercise tends to work best as a downward slide (starting on a high note going down to a lower note).

Make sure that you don't tighten or strain anywhere. Like the *Brrrr* "Car Slide," this exercise tends to take all attention away from the throat area and lift it up into the nose and mask. N*inging* along to songs using this sound is very good for expanding the top end of your range.

Exercise 24: Siren Slide (Downward)

- Place the tip of your tongue behind your upper front teeth, with the front part of your tongue pressing softly up against your palate.
- Again, mainly through your nose but with your mouth open, produce the sound *nnnnng*.
- Keep producing the sound while opening your mouth more widely and allowing your tongue to drop to its natural position resting with the tip behind your lower front teeth.
- Without pausing, gradually change the sound into *aaaarhhh*.
- The full sound becomes *nnnnnn(g)aaaaarhhhhh*.
- Slide down from random notes on this sound.
- Release support when completely finished.
- Repeat, changing the start note. Keep it easy and comfortable and expand your range as it becomes even easier.

Exercise 25: Free Sliding

And now for the real full-blown slides.

We start with a free slide. A free slide means *freestyle;* there is no set tonal point of start and finish. Look at it as pure play and indulgence for your voice.

- Start on any *random* note of your choice and gradually slide upward and then back down *in one flowing, uninterrupted movement.* Do not jump straight from one tone to another—sliiiiiiiiiide!
- *It does not matter where you start and where you finish.* Play around; vary the *volume, pitch, range, and length* of your slide and see how your voice behaves. I bet you'll surprise yourself.
- Pay attention to your body. How are your breathing and your support working? Do you remember to focus and project your voice forward like you've learned?
- Gradually expand your range, going as deep and high tonally as you can *while still feeling comfortable.*

Use the following examples for all your maintaining slides and other exercises.

When doing double slides or combos, simply pick from the list to make your own combinations. An example follows in Exercise 33. Notice how different vowels seem to sit in different places in your mouth. You will soon find that some sounds merge more easily than others.

Neutral

When doing exercises, *always* make sure to apply the Basics.

When doing exercises in Neutral, always remember to apply the Neutral settings of the jaw, tongue, etc. as described in chapter 7, "Vocal Modes."

- *Heeeeehh . . . E,* as in "h<u>e</u>" or "f<u>ee</u>ling." Tone long and drawn out, slide. Emphasis on the vowel sound.
- *Huuuuuhh . . . U,* as in "y<u>ou</u>." Tone long and drawn out, slide. Emphasis on the vowel sound.
- *Haaaaaahh . . . Ah,* as in "<u>A</u>hhh, this is nice." Tone long and drawn out, slide. Emphasis on the vowel sound.
- *Eeeeehh . . . E,* as in "h<u>e</u> or f<u>ee</u>ling." Without H, tone long and drawn out, slide. Emphasis on the vowel sound.
- *Uuuuuuhh . . . U,* as in "y<u>ou</u>." Without H, tone long and drawn out, slide. Emphasis on the vowel sound.
- *Aaaaaaahh . . . Ah,* as in "<u>A</u>hhh, this is nice." Without H, tone long drawn out, slide. Emphasis on the vowel sound.
- *Puuuuuuuh . . . U,* as in "b<u>oo</u>" Notice how the added P in the beginning places the U slightly differently in your mouth, and makes the sound *feel* different as well. Tone long drawn out, slide. Emphasis on the vowel sound.
- *Peeeeeeeh . . . E,* as in "f<u>ee</u>ling." Tone long drawn out, slide. Emphasis on the vowel sound.

Curbing

When doing exercises, *always* make sure to apply the Basics.

When doing exercises in Curbing, always remember to apply the Curbing settings of the jaw, tongue, etc. as described in chapter 7, "Vocal Modes."

- In a moaning, complaining way, say *Eeeeeeehh . . .* like you are about to cry or like the cry of a baby. Maybe imagine the evil laughter of an old witch, like *heh, heh, heh.* Tone long drawn out, slide. Emphasis on the vowel sound.

- In a moaning, complaining way, say *Ooooooooohhhhh* . . . like "Ooohh, my tummy hurts so bad." Tone long drawn out, slide. Emphasis on the vowel sound.

Overdrive

When doing exercises, *always* make sure to apply the Basics.

When doing exercises in Overdrive, always remember to apply the Overdrive settings of the jaw, tongue, etc. as described in chapter 7, "Vocal Modes."

- In a loud voice, shout *HEY!* (Haa-yyyy-eeh), as if you are calling someone in the street. Tone long drawn out, slide. Emphasis on the vowel sound.
- In a loud voice, shout *EY!* (Aaa-yyyy), as in "<u>a</u>men!" Tone long drawn out, slide. Emphasis on the vowel sound.
- In a loud voice, shout *WOH!* as in "I w<u>o</u>n't do it!" Tone long drawn out, slide . . . like "I wooooooooon't do it!" Emphasis on the vowel sound.
- In a loud voice, shout *OHHHH!* as in "h<u>o</u>me," like "Go hoooooooooooooome!" Tone long drawn out, slide. Emphasis on the vowel sound.

Belting

When doing exercises, *always* make sure to apply the Basics.

When doing exercises in Belting, always remember to apply the Belting settings of the jaw, tongue, etc. as described in chapter 7, "Vocal Modes."

- In a very loud voice, shout *AI!* as in "t<u>ie</u> or <u>I</u>." Tone long drawn out, slide. Emphasis on the vowel sound.
- In a very loud voice, shout *EE!* as in "h<u>e</u> or f<u>ee</u>ling." Tone long drawn out, slide. Emphasis on the vowel sound.
- In a very loud voice, shout *EY!* as in "h<u>ey</u>!" Tone long drawn out, slide. Emphasis on the vowel sound.
- In a very loud voice, shout *AY!* as in "<u>a</u>pe" or <u>a</u>men!" Tone long drawn out, slide. Emphasis on the vowel sound.
- In a very loud voice, shout *AH!* as in "<u>Ah</u>hh, this is nice." Tone long drawn out, slide. Emphasis on the vowel sound.

Use the above sounds as directed for all the following slides.

Exercise 26: Upward Fifth Slide

- Start on a reasonably low note of your choice and slide a fifth (five notes) upward.
- Hold the top note for a second.
- Then slide back down to the same note you started on.
- Then move a semi-tone or one full tone up the scale and repeat the exercise from there.

Continue doing this till you reach a point where the top note becomes difficult. This is the top of your range for now, and you shouldn't push your voice into areas where it doesn't seem to want to go. However, this doesn't mean that it is not possible for you to get there ever. Go back and readjust your technique and try again. But remember—it must not be uncomfortable at all! If it is and you still can't do it, lay off for now. Maybe you can do it tomorrow or the next day or next week. Have patience and remember that Rome wasn't built in one day. Your voice needs gradual stretching, just like any other muscle, to expand fully. If you were learning to dance, you wouldn't expect yourself to go into a full split on your first day either.

Exercise 27: Downward Fifth Slide

Same as above, only move down the scale instead of up.

Exercise 28: Fifth Slide—Both Ways

Now combine the two. First slide up a fifth—then back to your starting note—then down a fifth—then back and land on your starting note—all in one go, on the same breath.

Exercise 29: Upward Octave Slide

Same as the fifth slide, but using an octave (twelve semi-tones) range instead of a fifth range.

Exercise 30: Downward Octave Slide

Same as the above, only move down the scale instead of up.

Exercise 31: Octave Slide—Both Ways

Now combine the two. First slide up an octave—then back to your starting note—then down an octave—then back and land on your starting note—all in one go, on the same breath.

If you find that working with an octave is a bit much, stick with the free and fifth slides.

If you need variety try the following slides.

Exercise 32: Fifth and Octave Slide

Combine a fifth and an octave slide like this:

Choose your starting note—now slide up a fifth—and then back to your starting note—then slide up an octave—then all the way back down and land on your starting note again—all in one go, on the same breath.

If you combine two or perhaps even three different sounds, still binding them together, you have yet another variation of the fifth and octave slides. Use the example in the following exercise.

Exercise 33: Double Slides and Combos

Simply put two or more slides together as one in one long movement—then back and land on your starting note—all in one go, on the same breath.

Double slides are a little more challenging than single (one up, one down) slides and demand more support. They are good for training smooth transitioning between sounds and overall control. Notice how different vowels seem to sit in different places in your mouth. You will soon find that some sounds merge more easily than others.

If you combine two or perhaps even three different sounds, still binding them together, you have yet another variation, such as *Hah-ah-ey-eeh-yuhhh.*

Please note that even when you have two or more slides (see below) bound together and move tonally up and down the scale two or more times in a row—it *must* still be *one, smooth, continuous, sustained movement without breaks!* Keep the airflow and the sound steady all the way through. This is very important. If you can't handle it without breathing in between, it simply means that you are not strong enough in your support and not ready yet for this exercise.

Exercise 34: Multiple Slides

Use multiple slides to boost your stamina and push your lung capacity to the limit!

See how many slides—fifth or even octave slides—you can do while still binding them together, *all in one go, on the same breath.*

Use one or combine several different sounds as you do this. Use the same procedure as above.

Example: *Hah-ah-ey-eeh-eeih-eeh-ouu-uuh-ooooh.*

This exercise is also very suitable to perform as a scale.

OTHER EXERCISES AND SCALES

All slides can be converted into scales. If you like, you can include scales in your exercise program. This works best if you have a musical instrument such as a piano, keyboard, or guitar available. For a scale to sound balanced and for your pitch to sound clean, your breath control and support need to work properly. If pitch problems occur, it is likely that either these do not work or that you are straining—or both.

Scales are slides cut into small bits or steps. You can use the same intervals and the same sounds as with the slides and all the other exercises in this chapter.

Use any vowels, vowel combinations, or vowel-consonant combinations of your choice. Or simply use words and sounds relevant to any speech that you are working on.

It doesn't matter as long as it makes sense to you, is relevant to what you need to learn and what you are doing, and is helping you improve.

In fact *you can apply any sound or word to any exercise of your choice*—it doesn't have to be a scale or a slide. You can work with just one note if you like.

For example, a fifth slide:

- *Hah, ah, ah, ah, ah, ah ah, ah, ahhhhhh . . .*
- *Me, me, me, me, me, me, me, me, meeeeeeh . . .*
- *You, ou, ou, ou, ou, ou, ou, ou, ouuuuuhhh . . .*

Then as a double fifth slide (in one long movement—up, down, up, down, rest):

- *Hah, ah, ah, ah, ah, ah, ah, ah, ah, ah, ah, ah, ah, ah, ah, ah, ahhhhh . . .*

There are, of course, numerous more exercises available than what I have presented here, but by and large they all tend to do the same things. Ultimately, you are training your voice for speaking purposes, not with the intention of joining the National Opera or auditioning for *American Idol.*

For pure technique, I also strongly recommend that you study *Complete Vocal Technique* by Cathrine Sadolin. It is, in my opinion, the best, most logical, and most comprehensive pure vocal technique bible around. It is a *must* for singers. Find it here: www.CompleteVocalInstitute.com.

But for now, the exercises in this book should do the job for you. It is crucially important that you enter into these exercises with the right mindset. If you need help with that, look forward to part 4, "Persuasive Speaking through Inner Power," where you will get some great tools to add to your training and development process.

For audio exercise samples, please visit www.SuzannRye.com/audio.

CHAPTER 12

The Voice Doctor: Problems, Cures, Prevention, and Maintenance

Many people neglect to support their voices properly when they talk. As a result, voice problems are more common than you might think, not only among speakers. Often people like schoolteachers, consultants, salespeople, telesales people, switchboard operators, dance or aerobic instructors, childcare assistants, and so on—any people who need to speak for hours on end and perhaps even shout occasionally—are also in the red zone and need to pay extra attention to their voice technique.

The simple truth is that *prevention is better than cure!*

If you take the time and make the effort to establish correct technique and maintain good physical and mental health, you will reduce the risk of problems. It is probably nearly impossible to avoid minor problems altogether, particularly in the beginning phase of your training, but you can certainly avoid serious incidents and thus keep from wasting time curing and recovering from problems that could have been avoided.

It is important to heed the warning signs and detect faults early so that they can be rectified and problems eliminated. Once troubles start, there is a danger of falling into a vicious cycle where things can escalate and a relatively minor problem can result in something far more serious and perhaps ongoing. This will set you back unnecessarily and can be expensive. Moreover, there is always the risk of causing serious damage that can lead to permanent problems. You do not want this to happen. Follow the principles of the Basics and pay attention to and trust your voice's and your body's signals.

Like I've said before, *if it feels right—it probably is. If it feels wrong—look into it immediately!* Don't try to *force* your voice to work normally if, for some reason, it doesn't. Look at your overall technique *and your thinking—your state of mind.* Is something bothering you?

If so, it might be affecting your voice. *Learn to feel and distinguish correct from incorrect technique.* You do *not* save time by ignoring problems and trying to avoid dealing with them. So do not postpone correcting your technique— the longer you spend nurturing bad habits, the longer it will take you to de-learn before you can re-learn.

Your voice is pretty tough—it will allow you to experiment, and a worn-out voice can be repaired, but it will not allow continuous or repeated abuse. A few mistakes are OK—learn from them and improve—but try not to make the same mistake twice. Although your voice is tough and *can* take a little bit of beating up, it can't take it forever. And as you now know, once you get serious problems, it can be a nightmare. You don't want to go there if it can be helped. And it can—easily.

If you make mistakes and encounter problems and you are not sure why and what to do—don't panic! Help is always at hand.

Depending on the seriousness of your condition, there are people that you can ask; please do not be afraid to do so. The good health of your golden voice is too important to ignore. Most problems are easily cured by rest and correct technique. If the problem is not easily handled by correcting your technique, you may want to consult a voice coach or a speech therapist. If problems persist and you suspect an ongoing *physical* problem, see a throat specialist— preferably one who actually specializes in the voice and has experience working with voice professionals and is used to dealing with voice issues.

Please be aware that *not all* throat *specialists are* voice *specialists.* Unfortunately, many doctors know very little about voice mechanics and tend to be hopelessly outdated on the subject. So do yourself a favor and spend some time finding a doctor appropriate to your needs. (See note at the end of this chapter.) A good voice specialist will insert an optic camera and actually look directly at your vocal cords and video record them in action. This helps the doctor make an exact diagnosis and determine the best course of action if indeed a serious physical problem is detected.

Following are the most common problems or symptoms that you can encounter, ranging from not so serious to very serious.

We will look at:

- What is the problem? How does it manifest? What are the symptoms?
- What are the probable reasons for the problem?
- What should you do about it?
- How can you avoid it in the future?

CONSTRICTIONS

Constrictions and problems caused by constrictions are undoubtedly the most common reasons for both sudden/acute and ongoing voice failure. Constrictions can be purely psychological, or they can be physical in the sense that they have ingrained themselves in the muscles as muscular memory—a continuous and automatic muscular dysfunction which, if not detected and dealt with, will eventually result in more and ongoing problems. In theory, the symptoms could be anything from "frogs" in the throat, hoarseness, or loss of voice to infections or even, worst case, nodules.

Often people are not aware that they have constrictions. They just have a sense that something's not quite right, and speaking often feels tiring and uncomfortable. They are surprised to find that their problems are fairly easily solved by applying small changes and thinking differently (learning not to hold back because of insecurity or fear).

Especially when experiencing a very real physical and perhaps even painful problem, it is sometimes difficult to understand how it can be largely psychologically rooted—and solved. By learning to use the voice freely and naturally with the right thinking and the correct techniques as explained in the Basics in chapter 6, you can avoid constrictions completely.

Right thinking and the implementation and consistent use of correct technique are the cure for constrictions and constriction-based problems. *You have to get rid of bad habits, learn correct technique, and recondition your voice.*

I cannot stress this enough: your emotional and psychological health is directly linked with your physical health, including the health of your voice. Overall harmony and awareness will be your strongest weapon against constrictions and any other problems. Together with the right action, they will act as prevention, maintenance, and cure anytime.

Most symptoms can be traced back to attitudes, beliefs, and thinking patterns. For instance, being horrified of getting ill just before an important speaking engagement might actually cause you to become ill. Reluctance to do a particular engagement might make you ill to provide you with a suitable excuse to cancel. Or perhaps severe nervousness or insecurity might impair your voice temporarily in order for you to have a good excuse should you not live up to other people's or indeed your own expectations.

In general, we have a tendency to attract problems to the areas where they are the least desirable; people who are professionally dependent upon their voices seem to be mysteriously more prone to throat infections and other throat problems than others.

These kinds of symptoms can either sneak up upon us gradually or occur out of the blue. Always try to find the root of the problem and deal with it quickly. Often you'll find that there isn't actually anything physically wrong. If you suspect that you have constrictions, look into it. First use the techniques, the advice, and the exercises in this book to resolve the problem. If you don't see any positive results and you remain unsure, seek advice. Better to be safe than sorry.

If you take good, loving care of your voice, it will behave very nicely indeed. Be sure to get enough rest, eat properly, and exercise regularly. Visualize yourself and your voice strong and healthy. Create a suggestion or positive affirmation about ultimate health and strength, and remind yourself of it every day.

SUDDEN ACUTE VOICE PROBLEMS

If you experience sudden, acute voice problems, you're either ill with a serious infection—in which case you probably feel terrible and should stay in bed—or you are suffering from self-induced vocal problems, probably caused by fear.

Fear of failure or serious nervousness can cause your voice and your throat to lock. This normally feels like you have a piece of string or wire tied around your neck with a tight grip on your larynx. *This is a sign of psychologically induced constrictions.* It could also be a sign of a *very* tired, exhausted voice.

You need to use whatever methods you have available and are comfortable with to calm yourself down. In parts 3, 4, and 5, I will give you several strategies for dealing with fear and nerves.

For physical relief, use the same cures prescribed for real illnesses later in this chapter (such as steaming). Use gentle exercises like low, well-supported humming to massage and warm the voice (see chapter 11).

In the unlikely case that there *is* a real sudden physical problem like severe swelling of the cords and you absolutely need to talk, have your doctor give you a steroid boost. This will take down the swelling immediately. But please consider this an absolute emergency; it really should be the very last resort. Steroids are extremely unhealthy and will sit in your system and affect it for a long time. You can only do this once or twice a year, and I really don't recommend it. I'm just telling you that it is an option, albeit a risky one. You're obviously better off dealing with your problems in a more natural and healthy way. A steroid shot is a quick fix, not a long-term solution. It gets rid of the symptoms, but it doesn't *cure* anything. You have to find out what caused the problem in the first place. If it was self-induced, what did you do and why? Learn how to prevent yourself from doing it again. Deal with the real issues long-term.

MORNING VOICE

When you've just waked up or maybe even for the first few hours of the day, your voice may sound a bit husky or different. It may even feel weak and powerless. You might have the urge to constantly clear your throat.

Don't worry—this is completely normal. You do not need to do anything about it. Your voice will naturally restore itself back to normal over a few hours or less.

If you sleep with your mouth open, air passes back and forth over the mucous membranes all night, causing them to dry out. Snoring affects your membranes as well. To function properly, the membranes need to be moist, so until moisturizing has taken place, the voice can sound rough and feel slightly irritated.

Dry heat or air conditioning can have the same effect. It is not uncommon for voice professionals to avoid air conditioning like the plague not only because of the dryness but also the added cold draft. Don't be surprised if you find sleeping in an air-conditioned room slightly bothersome.

If you have an early morning session and can't wait for your voice to restore itself but desperately need it to function quickly, give yourself a little extra time to get all warmed up. Have a nice hot drink, relax (meditation is good), perhaps go through your presentation in your mind (no sound).

Massage your throat lightly and do a few soothing warm-ups or exercises, starting with deep breathing and going into *ahhhs*, relaxing the face muscles, jaw, and shoulders. Next do some comfortable deep humming sounds, *hmmmm*, which will massage and warm your voice. Then go about your normal business. You voice will be fine.

"FROG" IN THE THROAT

A "frog" is an expression used to describe something tickling or irritating the voice/throat, prompting you to constantly clear your throat or causing you to cough. It is normally harmless and will pass. It can be caused by anything really, but often it is due to nervousness or holding back emotion. Especially if your throat suddenly closes up or tightens so that you can hardly speak, the cause is likely to be psychological.

Illustration 10 -
Frog In The Throat Clerk

If you keep having frogs, they might indicate the beginning of other problems. See if the symptoms match any of the other symptoms described in this chapter.

COLDS, STUFFY NOSE, AND SINUS PROBLEMS

These are, of course, irritating symptoms and conditions that can make speaking very uncomfortable indeed. It's not unusual to get a headache if you speak, particularly with blocked sinuses. However, it doesn't necessarily affect the voice in a bad way as such, but you can hear a difference in the sound.

The best trick I know is to *steam* for about 10–15 minutes. Pour boiling water into a large bowl and add chamomile and Japanese peppermint oil (only 2–5 drops; it's very strong and can irritate your eyes—available in the pharmacy or health shop) or perhaps eucalyptus oil and thyme. Place your face directly over the bowl and put a towel over your head. Close your eyes! Inhale steam, which soothes the mucous membranes and the vocal cords.

As you inhale, imagine a cool blue mist or cloud of steam swirling in, up, and around your nose and sinus (upper) cavities, clearing them out, flushing out all the annoying stuff, and leaving you clear and fresh.

If you can, steam for 15 minutes. Then keep quiet for half an hour afterwards.

After that, begin making sounds, first using soft, soothing exercises like humming (*hmmmm*) and soft *ahhhhs*.

Do not steam immediately before an engagement—leave at least a few hours. The steam affects the membranes and the cords, and they need to settle again in their own time.

Do not interfere in the process by using your voice unnecessarily or clearing mucus off the membranes by clearing your throat. Steaming usually works wonders.

If you have a bad cold or oncoming flu, try this recipe: Add the fresh juice of a whole lemon to hot but not boiling water. (Boiling kills the vitamin C.) Add some freshly chopped chili peppers, puréed fresh ginger, and honey. Drink with delight! You'll sweat like a pig and soon feel better. If you're really hardcore, add a clove of garlic to the mixture as well. It might not be the most delicious drink that you ever had, but it'll clean you out in no time!

Or try the soup version: Make any kind of soup of your liking. Add *loads* of the above ingredients (do not boil!), and voilà! Your face will light up purple, and you'll sweat it all out. Make sure to warn your spouse in advance though. Better still, have them join you, and they won't have to sleep on the couch. Well, it works for me.

DRIED-OUT MUCOUS MEMBRANES

Please also see the "Morning Voice" section above.

If your mucous membranes are dry, they will immediately seek to moisturize themselves by producing mucus because they need to be moist to function properly and because it is their job. Mucus is basically produced to protect the vocal cords.

If the dryness is consistent and goes beyond the normal few hours in the morning, it can cause severe irritation to the cords. Contrary to the usual "morning voice," this is not normal and you should look into it. You could have an infection or an allergic reaction.

EXCESSIVE MUCUS PRODUCTION

Please also see the above section.

If you tend to consistently produce too much mucus, it might be a sign that something is not quite right. Since mucus is produced in self-defense, you might want to find out what exactly the membranes are defending themselves against! What is causing the excess mucus production? You could be causing damage to your voice by using incorrect technique. Your vocal cords could be seriously irritated or wounded. You could be experiencing an allergic reaction of some kind, or perhaps you have an infection.

Try to avoid clearing your throat to scrape the mucus off the membranes, as this can be rough on the cords and will only prompt the membranes to produce *even more* mucus to moisturize and protect the dry, irritated area. The best way to clear the voice is to use it.

Try steaming followed by *humming* or *chanting* in a comfortable low voice. A comprehensive warm-up and/or an extended exercise routine would certainly help too.

If the excess mucus production continues, you must look into it. See your doctor or a homeopath. You probably have an allergy, most likely dairy.

PROBLEMS CAUSED BY ALLERGY

If excess mucus production persists but you do not feel any discomfort or pain and you cannot detect any other symptoms, you might be suffering from an allergy. Lots of people have allergies—and lots of people think that they have allergies but they really don't.

If you think you might have an allergy, look into it. Try eliminating certain food groups and see what happens. The most common allergy to cause excess mucus is dairy products. If you can't figure it out, see a specialist. If something is continuously upsetting your system, you need to find out what it is and deal with it. People deal with allergies in different ways. You need to decide what works for you. I suggest that you consult with your doctor or a homeopath.

INFLAMMATION OF VOCAL CORDS

It is not unusual for the cords to get a little irritated or inflamed even. This is nothing to worry about. Just try to make sure that it doesn't get any worse than it has to and that it is not a recurring thing. Ultimately, your cords are not supposed to be anything less than perfect.

You have to consider that you might simply be ill and perhaps in need of antibiotics or other treatment. If you are, relax and get better. Rest your voice.

Make yourself a hot super-drink and some soup as described earlier. They really work magic!

SWOLLEN VOCAL CORDS

If your vocal cords are swollen, either you have an infection or your voice is very seriously strained and worn out and you may be in danger of developing nodules. Either way, you must not use your voice, if at all possible. You need rest and pampering!

If swelling persists, see a throat specialist, preferably one who is also a *voice specialist* and who can film your cords before and after to track the situation. (Remember earlier when I said that not all throat specialists are voice specialists?) If the swelling is caused by an infection, you may need medication.

If you really desperately need to work (speak) and there is absolutely no way out, you may be able to persuade a throat specialist to administer steroids. Steroids will take down the swelling almost immediately, but remember that a steroid shot is a quick fix, not a long-term solution. (See "Sudden, Acute Voice Problems" above.)

Moreover, working successfully with a problem, whether suppressed by steroids or not, always requires extra support, strength, and above all a flawless technique. So if the actual problem stems from lack of support or otherwise poor technique, you are still in for a rough ride. If, on the other hand, your support and general technique work well, you should be able to go through with your speech/presentation without any major problems. I once did an entire concert with severely swollen cords. I could not speak a single word either before or after the show—but I managed to sing for an hour and a half! How?

Well, I'll have to admit that on this occasion I did the steroids thing, which I have succumbed to only three times in a very busy twenty-five-year career. Second, my technique was flawless from start to finish. If it hadn't been, I would not have able to do it. The second I would ease off and be just a tiny bit slack, my voice would go.

Sound is created by vibration. Swollen cords cannot vibrate normally. That's why you can't speak normally with swollen cords. Steroids will reduce the swelling, but it won't last. It doesn't *cure* anything. It is a temporary emergency solution that you should resort to only if absolutely necessary. The best thing is to rest and leave the voice to recover till the swelling has subsided. If you do want to medicate, choose wisely.

LARYNGITIS OR OTHER INFECTIONS

It is fairly easy to distinguish a genuine infection from constrictions and self-inflicted tear and wear; with an infection, you will feel ill and probably have a fever.

If you have an infection you should avoid working if you can and, in general, use your voice as little as possible. Relax and spend time recovering. Snuggle up in bed and be pampered. Get lots of vitamins and water. Get somebody to make you a big pot of my infamous soup and have some of my hot drinks (see "Colds, Stuffy Nose, and Sinus Problems" above).

Perhaps you should see a doctor and get some antibiotics.

Illustration 11 -
Poorly Clerk

HOARSENESS

There's a difference between *husky* and *hoarse*. A husky voice has a certain underlying softness and breathiness, whereas a hoarse voice sounds more rough or rugged and constricted.

Unless hoarseness is produced healthily as an intentional effect, it is a sure indicator that something is wrong. It might not necessarily be serious. If the hoarseness is created by constrictions that haven't yet manifested physically, you can get rid of it by doing healthy, soothing, well-supported exercises, starting with soft, low *humming* sounds and also very open sounds, like *ahhhh*. If you don't need to work, see if completely resting your voice makes a difference (no speaking, not even *whispering*). Another really good remedy for hoarseness is steaming (see "Colds, Stuffy Nose, and Sinus Problems").

If the hoarseness continues or if it is very uncomfortable or painful, you should look into it. Perhaps see a throat specialist. You might have an infection. Or your voice may be seriously strained or worn out, and you might be developing nodules, in which case you need to take it very seriously.

LOSS OF VOICE

If you don't listen to the early signals from your voice that something is wrong—if you continue to push a tired, strained, worn-out voice to work—it might cease to function completely. In other words, you lose your voice.

Again, it might not be as serious as it seems, and a lost voice may be regained fairly easily—but then again it could be more serious.

Proceed with caution. Rest your voice and follow the same guidelines as described in the previous sections. If your voice doesn't recover—seek medical attention.

Do *not* try to force your voice into action—it will only make matters worse!

SERIOUSLY STRAINED/WORN-OUT/EXHAUSTED VOICE

If your voice is tired, it needs rest.

If your voice is seriously strained and worn out, you haven't been listening to it and you are not treating it very nicely! *A voice in this state needs* <u>complete</u> *rest!*

Respect your voice. Don't abuse it, please. It is so not worth it!

If you have a wound and you keep banging against it or scratching it, it won't heal—it will get worse. It is no different with your voice.

You also need to avoid allowing your voice to partially heal and then creating the same problem over and over again. This way you will develop nodules, and the healing process will be longer and could include surgery. You do not want this to happen!

Rest, rest, rest!

DEVELOPING NODULES

If you ignore voice problems and refuse to listen to your voice's signals, you will start to develop nodules—little bumps of swelling on the vocal cords. When both cords have swellings in the same place (opposite each other) constantly banging against each other, you have nodules.

If you think you may be developing nodules, see a specialist straight away! The earlier nodules are diagnosed and dealt with, the better the chance of a quick and successful recovery.

Unlike the general swelling of the cords discussed earlier, nodules specifically indicate abuse. Furthermore, they are unlikely to calm down by themselves, and they cannot be medicated away. They *will* develop into permanent nodules if you do not take action by first dealing with them and then correcting whatever you were doing wrong to cause them in the first place.

Nodules prevent the cords from coming together and closing properly and severely impair the normal vibrations of the cords. Eventually they cease to function, and speaking goes from being very difficult to being impossible.

In the beginning, you might not be aware that nodules have actually begun to develop. You may have become so accustomed to speaking with irritated, inflamed, or swollen cords that you don't realize the severity of the condition. Persistently speaking with developing nodules intensifies the problem.

You need complete rest till the cords are back to normal. This means *do not use your voice* <u>at all</u>! Do not speak; do not even whisper for at least one to two weeks depending on how severe your condition is. You *must* wait for your voice to fully recover. Write notes to people instead of talking. Aid your own healing by healthy living and positive thinking.

Then you will rehabilitate. The rehabilitation process should be gradual and very gentle. Start by doing soft warm-up exercises—well supported *hummings* and *aaahhhhs* every day. *Make sure it feels completely comfortable all the time!*

Restrict speaking. Speak only when necessary, and when you do speak, *make sure that you are supporting properly.* Gradually, as you feel your voice getting better, you can speak more and more.

Then correct your technique so that you won't set yourself up for the same problem again! If you don't know what to do, ask a voice coach or a speech therapist.

PERMANENT NODULES

If nodules are not detected and dealt with, they will get worse and worse and can in the end become permanent as opposed to developing.

For any voice professional, this is a nightmare, the worst-case scenario next to being seriously ill or having your larynx ripped from your throat.

However, despair not, my friend. In most cases the nodules can still be gotten rid of by *complete* rest (see above) for up to two weeks, followed by speech/voice therapy during and after rehabilitation. A speech therapist will work with you and teach you exercises that can assist you in alleviating the nodules and prevent further abuse. You will work on basic voice technique as described in this book, only instead of being preventive learning that you are engaging in by your own choice, it will now be a crucial part of recovering from problems that could easily have been avoided in the first place.

Take heed of the undisputed fact that *permanent nodules clearly indicate some wrongdoing on your part.* They stem from and are aggravated by wrong, lazy speaking habits (such as lack of proper support when speaking).

In some cases, the nodules become so hardened that they require laser surgery to be removed. Surgery is optional, but the specialist might advise you that this is the best solution for you. Certainly, as a voice professional, living with permanent nodules forever would be unacceptable. So consider your options carefully.

After surgery there will be an approximately two-week healing and recovery period. During this time you must also not use your voice *at all!* (See above.) You must wait for your voice to *fully recover* before you start using it again. Your surgeon/throat specialist will examine your cords regularly to make sure everything is OK and progressing.

Again, you need to follow the procedures described in the previous sections. Hopefully, however, you will only need *one* silent period (starting immediately after the operation and lasting for two weeks). After that, take it *very* easy. Recovery from permanent nodules is a lengthy process that should be carefully monitored. Take it seriously. The amount of time and energy you put into your recovery process will, without a doubt, show up as an investment in your future speaking career.

When you do get back to work, *do so with awareness of what caused the problem in the first place and be sure to put it right.* Remember—nodules come from abuse only, so you must have been doing something wrong to develop them in the first place. *Pay careful attention to your support and overall technique.*

GENERAL VOICE MAINTENANCE AND PREVENTION

First of all, get very familiar with your voice—"listen" to it.

If something feels wrong and you are really worried, get it checked out. Perhaps get regular voice checkups—once a year is fine or perhaps every six months if you are very busy and work all the time. Most singers get regular checkups; why shouldn't you as a speaker? After all, more problems occur from speaking than singing.

Stick with proper voice technique—all the time—and avoid constrictions.

Use the Basics, the voice exercises, and the rest of the program in this book to stay in good vocal shape.

Respect your voice like a good friend and treat it accordingly.

Remember: *your voice is your calling card.*

Live healthily. Get plenty of vitamins and water and everything else a healthy, happy body needs.

Get enough sleep and rest. Especially allow your voice to rest between gigs.

Build up strength and stamina. Keep in shape—it makes you feel good and look good and gives you extra energy. If you don't like the gym or if you're not into heavy sports or running around, try yoga or tai chi, which will work wonders for your breathing too!

Think positive. Your attitude affects your overall health and the health of your voice. Use positive affirmations and suggestions for prevention, cure, and maintenance. Imagine your voice and the rest of your body strong, healthy, and powerful!

Expect your voice always to work optimally for you, and give it the best conditions to do so. Build up confidence to make you and your voice grow stronger.

Avoid bottling things up—express yourself as openly and freely as possible. Suppressed emotion can impair your ability to function both mentally and physically. Unreleased energy forced to stay in the body will eventually need an outlet. If it is not released normally through expression or physical activity, it will accumulate somewhere in your muscles and create tensions or disease.

Practice relaxation and do a few deep breathing exercises every day; at best do some light physical exercise or warm-up as part of your daily routine to loosen up any tension. The more relaxed and open your body is, the less tension; the less tension, the less restriction. See yourself as an open channel through which energy needs to flow. If you have blockages, the energy cannot pass through freely and your optimal functionality is impaired. For your voice to feel well and perform well, it must be energized in the appropriate way, as must your mind and the rest of your body.

Perhaps it is very ambitious to aim for a state of constant and total balance in body, mind, and Soul. However, if you can achieve and maintain a reasonably healthy balance, you will have fewer problems.

More information regarding voice health and the importance of physical strength, as well as issues like eating, drinking, and smoking, is in chapter 15, "Frequently Asked Questions."

Note: There are other and even more serious voice problems than the ones described in this chapter. If in doubt, always consult a medical expert, preferably a laryngologist, who specializes in the diagnosis and treatment of problems of the larynx and voice. A laryngologist can perform a "transnasal fiberoptic laryngoscopy," a technique for examining the larynx in which a small fiberoptic instrument is placed above the larynx, through the nose. The technique allows examination across the dynamic range of the voice and during speech.

Part 3
The Art of Performance

CHAPTER 13

Great Showmanship

As a speaker/presenter, you are a communicator. Your job is to successfully communicate a message in an interesting, engaging, and entertaining enough way for people to stay focused during the entire presentation. That's no easy task. The average attention span of human beings is said to be no more than ten minutes. Then the brain simply needs to switch channels at least for a few seconds—enough to lose track of what's being communicated.

Strong communicators are excellent performers, astute observers, and proficient energy translators. They read their audience, pick up hints, and move and sway with the mood. They dance gracefully, every step carefully planned but effortlessly executed, like pure play, holding the audience captive and eagerly awaiting their next move. Their words, flowing naturally and with poised ease, are just right—no more, no less—the perfect recipe, every sentence not too sweet, not too bitter.

The above describes what I would classify as *great showmanship*. Obviously it takes time, effort, and experience to arrive at this stage and become an accomplished speaker like this. And it takes courage. It requires you to completely let go of any restrictions and to trust blindly in your own skill and divine inspiration. It is much like playing music, improvising. There is a difference between playing an instrument and playing *music*. One is craft; *the other is art*. When the two come together, you have magic.

Illustration 12 - Super Clerk

RELATING TO THE AUDIENCE

Speakers use their voice and their body to convey messages, express opinions, etc. The more convincingly they do this, the better the show—the more successful and the greater the reception.

Any grand performance needs to have life and excitement and passion. The audience should walk away from it with some sort of bonus, something new that they've learned, something to think about, an emotional reaction, something that makes their life just a little bit different than before. Watching the performance needs to be worth their while because if it's not, they will never come back.

Think about it: what is it in other speakers that inspires you? What makes you eagerly anticipate a particular speaker's next appearance? Any chance you get, watch other performers work; pay attention to what they are doing and why. Merely observing others can teach you so much.

So how do we get there? How do we learn to create the kind of magic that will spellbind our audience and make them cling to our every word?

Well, one good step is certainly to *speak from the heart*—to speak *with sincerity*, display empathy and compassion, and *show a genuine interest in our audience.* We need to connect with them and relate to them on a heart level.

People like to feel important and appreciated, and they like to feel loved. Show them that you are genuinely happy to address them, that you believe in what you are saying, and that you believe *what you have to say is of real value to them.*

Consider your audience your friends. Bond with them, offer a warm smile, and use eye contact and inviting gestures.

Show emotion, if appropriate, and add soul and character to the performance, drawing on your own experiences. Use personal stories to create rapport and give them a real glimpse of you, the person. Relate to the audience and they will relate to you.

Touching people's hearts in some way will always make them listen to you more intensely and connect with you. Remember, *people are people,* no matter what kind of high-profile jobs they have. So meet them on a person-to-person level, even if your presentation is of a serious nature. A friendly, pleasant, and relaxed (but not sloppy) approach will come across as confident, competent, and in control. Your audience will trust you and pay attention to your message. If you are relaxed, calm, and comfortable, you will project it and inspire the same feelings in your audience.

But the opposite is also true: if you are anxious and uneasy, your audience will react to it and become anxious and uneasy too. The audience will mirror you. That's why it is so important to take the time and make the effort to learn how to control anxiety, extreme nervousness, and so on. It is not only unpleasant to feel anxious; it also impairs the quality of your performance and certainly affects the audience's perception of you.

Exercise: Be Inspired—Create Magic

- What is it in other speakers that inspires you?
- What makes you eagerly anticipate a particular speaker's next appearance?
- What is great showmanship to you?

- Do you live up to your own definition of great showmanship?
- Have you ever felt yourself being completely in the flow of a great performance, almost watching from the outside as the magic of skills combined with divine inspiration unfolded, effortlessly and beautifully—*moving and swaying with the mood—like pure play?*
- If you have, hold on to that feeling and begin to nurture it every day as you practice. Remind yourself of it and imagine that it is already a natural part of your performance—every time. If you have not yet experienced this state of being, don't worry—you soon will.

I am going to introduce you to a couple of exercises later on that will boost your ability to induce an optimal state of mind for excellent performance.

PREPARATION—HOW TO SET YOURSELF UP FOR A GRAND RECEPTION!

Obviously you need to be as well prepared as you can. Know your presentation inside out. Knowing that you are well prepared and have earned your right to be there in the first place makes you confident and makes it easier to relax and give a super performance.

Speaking style is an individual choice. You need to find out what works best for you. People prepare themselves in different ways and use different kinds of notes or prompters. Many speakers approach speaking like an act and learn the entire speech—word by word, move by move—by heart. Personally, I prefer a less rigid approach; I generally advise against memorizing an entire speech word for word like this. But I have to tell you that in some circles it seems to be "the done thing," especially for keynote speeches. A speaker will do the exact same speech in exactly the same way over and over again, like a theatrical performance. I guess it makes it easier to book a speaker like this because the client will know in advance exactly what they are going to get. Personally, I stay away from memorizing entire speeches word for word. I find it restricts me and weakens my performance. I also prefer listening to other speakers when I don't know what to expect rather than hearing the same keynote over and over again.

Practice working with an outline and as few notes as possible. You'll find that it increases your confidence and improves your overall performance, not least your ability to think fast on your feet. And you won't get lost in your text. Free yourself as much as possible from your notes and papers. Often they are nothing more than a pair of old crutches, crippling you more than helping you, and preventing you from learning to walk by yourself in the long term.

Be well prepared, research your topics, know your material, and plan and rehearse till you feel that it's done, till you feel at peace. Once your mind is peaceful, everything will come to you; everything will flow naturally and unrestricted.

Practice the things you've learned in this book till they become second nature to you. Then forget about them—release them and allow them to work by themselves. Forget about the rules and trust your mind to work by itself. Believe in your own abilities, skill, and experience. Relax, let go, and trust your body and your voice to do their jobs naturally and easily. Follow and trust your natural impulse and instincts.

Remember, if you hold back, your voice will suffer. If you think about your gestures and movements *too much* you will become tense, rigid, and awkward.

Great performance is an art form; it's like a dance. Once you've learned the dance—once you find yourself moving and swaying with the mood, dancing gracefully, playing, captivating the crowd—you know that you're definitely onto something. You're on your way toward becoming not just a good speaker but an excellent one. Congratulations!

Earlier we spoke about how body language, nonverbal communication, and vocal inflections affect how you and your performance are perceived. When you prepare yourself for a presentation, thinking about suitable body language and vocal inflections should be part of your initial preparation as well, just like actors immerse themselves in a manuscript and research a character. Think about it, perhaps decide on a few strong moves that you are definitely going to use, then let it go.

You should also make an effort to research your audience. What type of people are they? Are there any cultural or religious issues that you need to pay special attention to?

Finally, consider your appearance. Decide in advance what you would like to wear. It gives you time to make a great choice and it gives you less stress on the day—especially if you're a woman.

THE STAGE PERSONA

Feelings and emotions are energy. You can learn to transform that energy into almost anything you want—to turn inconvenient feelings to your advantage. If you are incredibly nervous before going on stage, you can use that energy as fuel for your brain, making your memory and your focus sharp.

Directing/focusing energy is very powerful. You can learn to project almost anything you want, like switching on a light bulb. Being aware of what you project adds to your palette of expression. This is much like acting, only you are not pretending to be someone else—you are allowing yourself to be *the best possible and most powerful version of* you.

Having this kind of control enables you to actually *let go of control*, lean back, and allow the words to flow, almost automatically, through you. In this state, speaking/performing can be an incredibly empowering experience. But in order for you to achieve this, you first need to master the basics, and you need to be *very aware* of your own inner workings and your signals. You cannot possibly achieve this kind of laid-back observational state of mind without being reasonably calm in the first place.

Experienced performers tend to develop certain rituals that help them focus their energy and put them in the right state of mind. They develop an almost automatic "super-personality" that switches itself on minutes before a performance and stays put till after the show. This personality is the *Stage Persona* that I mentioned earlier.

Being able to focus your energy in this way is crucial in order to perform well and also to enjoy the experience. The good news is: *everybody can learn how to do this.*

Does that mean that you will have to become someone else? *Absolutely not!* You simply must become better at *bringing out the best* in you at your own command, instead of having to rely on luck, circumstances, having a good day, etc. It simply puts the control back in your corner so that you can consciously *decide* to have a good day.

Knowing that you can do this, that you are not at the mercy of any outside influences, and that you have the power and the ability to switch on that bulb wherever and whenever you please gives you immense peace. When your mind is peaceful, it works much better and faster, and you open up the channels for truly inspired knowledge, intuition, and excellence to flow through.

Illustration 13 - VIP Stage Persona Clerk

It allows you to *truly* be yourself—a better version than ever before. This is what we all aspire to achieve.

But make no mistake about it: there is a *huge* difference between genuinely being *in the flow* and putting on a great performance and *pretending* to put on a great performance. So please pay attention to the following because it is very important: *Don't <u>ever</u> underestimate your audience*—they are not stupid. They will not buy into a fake image or false pretenses. They will get impatient and find you awkward, embarrassing, tedious, and frustrating to watch. Your audience likes it when *what they see is what they get.* Pretense glares through. It makes you appear false—suspect even. It somehow indicates that not only are you trying to convince others—*you are trying to convince yourself as well.*

It won't work. If *you* are not convinced, how on earth do you expect to genuinely convince anybody else?

Pretense comes from insecurity, as does arrogance. Arrogant, condescending speakers are tedious to watch too; they tend to push the audience away rather than bonding with them; they create distance and leave people feeling undervalued and unappreciated. Maybe deep down these speakers don't feel that they have earned the right to be there or believe that they deserve the attention. If you don't feel like you deserve the attention, *how are you going to be comfortable demanding it*, which is what you have to do as a performer?

I would like to tell you a little story from my past. Some years ago when I signed my last record deal, I had an experience that really made me think and reflect on my own values and work ethic.

A deal was in the offing. I was a very confident and experienced performer at that time, so when the label manager asked to see me perform live before making any final decisions, I had absolutely no qualms about inviting her to a show. One evening she and a colleague came to watch what I felt was quite an excellent performance. However, they didn't seem too impressed. I couldn't believe it! How could they not *love it?!*

Next I was shocked to find that apparently the record company didn't feel entirely comfortable sending me out on tour before making sure I had what they called "performance lessons." I was very confused (and, admittedly, slightly miffed).

I knew I was *very* good at my job. I knew that I was an excellent singer and that I moved well. I knew that I could work the crowd like no one else. And the response that I had received on that particular evening had been amazing! What was there not to like?

It turned out that they didn't like my Stage Persona. It wasn't that they didn't recognize that I was a good performer; they just felt that my manner and attitude didn't quite fit the idea that they had in mind. In their opinion, I was too friendly with the crowd. I was being *too natural*—too much myself. They wanted me to have a more sophisticated and "awe-inspiring" image. I had to create more of a distance between me and the "common people." I had to give out an air of superiority, arrogance even, for now I was a "star."

This was good advice—just not for me. I was so completely not that kind of performer. Nevertheless, they genuinely felt that this image was what was best suited to the project, so after some soul searching I agreed to give it a try. I embarked on performance lessons.

As it turned out, this meant spending just one day with a very entertaining French choreographer—François, I think his name was. François was very intense and certainly very theatrical. He showed me how to perform as my new improved super-star self. After a few hours, he felt confident that I had been transformed. It was time to show the world his fabulous new creation!

I have never been more embarrassed than when I was asked to perform as my new sophisticated self to a tape recorder in front of a large mirror while the entire staff sat on chairs behind me. Anyway, I did what I had to do. I felt very uncomfortable, but I survived it, and they were happy. God knows why, for as I recall, it was appalling!

And so I went off on tour and did my thing—exactly how I'd always done it. The tour was a huge success, and the label manager was very happy and congratulated me on my new skills.

Truth is, had I done what she'd wanted me to and gone completely against my personal style, the tour would have been a disaster. I wouldn't have been able to pull it off because the Stage Persona that she had wanted me to adopt was so far removed from what I was about that it would have been nearly impossible to make it look anywhere near right. I would have felt and looked ridiculous.

As a speaker, you have to identify or create your Stage Persona as well— the one that reflects your personality best and comes most naturally to you. This will add strength to your performance and at the same time allow you to remain 100 percent genuine. If you have your own style, people will find you more interesting and pay more attention to your message.

Find your own voice (metaphorically). *Work* <u>with</u> *your strengths—not against them.*

In this particular story, the brilliance of the label manager's own vision kept her blind to something really essential: You cannot dress a wolf in sheep's clothes. (Well, you can, but it won't work for long.) What she failed to recognize was *my* strengths—*and* my weaknesses.

And I was reminded of something very important: Don't ever feel that you have to *change* yourself into someone else. You cannot force yourself to be something that you are not and expect it to work. You should never have to deny who you really are—not even on stage or in public. It is not emotionally healthy, and it will always cause trouble sooner or later. (Just look at the state of many of today's celebrities.) Embrace who you are and nurture your own personal style into the best that you can.

Having a professional front is not about being false. It's about being smart, playing your cards right, and staying in charge. So be cool, be professional, but whatever you do, *make it a natural part of you*. Be genuine. *Be yourself!*

Here are some things for you to think about when working with your Stage Persona.

Exercise: Identifying Your Stage Persona

- Do you feel that you have developed your own style on stage?
- If so, do you like your style?
- Do you have a Stage Persona already—a certain "character" you tend to become on stage?
- If so, do you like your Stage Persona?
- Are there things you would like to improve or change even?
- If so, what are they?
- How do you see yourself shining in your best light— your ideal self?
- Imagine your Stage Persona exactly how you want it! Keep the image in your mind's eye.
- Remind yourself of it every day from now on.
- Notice how that makes you *feel*.
- Remind yourself of this feeling every day from now on. The more feeling you attach to the character and image of your Stage Persona, the stronger it will become and the sooner you will find yourself merging with the Stage Persona and everything it represents.
- Do you have a pre-performance ritual? This could be anything from drinking tea to doing sit-ups—whatever

makes you feel good and ready. If you don't, develop one. Associate it with your Stage Persona.

In part 4 we will work more extensively with how to establish your Stage Persona, your *Dream Character*. You will learn how to prepare yourself and be able to enter into the ready state of mind before a performance. I will give you an example of a *Quick Performance Prep* later in this chapter.

BODY LANGUAGE, NONVERBAL COMMUNICATION, AND FIRST IMPRESSIONS

In order for you to come across as genuine and trustworthy, there needs to be harmony between what you say and how you say it. Your message must go with your signals. What you say with words needs to match what you don't say but still communicate using nonverbal and nonlinguistic communication.

Your facial expressions, gestures, and movements should have purpose and naturally support and emphasize your message. (Pay attention if you are speaking in a foreign country, as the meaning of some gestures may vary.)

Your posture, stature, and overall demeanor should be grounded and confident, with an air of natural authority (*not* arrogance though)—just enough to let the audience know that you are well informed and knowledgeable about your topic and that you are in control.

This goes for general appearance as well. As much as I hate to say it, first impressions count. You want to appear healthy, groomed, classy, and on top of things, as this *will* affect people's immediate opinion of you. So consider what would be appropriate to wear. Think about accessories and jewelry, what signals they send out, whether they could be too brash for the occasion. Could they be distracting, taking attention away from you and your message? By making a little extra effort and dressing up nicely, you will not only feel more confident, but you will also already have come a long way toward winning the audience's respect. I also like to look at it as a token of respect from me to the audience, saying: "You are important to me; I respect you; your opinion of me counts."

Set an example, show respect, and you will get the same back.

Be flexible. Aim to be the best version of you that you can imagine for that particular event. Then allow your own personal style to shine through in everything that you do. Again, be yourself, be genuine, be involved. If you show a genuine interest in your topic, chances are that people will be interested as well.

A PERFORMANCE IS ALWAYS NOW!

What happened five minutes ago doesn't matter. What is going to happen in five minutes doesn't matter either. Now matters! Concentrate on *now*.

Completely immerse yourself in the now! You've got to be right in there. That way your energy remains vibrant and your focus sharp. You can think ahead, but still stay present. This can be trained.

A performer seizes the moment—every moment.

When you're on, you're on—not in half an hour, but now. If you need time to warm up, do it before the show. If you spend half your performance getting into it, getting ready, you will have already lost half the crowd. The first few minutes are important. Give yourself 100 percent right from the start. Totally immerse yourself in the situation and completely *live* it, feel it breathe it, become one with it, and stay with it till you've walked out and closed the door behind you.

If you make a mistake or forget something, so what? Only you know what you were meaning to say in the first place. If possible, continue as if nothing happened. Chances are, nobody noticed anyway, and nobody's going to remember unless you keep reminding them. Don't let a mistake throw you off and ruin the rest of your performance. If you do, you ruin the *now*. You allow the past—something that has already happened and that you cannot change anyway—to affect not just the now but also the future, the rest of the presentation. This way, one mistake that probably no one noticed anyway can ruin an entire performance.

Stay in the now. Let bygones be bygones and move on. Keep smiling— everything is fine! *The show must go on.*

QUICK PERFORMANCE PREP

All performers have their own ways of getting ready, their own little rituals or performance prep. This is an individual thing. If you haven't already, you will develop your own personal ritual in your own time. My aim is to help you do that.

We will look at this more closely in chapter 15, where we will discuss warming up before a speech. In the meantime, here's an example of a quick performance prep that I often use myself. I use it with a Performance Trigger—a name that I associate with being ready, fired up, and calm at the same time. It helps me enter into the right state of mind. My name for this exercise is simply "Excellent Performance."

Try it and see how you feel:

- Close your eyes.
- Breathe deeply a few times.
- Shake your arms and roll your neck.
- Relax your body. Keep breathing calmly.
- Ground yourself.
- Take a moment to clear your head. Rid yourself of any outside influences that may disturb you. Relax your mind.
- Breathe deeply.
- Compose yourself. Calmly, in your mind, go through what you are about to do. Completely immerse yourself in it. As you do this, be sure to see yourself as your Dream Character, your ultimate Stage Persona self. Immerse yourself in that feeling.
- Stay grounded, keep your eyes closed, and keep breathing deeply. The increased oxygen flow to your brain will help calm you and increase your focus.
- Remind yourself of previous feelings of success and accomplishment. Remind yourself that you have been invited to speak because you have a valuable contribution to offer. Be grateful for the opportunity to share; look forward to it. Imagine the joy it will bring. Imagine the wonderful response you will get from the audience.
- Send love to the audience; thank them for welcoming you. Feel how they are already responding, sending love and gratitude back to you. Feel how you have already bonded.
- Now they are ready and waiting for you, looking forward to meeting you, looking forward to your sharing your

love and your wisdom with them. Allow yourself to feel the same way. Expect great success. Look forward to it!

- Breathe deeply. Shake your arms and roll your neck again to release any last bit of tension. Wiggle your face. Relax your jaw.
- Breathe deeply. Now you are ready. Feel it.
- Open your body.
- Walk in.
- Make eye contact. Acknowledge the audience with love and appreciation. There is already a bond between you and the audience, and now it is strengthening even more. Feel that bond, the familiarity, and the loving energy spreading in the room.
- Now, claim your space and naturally "demand" the attention. Take in the room. Settle. Maintain eye contact.
- Breathe deeply.
- Begin.

The Quick Performance Prep can also be found in chapter 21 at the end. That version has an added element, the Dream Character, which you will learn about in part 4.

CLASSIC PERFORMANCE DON'TS

Following is a list of pointers that I like to remind myself of every now and again. Generally, I am in favor of using "plus words"—focusing on what you *should* do as opposed to what you should *not* do. However, I do find these particular don'ts to be of good use, so here is my list of Classic Performance Don'ts:

Don't *excuse yourself.*

Making excuses immediately devalues your performance and makes people feel that they are getting less value for their money. It lowers your standard both in your own mind and in the minds of the audience.

The fact is, you are there, doing it. Get on with it—or don't do it at all. Halfway won't work.

Don't *ever let a mistake throw you off.*

If at all possible, continue as if nothing happened. If the mistake is too obvious to hide, simply apologize, then pick up and continue without creating a fuss.

If it is a really huge mistake that makes a big difference, then you'll probably have to stop the presentation, compose yourself, then pick up and start again. But in general, always try to ignore minor bloopers. Chances are, nobody but you noticed anyway. Certainly nobody is going to remember unless you keep reminding them. You know what was supposed to happen, but the crowd doesn't—that is, unless you make them aware of it. It's better to keep smiling and pretend that everything is absolutely fine. *The show must go on!*

Don't *be afraid of mistakes*—they are *good* for you.

Mistakes tell you where you can improve and become even better at what you do. They keep you on your feet and prevent you from falling asleep behind the wheel. They prevent you from becoming complacent.

Welcome mistakes as opportunities to grow. See them merely as *experiences.* Use every experience as an *inspiration* to move forward and learn more. *Get up, brush yourself off, and move on!*

Don't *ever give less than your best!*

Sometimes a gig can turn out to be a nightmare, or let's just be polite and say "less interesting" than you thought it would be. Things beyond your control might not work as they should or go according to plan.

If this happens to you—if for some reason you decide that a particular gig is not as interesting as you first thought it would be—that's too bad! It's your problem. Don't cheapen the gig in front of people; it's not their fault. You have agreed to do the job, so get on with it—end of story!

Once you've agreed to do something, be professional about it. Unless it's so bad that it's completely impossible for you to do your job, just get on with it, make the best of it, and, if it helps, think about your bank account. Besides, you never know who's there. Remind yourself that you do not have to go back there again if you don't want to.

Don't *devalue yourself or your work.*

Learn to accept compliments. If people enjoyed something you did but you didn't feel great about it—keep it to yourself! Just do better next time.

It is discourteous to other people's opinions, tastes, and feelings to cheapen yourself and something that you did which *they* seemed to appreciate. It takes away from their experience and makes them feel less enthusiastic and inspired about something that they enjoyed. What you're saying, essentially, is that they have poor judgment and poor taste.

A compliment is a gift. When somebody offers you a compliment, thank them and gracefully accept the gift. If your friend offered you a gift they really wanted you to have, would you refuse it? It's not big-headed to accept a compliment—it's polite.

Enjoy the attention and compliments, even if sometimes it may just be empty flattery. Who cares? Pretend you haven't noticed and thank them politely anyway.

Don't *look at your feet, and don't step on them either.*

And please don't try to imitate the Hunchback of Notre Dame. Stay grounded and strong. Keep your head up and your back straight!

Don't *fiddle with the mike lead or the stand—please!*

My pet peeve. More about this in chapter 14.

Don't *be afraid of the audience.*

They're your friends, remember? This topic deserves further scrutiny. Read on.

Illustration 14 - Hiding From The Big Bad Wolf Clerk

WHO'S AFRAID OF THE BIG BAD WOLF?

If fear is your first enemy, who's your second?

Some would argue that your second enemy is the heckler, the crowd vampire, the one who feeds on you and your insecurities to soothe his own. Do not attempt to feed him; his hunger is insatiable—the more he eats, the more he craves.

In my experience, most crowds are welcoming and appreciative. Most likely they are attending the event because they are already interested—nobody forced them to come.

But you *will* get hecklers from time to time. No matter how excellent a speaker you are, you can be pretty sure that at some point or another, you *will* come across people who are reserved and apprehensive and seem "hard to get"—and you *will* experience people who are opposing, disruptive, and downright rude!

So what? As long as you know that you're doing your job, then peace be with anyone who, for whatever reasons they may have, feels the urge to object.

Try not to make it personal. Please know that this is not *necessarily* because they are nasty, arrogant people by nature. They are just playing out their own insecurities, often not realizing that they are actually behaving very badly, making fools of themselves, causing you to struggle, tapping your energy, and distracting your focus away from where it should be—on your expertise, your well-prepared topic, your presentation, and the people who are genuinely interested.

Do not let the crowd vampires get to you. Don't allow them to project their emotions onto you and the rest of the crowd. Either ignore them, or, if the disruption continues, address them very directly and openly invite them to talk to you about whatever their issue may be *after* your presentation. Give them the center stage they so crave, and they will likely shy away from it. Their aim is to get people on their side, to feel like "somebody," to pretend they know better than you. Being put on the spot will *not* do that for them. In fact, chances are they will suddenly feel very silly indeed and retreat.

Know that this kind of behavior is just part of human nature. These people are in desperate need of attention, praise, respect, or acknowledgment themselves, and therefore they find it hard to watch others or *allow* others to get their fair share of *what they would like for themselves*. They are probably also of the opinion that they are there to be *entertained* and enlightened, and so they expect you to deliver, to do something that they can't do themselves—and do it right according to *their* ideas or standards. That is why you're up there and they are not. You are supposed to be superhuman! And no matter how well you deliver, it may not ever be good or exciting enough.

Well, too bad for them. *It is not your problem.* You can't ever please everyone in the entire world. Please don't waste your gunpowder on these people. Use it somewhere else where the fireworks are appreciated. I'm serious. Really, it's a common mistake to spend way too much energy trying to win over the one person *who doesn't want to know anyway.* Don't. Reserve your golden nuggets for the people who really want and appreciate them.

Be aware that often unfriendly, reserved people turn out to be the most appreciative of all. It turns out that they are just shy or simply in awe.

Don't ever be afraid of the audience.

If you are very nervous, either try not to show it or simply say that you are without making a big fuss out of it. Most people will find it endearingly human and take to you kindly for simply saying it. They know that what you're doing takes guts, and they're happy that they're not in your shoes!

If some people believe that you're insecure *because you don't know your stuff,* you'll soon prove them wrong. Once you've learned how to control nerves and take command of the stage with confidence and a strong presence, you will always be able to put your message across with unmistakable conviction.

CHAPTER 14

Using a Microphone

Sometimes when you speak at an event such as a conference, you will have to use a microphone. You are likely to come across four types of set-ups:

- Mike on a stand or on a lectern
- Handheld mike with cord
- Handheld mike, cordless
- Headset mike which will be cordless but probably with a little receiver box attached to your waistband in the back

Working with a headset mike takes some getting used to if you are accustomed to working with a handheld, and vice versa. It's good to be familiar with both and to be flexible. The sound and volume will probably be preset for all, normally to the highest level possible without the risk of feedback. It is up to you to adjust your own voice volume accordingly.

If you are the main attraction of the event, you will probably get to do a sound check—but don't count on it. Get accustomed to using a mike and learn to adjust your own volume instead of having to rely on others. Relish any chance you get to practice and become more comfortable with the mike.

Some people get a bit spooked the first few times they hear their own voice amplified. This is partly because you hear it differently, more from the outside (outer hearing) like when you hear a recording of yourself. It can take some getting used to. I will explain about outer and inner hearing later.

There are certain "rules" about using a mike, but fortunately it is not exactly brain surgery.

You have to pay attention to your own output and dynamics. You rarely speak at the same output level through a whole speech. Most likely your voice will move up and down in volume and intensity. Depending on how much, you might have to adjust the distance between your mouth and the mike head—basically move just a little bit closer or further away. If using a handheld mike this is easy; you just pull the mike in your hand slightly away from your face. If it's a stationary mike, you will have to just move yourself back and forward a bit in order to adjust input. But unless you are very fired up on the one hand or very timid on the other, chances are that you won't need to adjust at all.

If you are using a headset mike, you'll be more or less dependent on the sound technician. You can adjust the positioning of the mike slightly, but not much. Generally you should leave it in the same place and let the professionals control the sound. You're not in the best position to judge the front sound anyway, as you will be behind the speakers. If the mike comes too close to your mouth, it will create feedback.

As with the other mikes, stay well clear of the speakers. Be careful should you decide to "work the floor." If you move in front of the speakers, even at a distance, you might be in for a nasty surprise!

Bearing in mind that sound technology is forever evolving, at this point there are two types of stage microphone technology that you are likely to encounter: *dynamic* and *condenser*. Most technicians prefer dynamic mikes for live performances and will often go to great lengths to persuade you to use one. Dynamic mikes are generally more robust, less sensitive, and therefore less prone to feedback than condenser mikes, which are more difficult to work with as they are *very* sensitive and generally put higher demands on the technician. They are also more expensive. However, condenser mikes have a richer and more flattering sound and are better suited for speaking events because you don't have to hold them straight in front of your mouth as you speak. They will capture the sound well from all angles. This brings me to my next point.

When working with a handheld mike, *don't hold the mike right in front of your face* so nobody can see you. Keep the mike underneath your mouth so your face is clearly visible.

If you are working with a handheld *corded* mike, *please do not fiddle with the mike lead!* It's a dead giveaway—it screams of nerves and insecurity and takes the attention away from what you're actually there to say and do.

Illustration 15 - Fiddle Clerk

Problems can occur with the sound system. In that case, stay calm and rest assured that you are in the hands of professionals and that it will be taken care of; if not, well, then it's not your fault. In the highly unlikely event that the mike dies on you altogether and there is no replacement mike—you will simply have to make do without it. Remember the high volume voice settings (hard modes) in chapter 7? Now would be a good time to employ those!

When you get onto the stage, *please* do not start your speech by tapping the microphone and saying, "Hello, hello, can you hear me? Hello!" Assume first that everything is in perfect working order. Test the mike in front of everybody only if it is clearly *not* working. But in general, any type of microphone fondling is a real attention grabber, screams insecurity, and is unsettling to watch. So try to avoid any of that.

A microphone is likely to pick up little things that you might not notice at all when speaking acoustically, so pay attention to pronunciation and articulation.

If your pronunciation is very distinct and if your emphasis on so-called unvoiced consonants (consonants produced in the front of the mouth or with the lips) is too strong, it will create disturbing puffing or hissing sounds, which will force the engineer to turn your volume down. Strong *p's*, for instance can create minor "explosions." *K's* can scratch, and *tss* or *shh* sounds can even create feedback. You need to voice the consonants slightly—make them softer and less pronounced.

Working with pronunciation and articulation of consonant and vowel sounds is normally part of thorough vocal training. If you suspect that you need extra work on any of these things, I suggest that you work with a voice or acting coach or perhaps a speech therapist. Most speaking habits are easily corrected. If you have a real speech impediment, like a lisp, I suggest you see a specialist who works with breathing techniques and perhaps some type of mental training to reduce the effects. Today there are many such therapies available. I have seen many people go from not being able to speak a single clear sentence at all to giving public speeches with little or no problems at all.

Volume levels can sometimes be slightly difficult to judge because the monitoring (your sound fallback) at conferences is likely to be nonexistent. There will just be a PA front system (speakers that send the sound out in front facing the audience). You rely on the engineer/technician ("sound guy") to ensure the right balance.

Again, if you are a key speaker or the main attraction and the event is a big deal, it would be a good idea for you to go to the floor and test the sound for yourself beforehand. Bear in mind that an empty room will treat the sound differently than a room full of people, which will slightly eat off the volume and effects (like reverb, brightness, etc.—basically anything that enhances the quality of the voice) and also alter the frequency balance (IQ—bass, treble, etc.).

When working with an engineer/technician, don't be afraid to ask for what you want. Don't be too enamored with all the "magic" tools, though. When given the opportunity, some new speakers have a tendency ask for a bit too much "cream" on top. Don't. Too much reverb, etc. will blur your voice and take away from its presence and individuality. These things are supposed to complement your voice—not disguise it.

Once you are familiar with the mike, you will come to see it as a natural extension of your instrument. Your mike technique becomes automatic, especially if you know your voice and its strengths and powers well. You can use the mike to enhance your expression. Breathy, whispery, intense sounds, for instance, work great through a mike but rarely work at all acoustically.

If you have a high profile, you might have to do radio or even television interviews. In that case, be aware that there is a difference between working with a studio mike and a "live" mike (in a live situation, such as a conference).

RADIO

Studio mikes are very sensitive, requiring less output and more consonant control. You cannot puff and whissssstle your way through a radio interview.

Round your words. Perhaps use slightly warmer voice colors/deeper resonance.

Lean back and speak clearly and calmly.

Relax—concentrate on what you say and how you say it. Nobody's watching you and reading your body language right now, and they won't even notice if you're reading out of your notes (although try not to, as it will always sound much more natural if you don't).

TELEVISION

The television studio will be miked from above, and you will be speaking into the room as if you were just having a normal conversation with someone (which, in fact, you are).

Or you will wear a little mike on your clothes, probably attached to your collar. The mike will be cordless or with a lead attached to a little receiver box.

You will speak normally, like you would in any conversational situation, and the engineer will adjust the sound to suit your output.

Doing television is a subject on its own. We will talk more about that in chapter 15, "Frequently Asked Questions."

Last word on using a mike: *love the mike*. It is your partner, an extension of you. The mike amplifies your message for everyone to hear loud and clear—wonderful!

CHAPTER 15

Frequently Asked Questions

When I do my workshops, seminars, or speaking engagements—even when I teach in college—I always get asked the same questions. So I guess the answers to these questions are important to a lot of people.

I have compiled thirteen of the questions that I have been asked most often, along with my answers. They mainly concern things that have not already been addressed in this book, but some expand on basic topics already covered.

If you would like *your* personal questions to become part of my next book on voice, speaking, performance, and presentation, please submit your question to me by e-mail, and I may include it in an extended questions and answers book coming up.

Send your questions to: questions@suzannrye.com

SMOKING

I'm a public speaker, and I smoke. Does smoking really affect my voice? If so, how much? Should I quit?

Well . . . *yes!* Smoking is bad for you whether you are a speaker or not! But we all know this anyway. I don't think you really need anyone to tell you that. How much and how it affects your voice, however, deserves some scrutiny.

There is no doubt that when you *don't* smoke, you are generally more energetic, your body is healthier and stronger, and your lungs and *your vocal cords are generally less irritated.* That means that you are overall *less prone to throat and voice problems.*

Furthermore you can *enjoy the full trained range of your voice,* which seems to change when you smoke—you tend to lose the very top end of your range. This is not really a major concern for speakers, but it could be for singers.

When you inhale smoke, it comes into contact with the mucous membranes of the vocal cords. This aggravates the membranes and tends to dry them out, which will prompt them to overproduce mucus until they are so used to being dried out that they no longer function normally. If you are a consistent smoker, your voice will simply think that this *is* the natural state, and the overproduction of mucus will likely stop and then only recur *if you stop.* This is obviously not how it's supposed to be—it is not natural. Anything that is not natural, essentially, is not ideal.

Let me make this very clear: I'm not saying that if you smoke, you should keep smoking! But you may want to seriously consider *when* would be a good time for you to quit. Depending on how sensitive to changes your body is, you might want to incorporate it very carefully into your working schedule— not just for emotional/psychological reasons (you might feel a bit edgy to begin with when you stop), but for *physical* reasons as well.

It is not necessarily an advantage to stop smoking in the midst of a busy schedule or before an important project. As we know from the principles of practicing and conditioning, your voice is a creature of habit. So you see, it is not just *you* addicted to the smoking. You could say that *your voice is addicted or used to getting its fair share of smoke as well!*

If your voice is suddenly denied its daily fix, it may very well protest! This is because the vocal cords' mucous membranes need time to adjust to the new conditions. This can take anything from 2–3 weeks up to 4–6 months. In the meantime, your voice is likely to be agitated and unstable—just like you might be.

The membranes will keep producing excess mucus because they are affected by the changes in the bacterial flora. They are protecting against what they see as an attack on "normality" when in, fact, now is more "normal" than before. This will prompt you to constantly try to clear your throat. This, in turn, induces a vicious cycle where the more you clear your throat, the more mucus is being produced, and so on. As a result, you will probably get a sore throat from constantly irritating your voice. In order to make your voice function normally, you are then likely to tense up, which will then lead to new problems. So you see, short term, it's a catch-22.

However, you have to weigh these short-term effects against the long-term damage that smoking can cause, not just to your voice and your lungs but also to your general health. Having been on both sides of the fence, I can clearly say that smoking versus not smoking makes a huge difference to your general well-being. There's no way in the world that I personally would want to live with the daily effects that smoking has on the body—not to mention the constant feelings of guilt that tend be on any smoker's menu. Having said that, I (oh, my!) will smoke *occasionally* in a social setting; but few "real" smokers can get away with that. I guess once you've been seriously hooked, party smoking is out of the question. Having the occasional cigarette or cigar can easily take a few days for the voice to get over. It won't take weeks or months, as in the case of going from smoker to nonsmoker, but it *will* affect your voice. So if you do decide to party all out, maybe you shouldn't do it the night before an important gig.

Ultimately, it is an individual choice whether to smoke or not. It seems to affect different people in different ways. It is up to every person to listen to their own body's signals and decide what their priorities should be.

In general, *from a professional perspective*, I feel that there's no need to be hysterical about it. I know I shouldn't say this, but lots of voice professionals smoke, and they still can work very well indeed. *But* they would probably sound better, find performing easier, and get less hassle if they didn't smoke. They certainly would be healthier and in better overall shape. So . . . if you want to stop smoking, you should, of course. There is no doubt that in the long run you'd be much better off. But you knew this anyway.

WHAT TO EAT AND DRINK TO KEEP THE VOICE HAPPY

What should I eat and drink to keep my voice "happy"? Also, what helps if I get rough or hoarse?

This brings us to one of the greatest myths about the voice. Your voice does not care what you eat or drink!

Well, OK, that's not *completely* true; your voice cares, together with the rest of your body, about being healthy and well nourished. If you have allergies or are very sensitive to certain products (many people are sensitive to dairy products, which can produce swelling or an excess of mucus), stay away from those. Alcohol can also affect your voice by dilating your blood vessels, including those of the mucous membranes of the vocal cords, causing the cords to swell.

But apart from that, contrary to common belief, your voice does not favor ripe bananas, egg yolks, or spoonfuls of honey. If something smells nice and soothing, your voice might like it, but it certainly will not be "greased" or lubricated by it.

Your voice doesn't care so much what you eat or drink because it doesn't notice. Food and drink simply go down a different drain. Your vocal cords sit above your windpipe. You don't eat or drink through your windpipe. The only time food goes down your windpipe is when, by accident, you get something stuck in the wrong drain, choke, and need to immediately cough it up again!

So, once and for all, *food and drink will have little or no* <u>direct</u> *effect on the condition of your voice.* Your voice can, however, react to vapor, which is why some strong throat pastilles can have some effect. It also reacts to heat and cold, because the whole throat area is sensitive to temperature. If you really want to do something soothing for your voice, you should give it some nice hot steam, either natural or with added vapor, such as chamomile or peppermint (see chapter 12, "The Voice Doctor"). I find Japanese peppermint oil to be fantastic. This also comes in tablets that release a wonderful strong vapor of refreshing peppermint. Eucalyptus is nice too. I doubt how effective these tablets really are, but if they make but a small difference and they make you feel better then, hey, why not? At least they are better than bananas. Of course, if eating or drinking something specific has the *psychological* effect of making you feel better, then by all means, indulge!

What you should really be doing on a regular, long-term basis is getting the right vitamins that will give you strength and build up your immune system so you don't have to worry about illness and sore throat in the first place. This, together with the correct use of technique and your positive frame of mind, will keep you in continuous top form—no sweat!

PHYSICAL EXERCISE

Will exercising regularly help my voice?

Yes, definitely! The stronger and fitter you are, the better the energy supply in your body (and mind). Energy is fuel for your engine, and the strength helps your engine run more smoothly. When you are strong and fit, you are likely to have more power and more control over your breathing and your support.

Exercise forms like yoga, Pilates, and tai chi are particularly good for harmonizing energy flow, building physical and mental strength, and increasing flexibility and stamina. They will also do wonders for your breathing.

Vocal problems can occur simply because of lack of strength. If you lack physical strength and stamina and if you are tired, you might find it very hard to keep up your energy and your technique during a long presentation/performance, let alone an entire tour of engagements, which could mean several consecutive months with very few breaks in between. This is a tough lifestyle, and unless you stay fit and get enough rest, your energy levels are very likely to decrease. If this continues, you'll finally begin to feel worn out. This is the danger zone. When your body fails, your technique and ultimately your voice suffer. This is a frustrating situation, so you fight back, trying to force your voice to its limits in a desperate and somewhat illogical attempt to compensate for the lack of energy. Naturally, this only makes things worse and starts spinning a vicious cycle of increasing abuse that finally leads to more severe problems.

I think that answers your question: exercise is good. It generally makes you feel better as well and can help build confidence at the same time. So off to the gym!

IMAGE

How important is image?

First, let's distinguish between image and looks. Image is about style and includes personality or how that personality is coming across or being presented to the world.

Looks do not necessarily reflect somebody's personality. Looks are more on the surface—clothes, grooming, etc. A look can be created. A personality . . . well, that's a little bit more comprehensive. You could argue that a look *says or indicates something about the personality*—but it's just an assumption. You can't be sure to read somebody correctly by their look. It could be a "uniform," or the person could have made a conscious choice to dress a certain way for reasons unknown to you. However, most people would probably not think that far when considering first impressions.

You've heard the expression that you can't judge a book by its cover? Well, I'm an author, and as much as I tend to agree with that statement, I also know that it is not entirely true. It might be true that you can't *really* judge a book by its cover—*but most people do*. It's a fact. One of the first things taught in any book-marketing seminar is that the cover of your book is everything. It can make or break your book. Interesting—I wonder if it's the same with people?

We discussed first impressions, dressing the part, etc. earlier. Ultimately, I think that the *degree of importance* very much depends on your exact area of work. The amount of emphasis on image and looks varies. If, for instance, you are a distinguished scientist—the best in your field, people may forgive you for looking like the bag lady (or man) under the bridge (no offense to the bag lady, by the way). It might even add credibility to your "mad scientist" image. (Just an example—none of the scientists I know look like bag people or are madder than average.)

Illustration 16 - Bag Man Clerk

That aside, it is certainly no secret that in most areas of the *entertainment industry* not just image but also "good looks" (according to the commonly perceived definition) are extremely important. There seems to be a general consensus that if you look good, you will get more and better work and that generally you have a greater chance of *commercial* success if your looks are, shall we say, commercially pleasing. Unfortunately, I can't really argue with that. What I can't argue with either is the tendency for this attitude to spread into other industries as well.

It's safe to say that today's society is *extremely* visually based, no matter what kind of job you have. I'd even go as far as to say that we are bordering on obsession. Most people kind of think that it shouldn't be like this—but we all recognize that it is. We tend to accept and also to feed the notion that good looks are the be-all and end-all of our existence. (Ah, the glorious superficiality of the twenty-first century.)

So, yes, image is important. A strong image that includes a good look is your best bet anytime.

What that image should be, though, is largely open to interpretation. There are so many aspects that determine whether an image works or not. It is exceedingly difficult, if not impossible, to maintain an image long-term if that image conflicts with the person behind it. Therefore the task is to develop a persona that works in harmony with both the individual and the outside world. As a professional performer you are, whether you like it or not, a public figure. This kind of status gives rise to certain rules. They come with the territory. So you have to deal with that.

You have to consider that the entertainment and speaking industries are exactly that: industries. There is competition, and sometimes big money is involved. Whoever works with you will want to see sales and profits, and so will you. So be smart about it.

As much as personal taste comes into it, so do trends and clever, up-to-date marketing. Maybe you don't like to dress up. Well, do you want the gig or not? Speaking isn't the first job in the world to require some sort of "uniform." I'm sure it won't kill you. I'm sure your personality is big enough to outshine a suit anytime.

Ultimately, it's up to you as a performer and perhaps public figure to decide what works best for you. You must determine how best to incorporate all the necessary aspects of being a commercial commodity while, at the same time, upholding personal integrity. You need to find a healthy and fulfilling balance between the two. This is very important if you are going to be successful in all meanings of the word and if you are going to fully appreciate that success and continue to enjoy your work.

I would really like to think that *ultimately the personality aspect is more important than any given look.* But I know that first impressions count and that people don't necessarily spot my (wonderful, winning) personality within the first thirty seconds of meeting me. They do, however, have plenty of time to judge my appearance and make an assumption about my personality based upon it. And most likely, they will. If that assumption—true or false—goes against their grain, chances are that they may not want to hear what I have to say. Bummer!

THE MEDIA—AND THE PAPARAZZI

I resent the way the paparazzi and the media sometimes harass public figures and famous people. It really is off-putting to me. If my career seriously began to take off and I became more visible in the public eye, I'm not sure that I would be able to handle that very well. Have you got any advice?

(Note: In my answer, I shall use the term "the media" broadly to include any and *all* media, including the paparazzi and the press.)

First of all, I'd have to say that I really doubt that this will ever become such a big issue for you as a speaker. Ironically, very few speakers ever reach the kind of celebrity status where they will be more interesting to the public than the local pop idol contestant. But of course, there are some very high-profile people who also happen to speak as a result or byproduct of what they do, such as Al Gore, the Dalai Lama, and Nelson Mandela, or some of the very high-key, successful coaches or perhaps authors like Anthony Robbins, Mark Victor Hansen, or Paulo Coelho. I imagine that any of these people may have had a few run-ins with the press (and that's probably an understatement).

If you see yourself eventually belonging to that category of speakers, I appreciate your concern and I do understand where you are coming from. The whole media and paparazzi frenzy is, in my opinion, a sad reflection of today's celebrity- and gossip-crazed society. Nevertheless, as most sane celebrities will tell you, it simply goes with the job. It's the price of fame.

The question is, of course, how far is *too* far. When is it no longer OK? Where are the boundaries between general public interest, which is reasonable and perfectly understandable, and harassment, which is not OK, famous or not?

It takes a true professional (and a bunch of good people around them) to deal with the media in a way that is productive to all parties. I think generally you need to look at the media as sort of your "partner in crime." They feed off you—but you certainly need them as well. Without them you'll hardly create any public interest at all, and as a speaker, author, etc., you obviously do need the public to survive. The media need their stories, and you need attention and exposure. A good relationship with the media can provide you with that. A bad relationship can as well, only it probably won't be the kind of attention and exposure you're looking for!

Look at it as sort of a mutual agreement—a "You scratch my back and I'll scratch yours" kind of thing. It's all very civilized, really. The media is a very powerful entity that can either make or break you, so you are best off trying to get used to the media from the onset.

Sometimes it can be hard to accept the kind of journalism that is especially prevalent where the entertainment industry is concerned. Stories are frequently made up. One word for that: sensationalism. Sensationalism leads to increasing sales, meaning, of course, larger profit. And the media is no charitable institution, so profit counts. Usually it counts more than the desire to report genuine true stories.

I once did an interview with a very well known tabloid that took a whole day. The reporter asked loads of questions, and afterward I felt certain that this would be a great piece. However, when it was published, I didn't recognize a single word of it. It was sleazy and stupid and very embarrassing. I was new to the whole tabloid press game at the time, so I got very upset. I called the reporter and asked him what the deal was. Why had he wasted a whole day of my time to end up writing a sordid piece like that? "Well," he said, "your answers were simply too boring. I had to spice it up a bit!"

When talking to the media, I would advise you to be honest but very careful. There are probably some things you would like to keep to yourself, so when asked about them, either try to maneuver your way to the next question or firmly but politely decline to answer. Never think that you can just have a friendly, off-the-record conversation with a reporter unless it is someone you personally know very well.

Always decide in advance what you would like to focus on, and then try to turn any conversation or any question in that direction. If you have something that you would especially like to talk about, let the interviewer know in advance (send them a press kit), and often they're more than happy to comply—it eases their work. If they're not compliant, try to have it your way anyway. Simply seize any opportunity to turn the conversation in the direction you prefer.

Have you noticed how politicians never seem to answer the actual questions that they are given? Well, there you go! Perhaps there's no need to be quite that extreme, but a little helping of political tactics would definitely work in your favor. Politicians are *media trained*. This simply means that they have learned how to best deal with the media, how to have the media work *for* them and *not against* them, how to turn almost anything to their own advantage instead of leaving themselves bare and open for assault.

If you don't want to be misquoted, be extremely specific about *what* you say and *how* you say it. And know that even when you are this careful, you could still end up more than just a little baffled. Try to be relaxed about it. Getting upset probably won't do you any favors.

If you don't want to be caught acting like a mere mortal, try not to act like one. What do I mean by that? Well, people are people—celebrities too, you know. They have the same needs and they do all the same, sometimes stupid things as the rest of us. When that happens, the media goes into a feeding frenzy! They come down on the shockingly human celebrity like a ton of bricks. So here's some sound advice for you if you ever find yourself among the select few.

If you don't want to be seen in public without your knickers—keep them on and don't wear a belt for a dress, because you know they're gonna get ya! If you prefer your private life to remain private, don't make out in the local park. They're gonna get ya there too. If you don't want to read shocking stories about your own sudden fall from grace and possible plans for rehab, don't be seen at your local hangout downing excessive amounts of alcohol before staggering outside, clothes and hair in disarray. (Do it someplace where you can leave by the back door and throw yourself straight into the backseat of a cab with a huge paper bag over your head.)

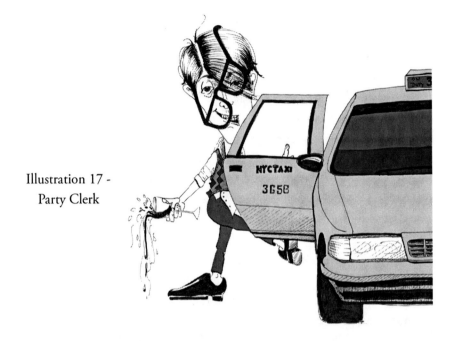

Illustration 17 -
Party Clerk

Basically, unless you don't care about having your less-than-glamorous escapades splashed all over the morning papers, be discreet about them. You're not supposed to be normal and have flaws like anyone else—sorry.

A few celebrities have fought cases against the media and won, but only after going through a lot of public hassle and parting with a lot of cash! For most of us, staging a war against the media is more trouble than it's worth.

So, however hard it may sometimes seem, try to make friends rather than enemies with the media.

RADIO INTERVIEWS

Lately I'm being invited to do radio interviews. Do I have to speak differently in the studio than I do live?

You don't necessarily have to, but you probably will.

When working in a studio (a good one, with an engineer who knows his job well), you have the ultimate conditions. It sounds great, you can hear every single little detail, and you really can utilize every means of expression available to you. But you tend to need much less power and perhaps less intense dynamics. Studio mikes, live mikes, acoustic speaking—three very different things indeed. For more details on this, go back and reread chapter 14, "Using a Microphone."

It is important to be aware that different situations call for different approaches and that what works in one place may not work at all in another. If, for instance, you are used to speaking acoustically in front of small crowds and then suddenly you are called upon to speak in front of a large audience all miked up, you might at first find this daunting—not least because of the mike. If you are used to speaking acoustically and you're suddenly handed a microphone, you might not quite know what to do with it or how to control your output. The clarity or the volume of the amplified sound might intimidate you. (See also "The Sound of the Recorded Voice" next.) The opposite could also be true: perhaps you are used to having a mike serving as an extension of you and your instrument. You might have become comfortable with the idea of having something to hide behind. If suddenly you no longer have the mike, you might feel more exposed—very naked and vulnerable. From a technical point of view, you have to project your sound much more strongly than you are used to in order to reach the back row. This could be daunting too.

Familiarize yourself with the various situations. What are the demands? That way chances are less that you will find yourself intimidated by sudden change of plans. We all have our preferences and weaker or stronger points, but they shouldn't make much of a difference. Once you know what's expected of you, it's all a lot easier.

THE SOUND OF THE RECORDED VOICE

I'm generally quite confident about my voice. However, when I hear my recorded voice played back, I always get really embarrassed and I think, "That doesn't sound like me, does it?!" My voice sounds so different, so strange—not at all like what I remember or expect. Why is that? What do you think is the problem?

The million-dollar question! First of all, there is *no problem.*

One of the great challenges for most people seems to be getting used to and accepting the sound of their own voice played back. This is a bizarre phenomenon with a surprisingly simple explanation. We are largely creatures of habit. If we are very used to something, it takes time for us to adapt to something else. This is true for the sound of your voice as well.

How you hear the natural sound of your voice is a mixture of *inner and outer hearing*. That basically means a mix of sound being projected out and then received back from the outside into your ears (outer hearing)—and sound being bone-conducted inside your skull to your ears (inner hearing). Try talking or singing while blocking your ears completely. You'll find that you can still hear yourself. This is your inner hearing.

You are the only person who will ever hear the inside resonance of your voice. Therefore, what you perceive to be your voice sound is not entirely identical with the pure outer sound that other people hear. The sound that they hear—or in the case of a recording, the sound that is being played back—is how you really sound to the outside world.

The reason why you don't like this sound is *not* because it is no good. You don't like it because *it is not what you are <u>used to</u> hearing* and so you don't entirely recognize it.

There is only one thing to do: get used to it! Learn to love and accept your sound. Record yourself and play it back till you finally become used to the sound and comfortable with it. Practice your speeches with a recorder running. Even better, video yourself. You can then work on body language and expressions as well. Most people are freaked out when they watch themselves on video the first couple of times. The first time I saw myself on a video recording, I cried!

Trust me: it does get easier with time. And remember, as always, you are your own worst critic. Work on improving the things that you don't like or that don't seem to work for you, but don't be too hard on yourself.

An additional factor could also be that we tend to have sound pictures in our heads of how we *would like* to sound. While this is not a bad thing because it can help us develop sound and style, it does tend to slightly blur our immediate perception. When we hear ourselves played back, our perfect picture cracks a little bit. I find that is true with dialects and accents too. I, for instance, didn't grow up in the States and spent most of my life in Europe, mainly in Denmark and Britain. I clearly have a Danish or at least non-British or non-American accent—but I no longer hear that. I would swear that I sound British or American, although, realistically, I know that I really don't!

This brings me to the last, cruel point—the truth—the awful fact that ultimately a recording never lies. You can of course get it treated, but nothing escapes the recording. Like an unfortunate photograph, an awkward recording is one dreadful moment forever captured for you to cringe over.

So practice, get feedback, but most of all get used to your own natural sound. If you don't already, learn to love your sound because, yes, I'm afraid you do sound "like that"—sorry. But I'm sure it's not half bad anyway.

VOICE PITCH, RANGE, AND COLOR

My voice is unnaturally dark for a woman, and my range is quite limited. What can I do, if anything?

Oh, I just love this one! I mentioned this phenomenon at the very beginning of the book.

Look, I'm sure that your voice is perfectly normal. In fact, I'm willing to bet!

I have lost count of the many clients who, when they first came to me, genuinely believed that their voices were somehow strange, limited, and different.

All I can say is this: Yep, your voice *is* different. All voices are. But I'm positive that your voice is in no way strange or limited. *You* may be limiting *it*—but that we can fix. After a few adjustments, most people quickly discover a voice they didn't even realize they had! When that happens, it is a wonderful breakthrough experience for both the client and the coach.

GETTING HOARSE

Why do I sometimes get hoarse when I speak?

You get hoarse when your voice gets tired or worn out due to poor technique. If your technique is insufficient, you will automatically try to compensate by applying pressure to your voice. Pressure equals strain, and as a result you may get hoarse or even lose your voice for a period of time. Go through the Basics again and review chapter 12, "The Voice Doctor," where you can find advice on how to deal with hoarseness and similar symptoms.

In difficult situations, an untrained speaker is likely to try to compensate for lack of volume and control by pushing their voice beyond its limits and therefore causing damage.

When your voice gets hoarse during or after a speech, it is a clear sign that something is not right. It is not natural, inevitable, or in any way necessary for the voice to become hoarse no matter how much, how long, or how dynamically you speak.

Practice your vocal technique to overcome problems and avoid these situations.

And get enough rest. If your body is tired, your voice gets tired too, and it takes much less for it to wear out.

SUDDEN "VOICE BREAKS"

I'm reluctant to use voice dynamics, high volume, etc. when I speak because when I do, sometimes my voice will suddenly "break." It's like it has a big gap right in the middle. It sounds ridiculous, and it is very embarrassing. It reminds me of when I was a young boy. It makes me nervous and insecure. What can I do?

First of all, rest assured that your voice inherently has no breaks or big gaps. It is perfect and whole and knows its job. It is *your* job to allow your voice to do what it is supposed to do without interfering.

If you experience a break in your voice, *you* put it there. So now *you* get rid of it by getting the Basics right. Great support and smooth transitioning between the voice functions will get rid of breaks for good.

A break sounds and feels almost like a change of gear. It is an abrupt change in sound and sometimes volume. Singers sometimes do this on purpose to accommodate a certain style. (Country singers and some pop singers often use breaks, for instance, not to mention the traditional yodeling singing style of the southern European Alps region.) But when breaks are not done on purpose—when they just happen by themselves when we least want them—they are often the cause of great frustration and embarrassment.

Breaks are often associated with change of register. Not so. This is one of the most common myths about voice technique. Breaks have nothing to do with change of register as such; they have to do with change of vocal function. Registers have their specific place on the scale, but they do not necessarily decide which vocal function we use, nor does the vocal function decide on a register for us.

An *intentional* break occurs when we *consciously*, on purpose, *change the vocal* <u>function</u>.

An un*intentional* break occurs when basic technique is not properly applied and when a change of voice function, *sometimes* along *with the change of register*, is not being properly supported. It happens when the voice is not allowed to operate naturally and make the changes that it is supposed to make. The voice will try to find a way to compensate. The cords will "click" into their desired state, resulting in an unintended break and loss or change of sound.

If you can't take your voice to a higher note without breaking, first look for tension, especially in the jaw and under the jaw. Then look at your support. Chances are that you are simply not lifting it well enough. If you add constrictions around the cords, preventing them from stretching, there is no way in this world you are going to reach that note! So there go your dynamics out the window. If, on the other hand, you support your voice properly, relax, apply the Basics, and allow the voice to work its wonders—it will. Reread chapter 6, "The Basics," and chapter 7, "Vocal Modes."

WORKING WITH A VOICE OR A COMMUNICATIONS COACH

Will working with a voice or a communications coach jeopardize my personal style?

No, absolutely not! Not unless you are working with the wrong coach.

I have often met clients that on the one hand wanted to learn but on the other hand seemed averse as if they somehow had the idea that I would attempt to strip them of their personal style.

I understand where this fear could come from. Public speaking has changed over the years—what was considered appropriate, respectable, and good public speaking fifty years ago is not the same today. We have certainly become more personal, less "old school," less authoritative than back then. So if your coach is coming from that sort of approach, they could surely teach you a few useful things, but chances are that they would indeed collide with your own personal style and how you would like to see yourself in today's speaking arena. So rather than not using a coach at all, find one who suits your style, who represents or at least understands and appreciates where you are coming from and where you would like to go. You need a coach who sees *you*. You and your coach need to be on the same page.

Coaches are not there to dictate your style. They are there to help you develop and enhance *your* style. They might give you good advice on what seems to work best for you, but ultimately style is about personal preference and taste. It is not the coach's job to decide what's right or wrong for you. Coaches are there to assist your growth and help you develop your skills further—nothing less, nothing more. Most coaches I know do this very well.

WARMING UP BEFORE A SPEECH

Should I always warm up before a speech/performance? If so, how?

I think that you should always get yourself in ready mode, psych yourself up before any performance—whatever that means to you. Most performers develop their own way of doing this and of knowing that now they are "on." This is what I referred to earlier as creating a Stage Persona that can be activated by a Performance Trigger—a personal ritual that switches them on like a light bulb. The Quick Performance Prep in chapter 13 is an example of a trigger like that. A trigger can be a single word that in itself contains an entire command, or it can be a whole ritual that you go through every time before a performance. It can be both. It can be long or short or whatever suits you and the circumstances you are working under. People have different triggers and things that they feel help them get ready and *feel* ready.

A trigger always works, if only because you have *decided* that it does and you *believe* that it does. As I said, it works almost like turning on a light bulb and you are ready to glow.

Some people rest or meditate for a few minutes or more.

Some people say a prayer.

Some people have a special drink.

Some people use a specifically programmed trigger.

Some people jump around.

And some people just internally turn their switch on.

The list goes on. There is no one way to do it—whatever works for you, really.

You probably really meant actual *vocal warm-ups*. Well, this may surprise you, but I don't actually favor doing a lengthy warm-up before a performance. At least I don't think that it is really necessary. I do like to get myself all fired up and ready and then save my gunpowder for when I get on stage.

But it really depends on how I feel. If I'm all good, I hardly do anything. If I'm a little bit under the weather, I might do a lot. I always do a few breathing and support exercises just to ensure that my engine is running smoothly and to get a nice oxygen high. Then I do a little soothing *hmmmmmmm* to shake up any mucus that might be lurking around. And then a few slides, starting nice and low down my range, just to make sure that I have no "frogs" and that my support is strong and my projection focused and clear.

If I really don't feel in top shape, I do some more low humming exercises with lots of overtone vibrations like a chant. This loosens any unwanted mucus on the cords and gives them a nice warming massage.

Warm up till you feel that you're ready. I'd say never more than 10–15 minutes *max* of exercises (not including ritual). Choose a few of your favorite exercises that work to give you physical proof that you are ready. This makes you feel in control and will, as well, help you cope with any nerves or insecurities.

Personally, I wouldn't do anything more. If pressed for time, I favor the trigger ritual (including deep breathing) over physical warm-up exercises anytime. The adrenaline would take care of the rest and get me warm in no time anyway.

Just remember that you do need to be "on" *straight away.* You can't spend half an hour getting there as you go along. If you generally find it hard to get going in the first few minutes, try incorporating something into your speech where it's OK for you to move a lot. That helps the adrenalin and pumps oxygen faster around your body, calms you down, and sharpens your mind. I find it helps me if I'm a bit weak or tired—it kind of jolts me into super action.

THE NEED TO LEARN VOICE TECHNIQUE

Is it really necessary to learn vocal technique? If so, why? It seems like a lot of work!

Is it really necessary? Well, it's certainly very *useful,* but I can't claim that it's *always* necessary. Not unless you have problems.

Now, as with anything, some people are naturals, while some need a bit of support. There are undoubtedly lots of speakers who have thriving, successful careers and who do not have any technical knowledge at all. And they never had any problems. Why?

Well, they probably never restricted their voice in the first place, or maybe they just managed to learn by themselves as they went along. However, judging by the number of people that I've seen over the years, I'd say that these natural speakers are in the minority. Most people who use their voice a lot seem to run into some sort of voice trouble once they start to get really busy. In order to avoid this—to remain successfully *and joyfully* in business in the long run—I would certainly advise you to make that little bit of extra effort. After all, you are very dependent on your voice; it is your instrument. Being aware of the right technique and practicing in the right way will immediately make a difference.

Create a routine that works in harmony with you and your life. You'll feel good about being in control and knowing what you are doing—and also what to do differently if something suddenly doesn't work.

Learning voice technique is really not very time-consuming. Remember, it is not the *quantity* of time spent but the *quality*. If you compare the short-term investment of getting informed to the long-term hassle of dealing with problems after they occur, you'll see that there is little doubt that learning the right technique is worth it.

Part 4
Persuasive Speaking through Inner Power

CHAPTER 16

The Inner Workings

If you struggle with lack of confidence, insecurities, stage fright, crippling nervousness, or the like, it can be extremely helpful to work on these symptoms—or *responses,* as I like to call them—directly rather than just doing the practical training (voice technique, etc.) and hoping that eventually improved skills will eliminate all the psychological effects. They probably won't.

In fact, it tends to work the other way around. This is why I always recommend that you take a more holistic approach. Work on your practical skills *and* your emotional state, your nervousness, stage fright, etc. at the same time to achieve the best results. It is the most enjoyable, the most fulfilling, and unquestionably *the most efficient* way to work.

Maybe you don't feel that you need any help in this area at all—maybe you are brimming with confidence and you relish every second of limelight that you can possibly get. If so, congratulations—good for you! You can skip this part. With all your newly learned skills on top, you are now officially superpower speaker of the year. Go out and kick some butt!

Just promise yourself that you are going to come back to this section if, at some point, you run into problems that don't seem entirely rational to you. Why? Because if they are not rational—if they are not easily explained and solved in a practical, technical way—they probably aren't practical or technical problems but emotional responses.

I am aware that a holistic approach is not for everyone. As I said, if you are mainly interested in all the technical stuff, it might not be for you. But if you struggle with stage fright, nervousness, and perhaps lack of confidence, this approach is a good choice for you.

It's really simple and easy to follow, and it works. You will get the tools to stay motivated, build confidence, and trust in your own abilities. When you feel good about yourself and what you do, your voice and your entire demeanor show it.

In chapter 1, "Make Friends with Your Voice," I mentioned what I refer to as the "Inner Workings."

The way we think has a profound effect on our lives. Most of us tend to be overly self-critical and choose not to fully acknowledge our own unique qualities and talents. Instead, we focus on all the things we don't like about ourselves and the areas that we feel we should improve in. It is important to remember that while constructive self-evaluation certainly is very helpful, never-ending critique and self-bashing will lead to nowhere. Progress will be slow to nonexistent.

What's happening on the inside reflects on the outside. What you believe about yourself, life in general, work, the world, and other people deeply affects you and your well-being. In fact, it affects everything around you and creates your life experience.

So in order to achieve the best results, we need to look at how we think. Is anything holding us back, preventing us from being the best that we can be? Are we keeping ourselves from exploring the brilliance and the insight that we truly have to offer?

If so, isn't it time to change that?

What if I offered you a way to combine the practical skills learning process with success and confidence building?

I have developed a very easy-to-follow and simple learning and development program that I have included for you here in this book. It is a program that I have been using for years. In fact, I rarely teach any of the practical skills anymore without taking this approach. To be perfectly honest with you, I'm not hugely keen on teaching pure technique anymore.

Luckily, there are plenty of brilliant voice coaches out there who are—there's something to suit everyone.

What I like about my program is that it offers more than just a quick first-aid fix. It actually gives you the tools to create lasting results—real change, once and for all. The fact that it's an all-in-one solution makes it really handy and comprehensive. Follow the steps, do the exercises, use the tools, and you are on your way. You have the practical training—the voice exercises on the one hand and the success- and confidence-building exercises on the other. And you have your own personal virtual coach to take you by both hands and guide you every step of the way.

Before I get into it, let me just quickly define what I mean by "success" building. Success to me is being fulfilled, being happy and at peace doing whatever it is that you're doing, feeling joy and excitement doing it, and having the privilege of being able to serve other people as well along the way, assisting them in achieving the same kind of success. Feeling at peace and joyful as opposed to feeling nervous, anxious, and stressed out has more to do with an inner state of mind than it has to do with outer circumstances. Both can be changed; it's a matter of deciding which one (or maybe changing both).

To put it very bluntly, if you are a speaker or you have to speak publicly in some capacity or other and you absolutely dread it every time, you have two choices. You can either find a new type of job where you won't have to constantly expose yourself to undue stress and anxiety—or you can decide that you actually do like your job after all and would like to keep it, and so you need to find a way to alleviate the stress and anxiety and perhaps even change it into excitement and joy instead. Which one do *you* choose?

The program speeds up and enhances the learning process by helping you create an environment to work in where you are constantly reminded of your own unique qualities, your achievements and successes, and your goals and prospects as a speaker *and as a person*. You surround yourself with healthy, positive energy, boost your confidence, and work in a passionate, constructive state of mind instead of a restrictive one. When we approach any given project with this kind of attitude, we learn, develop, grow, and accomplish our goals faster.

SO HOW DO WE DO THAT THEN?

Inspired by a concept known as the Dream Room—an environment where anything is possible, the words "no," "can't," and "impossible" are not part of the vocabulary, and absolutely no thought is dismissed as unrealistic—I decided to take the whole dream idea one step further and not only have a dream environment but also have my clients create and act out their *Dream Characters.*

My *Dream Character Program* or *DC Program* is a success and confidence-building coaching program. I use it for life coaching, *and* I use it for voice coaching when appropriate. Because most voice and performance problems stem from insecurities and emotional/psychological responses, I realized very early in my voice coaching career that this overall, holistic approach to voice performance training was the way to go. As I pointed out, these days it is rare that I am called upon to work only with voice technique. And I have to say that I relish that. The voice is a wonderful and fascinating instrument, but it is the person behind the instrument who adds excitement, flavor, and color to the music it creates. So while I am perfectly happy fine-tuning all the technical stuff, I really appreciate being able to work on the full picture too.

So that's what we will do in the DC Program. Then we'll finally fit it all into your own personalized training program, which will consist of your preferred vocal exercises, your DC exercises, and any other tips or guidelines that you feel will help you in your progress.

The DC Program consists of twenty exercises—twelve in the first part and eight in the second.

Add the DC Program to your Basic Voice Exercises from earlier, and you have your own virtual coach, your *Personalized DC Voice & Performance Training Program.*

Put your training program on your DC Vision Board so you can easily look at it and be inspired and motivated every day—and you'll never have to worry or buy another coaching program again. I'm sure that you are going to enjoy working with the Dream Character so much that you will want to use the formula for other things as well. And why not? The DC Program is for anyone and can be applied to any area of your life.

The *DC Vision Board* will have personal statements and specific exercises to suit your personal needs, as well as a structured and inspired Action Plan for you to keep track of your success and progress along the way. The board can be developed over time. Ideally, it should be constantly evolving. I have clients who have kept building and changing their boards as they themselves have evolved and changed over time. One client of mine bragged that after two years of constant building and training, his board took up an entire wall in his house. Now, that's what I call enthusiasm and dedication to the cause! (I wonder what his wife thinks of the new wallpaper, by the way.)

The *Dream Character* represents *your ideal self*. Add a specific situation or goal, and you have a very real prospective picture of your ideal self in the ideal (working) situation (enter the Stage Persona from earlier). Again, this is not about you trying to become somebody else—it is about becoming the best version of you.

You will learn how to do the *DC Visualization Exercise* any time at your own leisure to boost your chosen image and the effects of the program—or simply to have some special "you" time to relax and feel great.

You are going to learn how to create and implement your own personal ritual—your Performance Trigger—which is a simple and quick way of inducing the ultimate supportive state of mind just before an important speech or presentation.

You will get the tools to set up a very comprehensive daily routine that is guaranteed to give you great results.

The DC Program is simple and fast, and it makes you feel great about yourself and your work. And that's all you need to create progress.

DC is the ultimate training program for speakers who want to dig that little bit deeper and add that little bit more. When you follow this program, you are bound to see real, lasting results fast.

Using relaxing, inspiring exercises, the program is going to help you become clearer about what you would like to achieve. It is going to help you realize your true potential, strengthen your confidence, and learn to control nervousness. You will always be OK, regardless of the circumstances—it's a matter of choice. Once you realize this—not just on a rational but also on an emotional level—fear is no longer an option.

Becoming more aware of the inner workings and the effect that they have on you enables you to let go of old internal rules that no longer serve you and to replace them with new constructive ones. As your awareness increases, your confidence increases even more. At the same time, your practical skills are improving and you find yourself experiencing increasingly better results.

This is also going to help boost your confidence and your trust. On top of all this, you have one more thing working for you entirely by itself and free, and that is *time*. Over time, if you keep up the good work, it *is* obviously going to become easier. So you are all set—it can't go wrong! You're fast on your way to persuasive speaking through inner power.

CHAPTER 17

The Dream Character—
Bringing Out the Best in You

Perhaps you have decided to give the DC program a try, or maybe you are just curious to hear some more details. If so, now's the time.

Have you ever pictured yourself as your *ideal self*?

Have you ever played out a scene in your head where everything was perfect and exactly how you wanted it? Where other people reacted to you exactly like you would want them to?

Have you ever seen yourself doing all the things that you would love to do and imagined what life would be really like in your perfect fantasy?

Have you seen it, heard it, smelt it, felt it, and lived it so vividly that *for a moment you really believed that it was indeed happening?*

If so, your Dream Character is already part of you. If not, rest assured that it is certainly within your reach. It might be even closer than you think.

The Dream Character represents your *ideal self.* Not someone else's ideal, but *yours.*

For some people the Dream Character comes reasonably close to how they already see themselves. But for a lot of people, being their ideal self seems unreachable, something far out in the distance that they feel little or no connection with. They simply cannot comprehend how to get there.

The point of the DC Program and the DC Exercises is to create an optimal environment for you to work within, to help put you in and hopefully *keep* you in a state of mind that is conducive to enhanced learning and personal expansion. This way, learning and expanding are easier, faster, and more fulfilling.

You create that space for yourself. It is *your* truth on *your* terms—reaching for *your* goals. There is one rule, though, and that is *no objections!* In the DC environment anything is possible, so you *must* allow yourself to be the kid in the candy store. The shelves are full—you can pick anything you like. No room for modesty or limitations. You must adopt this attitude at least for now. You'll have plenty of time to be "realistic" later. Perhaps your perception of what realistic actually means will have changed by then, and you might see your dreams and goals in a different light. You are soon going to realize that your Dream Character *is* you—it already exists inside of you. Now bring it out, nourish it, and make it flourish!

OVERVIEW

Here's an overview of what's going to happen. Then, in the next chapter, we'll take each step of the exercise one bit at a time. It will all be explained very thoroughly, with guidelines and examples. So just read through it for now.

- **Goals List**

The first thing to do is to create a Goals List. You will be asked to think very carefully about your goals and dreams. You will have to write them down and *define* them so they become clear. What kind of situation do you see yourself in and how?

- **Obstacles List**

What do you see as your obstacles? What do you perceive as standing in your way? What is preventing you from getting what you want, getting to where you want to be, and *being* who you want to be? What makes accomplishing your goals "too difficult" or "not possible" even?

- **Obstacles Reviewed**

Review your Obstacles List. Do they serve you in any way? Are your obstacles as real as you think? Look closely, and you may find the very key to your progress. It's time to dig a bit deeper.

- **Positive Affirmations List**

Try replacing the word *obstacles* with the word *challenges*. Does it feel different? Imagine your obstacles to be just neutral statements with no weight either good or bad—just statements. Begin the process of creating positive affirmations out of negative statements. This is the first step toward *finding solutions.*

- **Goals Reviewed**

Return to focusing on your goals. Review them. Answer the questions as they appear in the exercise and observe how you respond emotionally. Write down your answers. Take your time, as this is very important.

- **Qualities List**

Write down the personal characteristics that you really like about yourself. This list can also include skills or abilities that you value or are proud of. Be bold. There is absolutely no room for modesty here. Write them *all* down.

- **Intended Qualities List**

This list should represent all the qualities that you *intend* to acquire. Intentions are very powerful. Fueled with strong emotion and passion, intentions become like heat-seeking missiles targeting your goals.

Note that there's a difference between the Goals List and the Intended Qualities List: The Goals List consists of things that you would like to *do, have, or achieve*. A goal is an *outer* component—something that happens as a result of something you *do*. A quality is an *inner* component—it describes something *within* you that will help you or compel you to achieve the goal. The Intended Qualities List describes *characteristics* or *skills* that you would like to acquire; it refers to *how* you would like to be or intend to become—the kind of person that you would like to *be*, not what you would like to *do*. They are of course connected, but both are important on their own as well. Now, perhaps you could argue that *skills* logically connect to something that you do. True, in one sense. You can have a goal that requires you to take a course that will *expand your skills*. That would be an *outer* goal. But the skills themselves still represent an *inner quality*.

- **Previous Successes List**

Nothing creates success more than success! Get in the frame of mind of being successful—and you will attract more of that.

Acknowledge your success. Be proud of yourself! Recognize that you have already achieved many things and that you have already been successful many times before.

Remind yourself of those things and those times, and write them down—even small things. How did they make you feel?

- **The DC Positives Selection**

By now you should have a nice Positives Selection consisting of your Goals List and Goals Reviewed answers, Positive Affirmations List, Qualities List, Intended Qualities List, and Previous Successes List. This selection is the basis for your continued growth.

Later you will add the Action Plan and the Basic Voice Exercises to complete The Personalized DC Voice and Performance Training Program. Finally, you will create a *DC Vision Board* to hang on your wall and use as your point of focus whenever you practice.

- **Create the Dream Character (DC)**

Using the Positives Selection, take the process one step further and create the Dream Character. Create an image in your mind's eye—the idea of your ideal self, a symbol, an *overall feeling* that fits your DC. You will use this image for your DC Visualization Exercise.

- **Your DC Name (Trigger)**

Attach certain words or statements to the feeling/image of your Dream Character and create your DC Name. This name is personal. It is yours, and it represents you as your Dream Character—in this case, as we're specifically targeting stage fright, etc., your (DC) Stage Persona. You will use the DC (Stage Persona) Name as your Performance Trigger.

• The DC Visualization Exercise

It's time to connect with your Dream Character at a deeper level. Through a comfortable and relaxing visualization exercise, you are going to create an even stronger connection with your DC. You are going to learn how to integrate it so it becomes an even more real and natural part of you. This is a wonderful experience that you will not want to miss. It is the pinnacle of the DC Program, and once you know how, it is such an easy yet effective tool to use.

Once you have created that space for yourself, you can go there again as often as you like—it is going to boost the identity of your DC even more every time. You will be given clear instructions on how to prepare for and carry out this exercise.

That's it. Follow the instructions, take the time you need, go through the program step by step, and enjoy yourself. Later on we will add your Action Plan and create your Vision Board.

Because this training program covers all the different aspects of healthy, strong voice performance, both practical and emotional, as well as giving you the option to continuously add to it yourself for your further development, it is probably the most comprehensive voice training program you will ever find. And, I'm willing to bet, the most efficient one too. I have seen so many people achieve much more than they expected in *a much shorter time than expected.* The DC Program inspires confidence, and *confidence creates success!*

By creating a dream environment, a restriction-free zone, and focusing on plus thoughts (positives) rather than minus thoughts (negatives), so much more becomes possible and so much more is achieved.

In my DC workshops I see people of all ages with different backgrounds and very different goals. It always makes for an interesting and open atmosphere. I put no demands on anyone, but I do ask this:

◊ Are you looking for a way to open up doors and explore new avenues?

◊ Are you open to dream about your ideal circumstances, your ideal self—*your ideal reality?*

◊ Do you dare to believe that your vision could be stronger than your current circumstances? Do you believe that it is possible to replace old thoughts and convictions with new ones—and are you prepared to try to do that?

◊   Are you willing to accept that your life, your current circumstances, and your future are your responsibility?

◊   Are you willing to take the few but necessary first steps toward an even better, even stronger, even more successful you—whatever success means *to you*?

◊   Are you prepared to acknowledge that in almost every problem of life, you are the problem—but you are the solution as well?

◊   If this program is right for you—if it works in harmony with your inner knowing—are you willing to commit to making a continued effort and to trust in your own progress even when, at times, it may seem to be moving at a slower pace than you might expect or want?

If you are, then the universe is going to give you everything you want, or should I say, *intend* to have.

The DC program takes you on a journey into your future life—the future meaning any moment from now on and onwards. It gives you the opportunity to see yourself do all the things that you love to do, to be the absolute best that you can imagine yourself to be, and to *capture the feelings that it gives you*. This is incredibly inspiring and motivating and it *is* going to generate real change. Feelings, emotions, and *passion* are incredibly powerful energy conductors. When you act on passion—when you add strong emotion to what you do and allow yourself to be present in that moment, to really *feel it*—you produce an enormous amount of energy. The more enthusiasm and pure intense energy you can put into the program, the more powerful and effective it is, and the sooner you are going to see results.

Work your way through the exercises from start to finish.

Before embarking on any exercise, I suggest that you read through the entire section first and make sure that you fully understand what you are supposed to do. At first you may not always be sure *why* you are doing it. I ask that you trust me on this one, as the reasons will become clear as we move ahead.

If you run into problems or have any doubts, go back and read the description of the relevant exercise again. Always make sure you know exactly what to do before you continue. Take your time. Don't rush through the exercises. If you feel like it's a lot of work, simply break down the program into smaller bits. Do an exercise or two a day or whatever—as long as you finish all of them and keep your focus. Make sure that you manage to maintain a feeling of continuum throughout the entire process.

Get a notebook, a folder, or a ring binder where you can work and expand on your exercises along the way and exchange or add pages when you need to. One important note: *Always* write in present tense or present continuous tense; this has a much stronger effect on your subconscious mind. Write "I am, I am going to, I am being, I do, I have, I am having," etc, instead of "I would like to, I could, I would, I wish, I will," and so forth. This is important. I will explain this further in Exercise 4, the Positive Affirmations List.

So now, let's get down to business—try out the DC Program for yourself! I wish you a wonderful and exciting DC time. Enjoy yourself, experiment, and have lots of progress, success, and fun!

For each exercise, first read through the entire exercise and the accompanying text, then go back and complete each step of the exercise in order.

Illustration 18 - Hhmm… Clerk

EXERCISE 1: THE GOALS LIST

- Think very carefully about your goals and dreams. What is it that you would like to achieve? (In principle, these could be any goals and not just speaking or career-related ones. But for the purpose of simplicity; when using this program in conjunction with your voice performance training, you might want to focus your attention specifically on goals related to this area. You can always expand on it later.)
- *Write down* your goals as they come naturally to you.
- Divide your goals into two boxes—one for *immediate goals*, the other for *long-term goals*.
- Now, *structure* your goals. Define them so they become clear. Make them look and feel clear and simple. Structure and clarity will make the process much more comprehensible and help you focus better. Rewrite if necessary.
- *Focus* on them. If you find focusing hard, perhaps your goals are not clear enough yet. If so, define them again but do not change the *essence* of the goals or dreams; do not make them smaller.
- Consider: Maybe you need to *divide* your goals into smaller parts.
- Finally, give your goals *deadlines*. Think about what would be realistic timeframes for reaching each goal.
- And then *commit* to pursuing your goals and keeping the deadlines (more about this in part 5, where you are going to make your Action Plan).

You know, sometimes, in order for us not to feel overwhelmed by all the things that we would like to do and achieve, all we need to do is to cut those things into bite-size chunks to make them more digestible. We need to take baby steps and perhaps focus on one or two things at a time. It is easier to climb a mountain one step at a time than to jump all the way from the ground to the top in one go. Reaching a big goal is the result of a vision followed by action—sometimes many actions. In other words, a goal is the sum of a number of smaller goals or steps. This is common sense and does not mean that climbing the mountain and reaching the top is impossible; it just means that taking it step by manageable step is more comprehensible.

If, say, your goal is to be a keynote speaker at a major prestigious event or conference, that is certainly achievable, but probably not as your first engagement. And the question becomes: If you only started speaking a few months ago, would you really *want* an obligation like that just yet? Would you feel comfortable? Maybe not—maybe you'd actually be better off speaking at a few smaller events first before you hit the major leagues.

We all do things at our own pace for our own reasons, and that's completely OK. Just never be afraid of the mountain. Climbing a mountain is a wonderful, enriching, and challenging journey. Standing on the top will be the greatest thrill and the most beautiful thing you've ever done or seen— till next time. Once you are there and you are enjoying the view, the thought of the next mountain seems a bit less daunting and a lot more exciting. And every time you become a better climber for it. But watch out—it's highly contagious. You're going to want to climb the whole time wondering what the heck your problem was in the first place.

Think big, but be prepared to take smaller steps. Make it a challenging journey but not completely inconceivable. If it is *completely unimaginable* to you that you could *ever* reach your goal, you will not be motivated. In this case, start smaller. Otherwise work with the notion that if you can imagine it, you can create it. Remember that this is a dream environment.

Albert Einstein once said, "If you can believe it you can conceive it." Today, this way of thinking is familiar to most people. Its principles are often referred to as the *Law of Attraction*. This law states that like attracts like—that we become what we think about. It states that you will attract into your life whatever you give your energy, focus, and attention to—whether wanted or unwanted. Thoughts and feelings are energy. You are constantly giving off vibrations of energy when you think and feel. These vibrations can be picked up and received by other people and the Universe. According to the Law of Attraction, the Universe responds to whatever you are offering by giving you more of whatever you are sending out. It does not care whether it is good for you or not; it simply responds to your signal.

Believe that you can succeed, intend to succeed—and you are going to succeed! Basically, believe it, intend it, create it! When you hold a steady focus on something and your intent to achieve it or to have it is clear and strong, then you *are* going to create it. *You are going to attract the people, situations, and opportunities you need. Be alert and ready to take advantage of these opportunities when they appear.*

Ever since I can remember, I have always found this to be true in my own life. In my school yearbook, we all had to have a statement or quote provided by our friends according to how they perceived us. My quote was "Anything you want to do—you can!" Even then, apparently, I very strongly felt this to be true. Actually, it often put me in trouble's way, as many grown-ups at the time seemed to be passionately against that notion and indeed very provoked by it. How utterly self-important and conceited of me to think like that! Well, perhaps so, perhaps not. The fact is—it worked. When most of my friends went on to do what was expected of them, I went on to do what I loved (music) without a thought for anything else. I heard a lot of condescending comments like "Isn't it time you grew up and got a real job? You can't be fooling around like that forever."

Well, a few years later most of my friends sang a different tune. I remember one conversation with a dear childhood friend of mine who was unhappy with her work situation, her marriage, etc. Life hadn't quite turned out the way she had hoped. She told me, "Look at you; you're so lucky. You love what you do, you travel the world, and you are your own boss and answer to nobody. If only I had had the opportunity to do that! Now it's too late; I've got the next twenty years or so cut out for me like this."

It hit me like a hammer. The second she said it, I felt devastated. I said nothing while she paused and thought about what she had just said. Then she laughed. She realized that she *had* in fact had the opportunity, *but she had made different choices*—choices that had seemed more appropriate, more attractive, or safer for her at the time. "Let me rephrase that," she said. "If only I had had *the courage* to do what you did and had *followed my heart*." "You still can," I told her. "I guess you're right," she said—and eventually, she did.

Our choices make us who we are. No matter what kind of choices we make, though, there will be rough patches. Those are valuable lessons. They tell us about ourselves, our needs and passions, and our ever-evolving place in the world. Relish those choices and those lessons. Be grateful every day for the wisdom they represent. It's yours for the keeping *and* for the sharing with other people.

Now, set your goals and make the choice to pursue them.

EXERCISE 2: THE OBSTACLES LIST

What do you see as your obstacles? What is keeping you from achieving your goals now? What do you perceive as standing in your way? What is preventing you from getting what you want, getting to where you want to be, and *being* who you want to be?

What makes accomplishing your goals "too difficult" or "not possible" even?

During the first exercise, I bet a lot of thoughts came up, some of them perhaps telling you to calm down a bit, take it easy, *be realistic*, don't get your hopes up too high, etc.

These are all valid thoughts and deserve looking into. We cannot just ignore the way we intuitively react when talking about our own dreams and goals. These reactions are firmly rooted in our subconscious. They are thought patterns that most of us have been conditioned throughout our entire lives to accept as truth. And maybe they *are* true—but maybe, just maybe, they are not.

In any case, let's not pretend that we can just ignore those thoughts and then they'll magically go away all by themselves, because that's probably not going to happen. And maybe that's not such a bad thing. They could be useful. They could show us where our real challenges lie and help us find a way to overcome them.

So let's write these thoughts down too.

- Which thoughts appeared as you wrote down your goals—none, loads, or a few? Write them down.
- Did you perceive any obstacles? Make a list of all the obstacles you see standing in your way—all the things that, in your opinion, make achieving your goals difficult or impossible even. Be honest.

Done? How did the Obstacles List make you feel in comparison to writing your Goals List? My guess is not so great, right?

OK, so why spend time on something that makes you feel bad? I'll tell you why: When something makes you feel bad—when you recognize something that represents pain to you—you are more likely to commit to moving *away* from it. Human beings respond naturally to either pleasure or pain. We are instinctively drawn away from pain and toward pleasure. So why do we not all live a life of total ecstasy? Well, because we tend to focus more on the pain aspect, thinking about and defining what we can *not* do and what we do *not* want rather than on what we *can* do and what we *do* want. And as we tend to get exactly what we focus on, *focusing on what we do not want will simply give us more of that!*

So we won't focus on your obstacles for long. Before you put your Obstacles List aside, though (put it in the back of your notebook, folder, or binder away from the other exercises), let's first answer a few questions about your obstacles (the next exercise).

After that, unless you want to keep your Obstacles List as a reminder of your progress, you could perform a little ritual to mark the change or transition that is about to take place in your life. Rituals can have a lot of powerful energy because they tend to strengthen our commitment to whichever cause we are choosing. Some people like to literally bury a part of their past that no longer serves them or even to burn it. Would you find it helpful to do the same? Thank the past for what it has taught you and given you, then send it on its way, as it no longer serves you and your purpose. But for now, you need your Obstacles List to do the next exercise.

EXERCISE 3: OBSTACLES REVIEWED

Now look at your Obstacles List. How does it make you feel?

Heavy, right?

So, I guess you might as well give up?

Hang on a minute—hold your horses! Let's answer a few questions first. Let's say, for now, that most of your obstacles could be *perceived* obstacles. What if they could be merely *convictions or beliefs* that you at some point have adopted? What if they are not as real as you think? Now, is that a scary thought or an empowering thought—or maybe both?

Ask yourself the following questions, and try to answer as honestly as you possibly can:

- Is it possible that these obstacles could simply be *convictions?*
- If so, what do these convictions give you? What do they do for you? Do they serve you in any positive way?
- If they do not serve you, why are you holding on to them? Do you need them? Are you perhaps more comfortable and safer staying where you are instead of moving forward?

- Is it possible that these obstacles could simply be reflections of your own inner fear? Could they perhaps be excuses, rather than *real* solid obstacles, keeping you from taking action?
- Is it possible that these obstacles could hold the very key to your progress? Is it possible that by identifying the fear and what caused it in the first place, you could dissolve the obstacles?
- What is the worst that could happen if you did decide to move forward with your goals and dreams?
- Is it worth it not trying? Is it worth staying stuck versus taking a quantum leap?
- What are the costs of these obstacles on a daily basis? What are the costs on a long-term basis? What were the costs in the past?
- If you choose to admit defeat to the obstacles and choose to stay where you are, not to move forward, what will this mean for your future? What are the consequences? What will your life be like? Who will you be, in your own eyes, in the eyes of others?
- What will it mean to you *and* to others around you if you keep holding part of yourself back?
- Who is responsible for these choices and the outcome?

Write down your answers. Then ask yourself these things:

- Are you still absolutely certain that the obstacles are as real as you perceive them?
- Do they represent the ultimate truth?
- Are they based on *your* truths or perhaps the truths of others?
- Compare to your past. Is there perhaps a pattern emerging? Do you recognize obstacles that have kept you from moving forward and achieving goals in the past?
- What are your three most limiting beliefs?
- Why are you holding on to them? What is holding on to them doing for you?
- What would happen if you chose to let go of those beliefs?
- Would you be willing to do that?

Write down your answers.

Here's my take on obstacles that I invite you to consider: there's a difference between real, actual, immediate obstacles—and perceived, "imaginary" obstacles.

Real obstacles, or "solid" obstacles as I call them, are things that are physically impossible to immediately overcome or move out of our way or change—they cannot be *immediately* dissolved. We need to create a way *around* these obstacles so that we can continue on our way forward. We might have to take a detour to get to our next destination, but we are going to get there, nevertheless.

Imaginary obstacles are ones that we perceive as being real, but in fact, they are not. They are barriers that we set up for ourselves. Their main job is to provide us with suitable *excuses* not to act upon our dreams and goals. Often, when we are faced with an imaginary obstacle, what seems to be the immediate problem is in fact not the real issue at all. It is merely a *response*, an effect of something else, some underlying event or issue hidden from our direct view. It may just take a change of thought or perception to dissolve these obstacles, to open up and create a way forward.

Imaginary obstacles are restrictions in our own beliefs and thought patterns that are blocking our way forward. They are not real. They are not fixed. They are imaginary obstacles that can be *re-imagined.*

Sometimes it's hard to tell the difference between the two kinds of obstacles. Does it matter? Well, not really. Effectively, if we choose to see all obstacles as imaginary—the solid ones merely causing a slight delay in realization—then we are well on our way.

Typical imaginary obstacles stem from any of the following: lack of self esteem, stuck internal rules (probably stemming from upbringing), habitual old patterns, inability to take action (procrastination, essentially caused by fear), confusion (inability to define goals and lack of focus and strategy), fear of being judged, fear of failure, fear of risk-taking, fear of responsibility, fear of losing an (often false) sense of control, fear of making the wrong choices and missing out, which in turn leads to, well, missing out, etc.

You've noticed that fear is a big factor here. We've discussed that earlier. Basically, once again we can conclude or *confirm* that fear is the biggest obstacle of all.

And guess what? Fear is a feeling. It is not a solid object, so it cannot be a solid obstacle. What that means is that *if we can overcome the feeling, we can overcome the obstacle.* I want you to consider this and keep it in mind. It is very important.

These are the most common excuses for being unable to move forward: *lack of money, lack of resources, and lack of competence. All* of these can be overcome.

Another excuse is *other people.* We sometimes feel that other people stand in our way of moving forward. Well, while we cannot control other people, we can certainly choose whom we surround ourselves with. It is also up to us to decide how much power we choose to give to those people—how much influence they should be allowed to have over our lives. Power needs feeding; if it is not fed, it starves and eventually shrivels away. We tend to forget that although we naturally make choices based on or involving the people around us, essentially we are all free individuals and can do what we want. And mostly we will—sooner or later.

If you really want something, it is very hard to suppress it for too long. And why should you? If you are happy and fulfilled, it reflects on everyone around you. If you're not, that reflects as well.

If you think about it, there is always something you can do to change things. Usually it turns out you have more options than you imagined. All situations, no matter how tough or complicated, can be changed. Some just call for more determination and diligence than others.

When faced with stubborn obstacles like that, we have to decide whether or not we have the urge, the motivation, the passion, and the energy to overcome it. Is the end result really that important for us? Are we willing to pay the price? What if we are facing an obstacle that implies a very serious challenge that cannot immediately be overcome, at least not till something else has been overcome first? Or we find ourselves in circumstances that, for the time being, seem to make it *physically* impossible to move toward a certain goal. This could involve a physical or mental handicap, a severe disease, or other difficult conditions like extreme poverty—circumstances that, for most of us, tend to make our own problems fade in comparison.

Well, of course, every situation is different and each person has to decide what is true for them. But we have all heard miraculous stories of little people taking giant steps against all odds—people faced with the most unforgiving circumstances. Most people naturally react to stories like this by saying, "I could never have done that!"

Are you absolutely sure? Do you think the other person planned it like that? Maybe at some point they couldn't imagine it either—but eventually they came through. It was possible, I would say, because they persevered and they believed and because something within them told them that they simply *had* to. This "something" added power to their faith and their ability to trust that if they really and truly committed themselves to the cause—if they did everything they possibly could on their part—the Universe would provide the rest.

Someone once said, "A problem is only ever as big or as small as you choose to see it."

I trust that when you have finished the DC Program, you are going to look at obstacles in a different light—that you are going to notice a difference, a shift in the "weight" of your obstacles.

Reconsider the terms "being realistic" and "being sensible." If we choose to believe that restrictions and limitations are necessary and "all part of growing up," then that is probably how it will be. But is it really that sensible? Is it sensible to blindly accept that placing barriers in front of us is the only way forward? I think not.

In any case, this is all about the *Dream Character.*

The Dream Character doesn't have to be "grown up." It has to be exactly what it wants to be. It responds only to constructive thoughts of endless possibilities, progress, and change for the (even) better. It chooses to believe in the reality that is a boundless source of free artistic and general expression and creativity.

I encourage you to join in. You might like it. And before you know it, you might, just might, find yourself taking some giant steps of your own.

EXERCISE 4: THE POSITIVE AFFIRMATIONS LIST

Try replacing the word *obstacle* with the word *challenge*. Does it feel different?

Imagine your obstacles to be just neutral statements with no weight either good or bad.

Positive affirmations are positive thoughts or statements that are repeated over and over. As you repeat them *and* infuse them with real emotion and passion, they go directly to your subconscious mind, where they begin to manifest as your reality. When you use positive affirmations, you decisively convert negative, restrictive statements into positive, constructive statements.

Begin with simply replacing minus words with plus words. For example, "*I'm not* smart enough" becomes "*I am very* smart—in fact *more than* smart enough!" "*I'm not confident* enough" becomes "*I am confident* and, in fact, *every day I'm getting more and more confident!*" "I'm too shy" could become "Every day I'm taking steps, moving forward, feeling more and more safe and comfortable with other people, in front of other people. I am finding communicating easier and easier, and I am becoming more and more open and outgoing so that speaking publicly is becoming more and more attractive to me, easier and easier, more and more fun, etc."

How to Construct Your Positive Affirmations

- Speak in the present tense and present continuous tense. Use the terms "I am," "I am being," "I do," I have," "I am having," etc., as opposed to "I would like to," "I could," "I would," "I wish," "I will," or "I will be," which indicate something that you either want but haven't yet got or something that "will be" sometime in the indefinite future. You need results now—not in thirty years or so! For example, say, "I am being completely comfortable regardless of the size of the crowd" as opposed to "I will not be uncomfortable because of the size of the crowd."

- Always avoid using the word *not*. Focus clearly on *what you want* rather than focusing on what you *do not want*. Use positive (plus) words. Formulate your statements in such ways that they clearly state what you *do* want to achieve, be, or become as opposed to what you *do not* want.

- Use passionate, *emotive* language—strong positive words, such as *fantastic, amazing, exciting, fulfilling, excellent, confident, comfortable, invigorated, energized, refreshed, brilliant, wonderful, incredible,* etc. These are all powerful words that will strengthen your positive affirmations even more.

- *Repeat, repeat, repeat! There is enormous power in repetition.* Strengthen your statements using repetitive phrases like "more and more, better and better, stronger and stronger, easier and easier," etc. You can also use the term "even more."

- Also use the terms *and therefore, and furthermore, so that,* etc., to strengthen motivation. For example, say, "I am more and more confident every day and therefore I am more easily inspired. I'm getting better and better at letting go and being in the moment, trusting my abilities and my intuition, and I am enjoying speaking in front of my colleagues every day more and more." Binding your sentences together, connecting them, and allowing them to back each other up adds reason and potency.

- Use the term *in fact* to underline a point. For example, say "I'm calm and confident on stage. In fact, I am so confident that every time I speak, I am enjoying it more and more."

Things to Avoid When Constructing Your Positive Affirmations

- In general, avoid words that have a negative feel, like *don't, can't, shan't, no, not, never, maybe, if, probably, could, should, might, may, perhaps, impossible,* and similar negatively loaded words.
- Avoid words like *try, want, hope, but,* and *hopefully* because they indicate that you are wanting something—but not having it, trying for something—but not making it, hoping for something—but not getting it, etc.
- Avoid terms like *always, forever,* and *in the future,* which are very diffuse expressions as well as indefinite time frames. Give it a specific time to start working. Say "from this moment in time (now)," "when I do this or that," "when I meet with this person," "when I arrive at this place," etc.
- Avoid adjectives that are not easily defined, such as *normal* or *perfect.* If you can ask yourself "What does *normal* actually mean?" it is perhaps not defined clearly enough.
- Avoid ambiguity. Be precise. Say exactly what you mean—and mean what you say.

Converting words and statements is an ongoing process. Practice doing this every time a negative, self-limiting thought enters your mind. Make a habit of it.

Begin right now to create Positive Affirmations out of negative statements using statements from your Obstacles List.

This may seem weird and perhaps difficult at first. Maybe you will even feel like you are lying to yourself sometimes, but that's OK. Fake it till you make it, as they say. And you are going to make it!

Just keep working on your list and watch it grow. Have fun with it. When you feel that you are done for now, put your Obstacles List in the back of your folder or binder, somewhere that you can't see it. If at a later stage you feel that you need to remind yourself of the heavy feelings it brought forth, by all means, knock yourself out—literally. You could also choose to dispose of it altogether with a little ritual like I described earlier. It's up to you to decide what is more powerful for you. Sometimes an Obstacles List can provide you with "proof" later on of what has been achieved "in spite" of those obstacles, and that can be very inspiring and motivating for some people. Do what you feel.

Whatever your decision, for now, make a commitment to part completely with your heavy obstacle feelings. You have allowed them to come out of your system, and they've had their say. Now let them rest in peace. Let them stay on the paper that you've put away or destroyed.

Keep your Positive Affirmations List and Goals List in front of you. Pause a moment. Then breathe deeply a few times. Clear your focus. Then *change* your focus to the next exercise.

EXERCISE 5: GOALS REVIEWED

Focus again on your Goals List. Read through it. Is anything missing? You can always add more things. (If you do and more obstacles appear, let them be heard—write them down, review them, convert them, and then let them rest in peace like the others before them.)

Now, focusing on your goals—how do you feel?

Ask yourself the following questions and write down your answers. Take your time. The Goals Review is very important. Answer every question and observe how you respond emotionally.

- Look at every single goal. Ask yourself first of all *why* you want this.
- What will it give you?

The answers may lead you to other goals.

- Add and/or redefine goals if necessary.

Then continue, asking yourself:

- What would achieving your goals and realizing your dreams mean to you? What would it give you, do for you? How would it make a difference in your life? What would it mean for your future? How would your life look different than it does now?

- How would it *feel?* How proud would you be? How grateful?
- Would it make a difference in the lives of others—the people closest to you? If so, how? What would it mean to them?
- Would you be able to contribute even more, to make a greater difference to others and the world? If so, how?
- How would that make you feel?

Write down your answers.

- Ask the same questions again, this time using present tense. For example, ask, "How *does* it feel?"
- Imagine that all your goals and dreams have already been fulfilled. Notice your reaction. Write it down.

Now answer this:

- Do you believe that you *deserve* to be happy and fulfilled?
- Do you believe that you *deserve* to be more successful and enjoy your work more?
- Do you believe that you *have the potential* to be happier, more fulfilled, more recognized, more successful, more _____ (you fill in the blank)?
- Do you believe that being happier and more fulfilled, having more joy and confidence, you would be able to contribute more to the world around you, to your family and friends, and at work?
- Do you have a sense of purpose—something that you would like to share with the world?
- Do you believe that you have the potential to do so?
- If so, who is responsible for fulfilling that potential?

Well done. That was a lot of questions, I know. Hopefully some of them ignited or inspired new thoughts or insights.

Now take a well-deserved break before you move on to the next exercise.

EXERCISE 6: THE QUALITIES LIST

Sometimes we tend to forget about our good qualities. We forget to appreciate them and cherish them, simply perhaps because, over time, we get used to them and take them for granted. Or maybe we tend to take on the idea that it's bigheaded to recognize our own qualities. We don't want people to think that we are "too big for our own boots."

I say, buy bigger boots!

- Think about any personal *characteristics* that you love or like about yourself. Write them down—all of them!
- Think about any skills or abilities that you value or are proud of. Write them down—all of them!
- Don't forget all the things that you have to offer that made you want to be a better communicator and performer/speaker in the first place. Write them down too.

Apart from that last one, your answers should be *general* answers. They do not have to do with your work, with speaking or performing. They could be things like "I'm a good parent, a good friend, a good listener," "I'm very understanding of other people and sensitive toward their feelings," "I have a lot to offer," or "I'm funny, smart, intelligent, and beautiful."

Put down anything that springs to mind—really *anything*!

And please, there is absolutely *no room for modesty* here! Write down *all* the good stuff. Allow yourself to be completely bold and honest. *Anything you value, like, love, or appreciate—write it down!*

Notice how it feels to realize that you already have so much value. Be grateful. Congratulate yourself. Love and appreciate yourself and all that you already have.

If you find it hard—many people do—or if it makes you feel funny, just remind yourself that it's your list. You don't have to show it to anyone if you don't want to. Remember that often—maybe because we're so used to our own good qualities—we tend to undervalue them and simply take them for granted. Until somebody reminds us, perhaps by praising us or paying us a compliment, we think nothing special of them. We often look at others and think "Wow!" We don't realize that they probably look at us in exactly the same way.

Try to look at yourself from the outside—look at yourself with the eyes of a stranger, or perhaps with the eyes of your best friend looking at your qualities. We are often kinder to our friends than we are to ourselves.

EXERCISE 7: THE INTENDED QUALITIES LIST

When you're done writing down all your qualities, it is time to make the Intended Qualities List.

This list should represent all the qualities that you *intend* to acquire.

You decide who and what you are—nobody else. So if you choose to have or acquire a certain quality, so be it.

How can you begin to attain these qualities and successfully apply them to your life?

You simply add qualities that you intend to be yours to the Qualities List. Since you intend these qualities to be yours anyway, you might as well decide that they are yours straight away. This is the first step toward acquiring them.

It may seem weird at first, but do it anyway. After a while, you are going to notice the boundaries between the two categories beginning to blur.

Looking at your intended qualities every day, thinking about them, and seeing them together with all your other qualities brings them closer to you every day more and more. Eventually you are automatically going to take the necessary steps toward acquiring the qualities that you need. You are going to call the right opportunities and the right course of action into your reality. The same process is true for your dreams and goals.

Remember that there's a difference between the Goals List and the Intended Qualities List: The Goals List consists of *things or outer circumstances* that you would like to do, have, or achieve. This could include a new job or an education of some sort that would provide you with new skills or abilities. The Intended Qualities List should describe *characteristics* that you would like to acquire. It refers to *how* you would like to *be* or intend to *become,* such as more open, more confident, etc.—not what you would like to *do.* Those are two slightly different types of goals, and we want them all in here—but on two separate lists for now.

If you have already put some qualities down on your Goals List in the beginning, don't worry about it. It doesn't matter—it's all part of the same thing. I just want you to dig really deep into all your secret lockers and pull out all the little gold nuggets lying around. We don't want to miss a thing.

EXERCISE 8: THE PREVIOUS SUCCESSES LIST

Nothing creates success more than success! So acknowledge your success. Be proud of yourself and be thankful!

- Define *success*: What is "success" to you? What does it mean to be "successful"?
- Is it possible that your definition of success is not entirely your own? If not, whose is it?
- If you'd like to redefine success, create a definition that fits your terms by asking yourself the following: How do I want to live? What do I enjoy doing? What is really important to me? What are my most important values?
- Think about the last time you felt successful. What did you do? Why did you consider it successful? How did it make you feel?
- Think about other times when you were successful. Recognize that you have already achieved many things and that you have already been successful many times before. Remind yourself of those things and those times. What were they? How did they make you feel? Write them down—even small things.
- See if you can spot a connection between what you did and how you thought *prior* to that success. Recall some of the feelings you had *before* you accomplished something really important—your excited, positive thoughts about it, your sense of focus, your inner knowing that you were going to accomplish it.
- See if you can spot a connection between what you did and how you thought *after* that success. Recall some of the feelings you had *after* you accomplished something really important—your excited, positive thoughts about it—your joy when you did succeed! Remember how that made you feel? Recall those feelings and know that success will be yours again—many times over! If you have succeeded before, you can obviously do it again. You have your list to prove it!

Absolutely anything can go on this list. Anything at all from, say, getting a job, getting a good grade, losing a few pounds, stopping smoking, being appreciated for an idea or an opinion, overcoming a fear or an obstacle of some sort, standing up for yourself and being noticed, gaining respect, saving enough money to buy something you really want . . . to giving your first speech/presentation, overcoming the nervousness, etc. Anything—big things, small things, the lot. Give yourself a huge slap on the back!

Illustration 19 -
Wanna Kiss Myself Clerk

In the wonderfully flamboyant spirit of the King of Soul himself, the Reverend Mr. James Brown, may he rest in peace, say it loud: "Damn, I wanna kiss myself! Ahhh!!!!"

EXERCISE 9: THE POSITIVES SELECTION

By now you should have a nice Positives Selection consisting of your *Goals List* and *Goals Reviewed* answers, *Positive Affirmations List*, *Qualities List* (including *Intended Qualities*), and *Previous Successes List*. (Remember, your Obstacles List should not be included here.)

From now on, unless referring to one specific sub-list, we shall be referring to all of these lists as one, which we will simply call the *DC Positives Selection*.

Good work! I'm sure you are a bit baffled right now. Maybe you didn't quite realize all the fantastic stuff that was already there. If so, I can certainly relate to that. Sometimes we tend to underestimate ourselves a bit and perhaps undervalue our achievements simply because it's "just us."

Well, we'll have none of that! There's no such thing as "just" in my book—literally. I hope that you have rediscovered how truly unique and amazing you are.

Be proud and happy and grateful for everything you are and everything you have managed to achieve so far. Just imagine where you can go from here! Remind yourself of those things that you are grateful for every day.

- Read through the entire *DC Positives Selection* again.

As you look through the selection, a fresh sense of opportunity is emerging. You are feeling inspired and motivated to move forward.

Maybe these goals aren't that far off after all. You have already achieved many things, and you have your Previous Successes List to prove it.

Take the time to immerse yourself in your DC Positives Selection. Merge with it. Enjoy it. This list will be the basis for your continued growth.

- Make a copy of the Selection or, if you like, pick out a few important things for now and pin them up somewhere where you can see them. Look at them every day!

Later on we will add the *Action Plan* and complete *The Personalized DC Voice Performance Training Program*. Finally, we will create your *DC Vision Board*. This will be your point of focus whenever you practice. I will explain this process in chapter 20, "The DC Vision Board."

EXERCISE 10: CREATING THE DREAM CHARACTER (THE DC)

OK, so far so good! Now comes the really fun bit.

Look, I know that there's a chance you might find this exercise a bit weird. But please, go along with me on this one—trust me, OK? You'll soon see why it's an important step.

Using the DC Positives Selection, we now take the process one step further and create the *Dream Character*, referred to as the *DC*, your ideal/ultimate self.

- How do you see yourself when shining in your best light?
- When are you in your element?
- When are you the most happy and fulfilled?
- When do you feel strong, successful, energetic, creative, open, expressive, confident, beautiful, comfortable, etc.?
- Basically, *how do you see yourself at your very best*, displaying all the characteristics from your Positives Selection, living out your dreams and goals?

Using your Positives Selection, create an image of your DC in your mind's eye. The image should represent the idea of your ideal self. You will use this image for the DC Visualization Exercise later.

See if you can capture an overall feeling that encompasses everything your DC is about—a feeling that represents your DC.

Play around with this. Try to be as creative and as visual as possible. Where are you? What kinds of situations do you imagine yourself in? What are you doing? How do you look? What do you wear? As your DC, act out some of the situations that you have on your Goals List.

Notice how it makes you *feel*.

Scripting

You can compare visualization with focused, organized daydreaming. If you are unaccustomed to daydreaming or playing with your imagination—or if you simply find it too weird or too challenging to imagine yourself being or "acting" as your ideal future self—you can use scripting. You simply write little stories or manuscripts, like plays, first and act them out in your head afterward as if you were rehearsing for a real play. Use words and statements from your Positives Selection This method can be a great help. Generally it is very powerful to write things down.

In all of these little plays you, as your Dream Character, play the starring role. Just like an actor would, you research your character and add more and more emotion and personality to it till gradually you completely merge and become one with it. The only difference between you and the actor rehearsing for a play is that your aim is to eventually *stay in character* the whole time. Why? Because the Dream Character is not a stranger that you portray. It is not an act. It is simply <u>you</u> *being who you really are*, who you can easily be, who you were supposed to be the whole time. It is you allowing yourself to shine, allowing yourself to be your absolute best, allowing your highest potential to manifest. It is you doing things exactly like you want to do them. It is not a false image because the Dream Character *is the ultimate version of you* that was there the whole time waiting to come out.

You decide who you are—nobody else.

Use scripting to create an image of your Dream Character. Create situations where you are being your ultimate best, doing things exactly how you intend. You can go through specific upcoming events or simply invent situations. Later you can implement your scripts into your DC visualizations.

This exercise is preparing you for later. You are fine-tuning your DC, making yourself more and more familiar with it. These small plays are like test-runs before the real deal.

You can make as many scripts as you like and do visualization exercises as much and as often as you like—the more the better. (I will explain in more detail about visualization in Exercise 12.) Give your scripts titles. If you have many scripts for different situations, name them differently. (See the following exercise.)

Scripting and visualizing are extremely powerful tools that can make a world of difference to your performance as a speaker. And I don't just mean the usual writing your speech and going through it in your head; I mean as a way to establish your *Stage Persona* and to be able to trigger it at a moment's notice, *anytime, any place.*

In this program, because our main aim is to work specifically with performance, *your Dream Character and your Stage Persona should eventually be one and the same.*

The fact that you have added things to your Positives Selection that are more general makes sense because your Stage Persona, as it is now and as it is going to be, is and will be extremely influenced by all other aspects of your personality and your feelings and beliefs about yourself and life in general. This is also the reason why creating a more overall DC image, as you've just been asked to do, is important before we finally direct our focus to our specific goal right now: dealing with nerves and stage fright and empowering your performance.

In theory, your Dream Character could be about anything. As I said earlier, you can use it to improve any area of your life; you can make it very broad or very specific. But for the particular purpose of this book, *your ultimate DC is going to be your ultimate Stage Persona.*

Do you see where I'm heading with this? Are you beginning to get the overall idea by now? I hope so—I hope you're still with me and enjoying the ride.

EXERCISE 11: CREATING YOUR DC NAME/TRIGGER

You've created your Dream Character. Now you need to find a suitable name for it. We need names and titles because they identify us. Some people even believe that names have their own energy attached to them and that they can somehow influence us. In any case, names are personal. When you think of your friend's name, a certain all-encompassing feeling of everything your friend is and stands for immediately comes along with it. It's like an instant mind movie is being played at the speed of light. This is what a name does.

And this is one reason why you need to name your DC. You've created the mind movie, the all-encompassing feeling of everything your DC is and stands for, in the previous exercise. Now you need to label it.

How? If nothing automatically springs to mind, perhaps look for ideas in your Positives Selection. You've already attached certain words or statements to the feeling/image of your Dream Character. Find something that you feel represents your DC well or take a few things and boil them down to create your *DC Name.*

This name is personal; it is yours. It represents you as your Dream Character—in this case your ultimate Stage Persona. Again, for the sake of this particular program, you should find a name that suits this particular use. You will use this name as your *Performance Trigger.*

The Trigger should sum up the idea of your DC in one to three words that you can always use to immediately boost your being the DC, doing and achieving your best. The more you connect with your DC (using the name), the more and the faster your mind is going to recognize the Dream Character as a real and natural part of you and associate this part of you with the DC Name/Trigger. Ultimately, it is automatically going to switch to DC mode as soon as it hears the name. What this means is that you can *call your DC into action anytime you want.* You simply take a moment to go into your own space (I will show you how to do this) and call the name; this will trigger the traits attached to the name.

Got it? I'm sure I don't need to point out to you how useful this is!

Use the DC Name/Trigger as part of your regular Performance Prep before any speech/presentation. I promise you, having this mental boost as part of your preparation—setting the right stage for yourself and putting yourself in the right state of mind, in "the Zone," as some call it—is extremely powerful!

The DC Name will probably be the sum of many qualities. However, try to choose a name that is *simple, easy to remember, and descriptive* of your DC.

Remember that in this program, the DC Name is meant to be a Performance Trigger. It will be used for a specific purpose—to enhance your performance as a speaker/presenter. Aim to find a name that somehow relates to or naturally symbolizes you in that capacity.

If you work with different scripts pertaining to completely different issues/situations, choose different, appropriate names for those scripts. Naming scripts adds power to them when repeating the names.

Later on, if you feel that it is right for you, you could choose <u>one</u> *name that simply empowers you in any situation of your life.* Some people choose to simply use their own given name; it really is a very individual choice. But for now, stick with the Performance Trigger name.

For years, before I developed the DC Program, my own Performance Trigger was simply called "Excellent Performance." Not very inventive, I know, but it certainly worked a treat. Now I have one name that acts as an all-around DC Trigger.

In chapter 21, "Meditation for Focus, Balance, and Relaxation," you will find a Performance Prep with the DC Name/Trigger integrated. Enjoy!

EXERCISE 12: THE DC VISUALIZATION

As the final exercise in this part of the DC Program, you are going to visualize yourself as your Dream Character. You are going to see yourself already in the ideal circumstances, already being that character, already having achieved your goals, already being successful. You already did something like this in Exercise 10, where you created your Dream Character and acted out little plays in your mind. This is not very different from that, only this is the biggie.

This is where you are finally going to imprint your DC thoroughly in your subconscious mind and connect it with your DC Name.

While in a relaxed and comfortable DC (dreamy) state of mind, you are going to introduce your subconscious mind to the DC and to the DC Name, the Trigger associated with the Dream Character.

Don't worry if this sounds confusing to you right now. I will explain to you very thoroughly how you do this.

Once you know how it works, you can do it as often as you like—the more the better. Not only does it make you feel great, but it also draws your DC nearer and nearer to you every time you do it. Finally, when you no longer see such a big difference or perhaps no difference at all between you and your DC, you know that you have reached the top of the mountain. You are standing on the top, enjoying the view, and looking for the next beautiful mountain to climb—another exciting journey. Only this time you are feeling even stronger and even more inspired because you now know that you can do it; you know deep in your heart that you can climb any mountain you like. Just take the first small steps and then continue walking till once again you reach the top.

So What Is Visualizing?

Visualizing is using your imagination to picture what you want in advance of getting it.

When you visualize, you work with inner images. The images *can* be strengthened and backed up by words and statements and vice versa—but not necessarily. You can visualize with or without verbal input. For your first DC Viz, though, I suggest that you use verbal input. I will show you how to do it.

You play out a situation or a sequence of events in your head, almost like watching a picture or a film with your inner eye. *The more real and vivid you make it, the greater the chances of generating similar circumstances in real life.* The more focused and real this vision is *and* the more feeling/emotion/ passion you add to it—the more likely or the more *certain* that you are going to attain it.

When your mind holds a picture long enough, you *are* going to manifest that picture in reality. Knowing this gives you a lot of power.

Visualizing is similar to what we call daydreaming; the difference is in the intensity. Where normal daydreaming is quite casual—you just drift on off into Never Never Land—visualization is more focused, more controlled. You work with *intentions*. Visualization is a *conscious effort intended to produce results*. It is taking a journey into your future life, feeling it, and living it completely as if it were already real.

In general it is best to focus on one particular event or situation and the circumstances surrounding it at a time. You can take as many journeys as you want, so you will have plenty of opportunities to concentrate on all the things you wish. Again, it is always a good idea to name your visualizations. The names should be simple, easy to remember, and descriptive of the main purpose/feeling of the visualization. This makes it easier to boost certain visualizations without having to go through the entire process every time.

In the long run, the DC Name/Trigger could be but one out of many such names/labels/titles. If, for instance, confidence is a big issue for you, you would certainly add lots of confidence to your DC, but you might also consider having an extra booster—a visualization called something like "Increased Confidence," where you concentrate solely on building confidence in any situation.

With the DC Visualization Exercise acting as a Performance Trigger to enhance your performance as a speaker/presenter, you should of course visualize yourself being your DC in this particular setting, adding the qualities that would empower you in this situation to create your Stage Persona.

When doing your DC Visualization for the first time, it is important to make sure that you have plenty of time on your hands and that you are in a *comfortable and undisturbed* environment—otherwise it might be difficult for you to concentrate. As you become more experienced, you are able to shut off the outside world and do your visualization anytime, anywhere.

Obviously, *the more you do this, the better you become at it and the more powerful the results are going to be.* Repeat, repeat, repeat—there is enormous power in repetition! Repetitions take your mind deeper and strengthen the effects of the visualization.

If you are using words or statements during your visualization—and I strongly recommend that you do—strengthen your statements using the following terms: *more and more, easier and easier, better and better,* etc. and the term *in fact* to underline a point—for example, "in fact, I am so good that . . ." as you learned in Exercise 4, the Positive Affirmations List. I have included a script for you to follow below. I have used it over and over again with great results.

How Do I Visualize?

Prepare yourself for visualization using the following preliminaries:

- Make sure that you are in a safe, private, comfortable space where you can remain peaceful and uninterrupted throughout the entire process. If you live with somebody, explain what you are doing and ask that they respect your privacy during this time. Put a "do not disturb" sign on your door. Switch off your phone, mail alerts, etc.
- You may want to play some soothing, relaxing music (no verbal input/lyrics unless intended for the script). If you wear headphones, you can shut out the entire world—great!
- Dim any electric lights. Perhaps light some candles. Be careful, though, that they are in a safe setting, as you should not have to concentrate on the possibility of accidents.
- Wear comfortable clothing, preferably no jewelry and no shoes—wear thick socks instead. Keep warm (especially your feet).
- Lie down, preferably on your back, or sit comfortably. In any case, your spine should be straight to allow a good energy flow through your body.
- Preferably keep your arms and hands by your side. Some people feel that they block their energy if they cross their arms and legs. Find out what works for you.
- Close your eyes.
- Completely relax.
- Breathe deeply.

If you find this difficult, join your thumb and your middle finger (long, third finger) as you learned back in chapter 6. Press them lightly together. This will help your deep breathing.

- Breathe in slowly, preferably through your nose. Feel how your lungs are filling all the way down. Breathe out naturally through your mouth, pressing your lips ever so slightly together, not closing your mouth completely. Repeat.

- Focus on your breathing till you feel really relaxed and comfortable.
- When you feel yourself slightly drifting off, your thoughts beginning to drift, you are ready to take the next step.
- Focus your mind—lead yourself into the space in which you intend to stage your play. Walk slowly, step by step, counting each step from ten to one. At one, you are fully present in the space you have chosen.

Note: For visualization in general, this space can be anywhere—a room, a stage, a garden, a mountain, the woods, a meadow, or by the sea—anywhere you feel is right for you and your purpose and where you feel safe, free, and at peace. For now, however, as your Stage Persona DC using your DC Name/Performance Trigger, a relevant setting like a stage at a conference is preferable.

- Know that this experience is yours and that you are completely safe and protected and in control. You are open only to your own intended suggestions that serve your own best interests. You are free to enter and exit this space at any time.
- Intend for your play to happen.
- Call your Dream Character in; invite it to join you. Expect it, feel it, identify with it, and merge with it.
- Don't worry if at first you are finding it hard to concentrate. Just enjoy the relaxation and take your time. Gradually you are going to find it easier and easier.
- When you feel ready, start creating pictures in your mind's eye. Picture yourself as your Dream Character using the images/symbols/feelings from Exercise 10, the DC created from your Positives Selection.

Imagine every detail. See it, feel it, identify with it, familiarize yourself with it, bond with it, immerse yourself in it, embrace it, feel it being part of you already, being the natural you—completely merge with it.

- How does it feel to be your DC? Record the feeling so you will remember it afterwards.
- When you're ready, completely slip into the role, the situation that you have chosen to focus on!

Purposefully and with strong intent and focus, play out the desired scene in your head. Make everything perfect and exactly how you want it! *Imagine every detail.*

Make your journey so real and vivid that when you return to the present, it feels *like a memory* rather than an imagined experience—like one of those really vivid dreams that stay with you for a long time, forever even.

See it, hear it, smell it, taste it, sense it, <u>feel it</u>—live it!

What are you doing? What are you saying? What kind of people are there? How are they responding to you? What is the environment like? How do you look? *How does it make you feel?*

See yourself doing all the things that you love to do and *capture the feelings that it gives you!* Completely slip into the role. *See yourself as already being that character, already having achieved your goals, already being successful.*

Be inventive. *Be boundless and completely unrestrained*—the more enthusiasm, pure energy, and emotion you put into your visualization, the more powerful and effective it is going to be and the sooner you are going to see results.

You are going to see changes in the way you think and in the way other people respond to you. Overall, you are going to start noticing changes in your life. A shift is taking place, and gradually a path opens up in front of you, becoming clearer and clearer. Soon more and more lights are going to shine on that path, and suddenly it seems the obvious way to go. Worries are replaced with feelings of joy, ease, and excitement.

When doing the DC Visualization, you use the extra component of the DC Name/Trigger. The purpose of this is to associate your DC with the Name/Trigger for a fast and efficient boost. If you are still not sure how this works, go back to Exercise 11 and read about the DC Name/Trigger. This is very important.

Again, since this program is focusing primarily on improving your skills as a speaker and the trigger in this case is meant to be used as part of your Performance Prep, the visualization that you do and the name that you use should reflect that. Remember, you can always add new scripts, topics, and names afterward if you like.

- When you feel ready, say quietly in your mind or out loud:

I am XX (Your DC Name/Trigger. From here on, XX will mark your DC Name/Trigger).

I am XX—this is my identity.

From this moment in time, whenever I say the word(s) XX, my DC identity is growing stronger and stronger.

XX is a natural part of me, at every moment merging with my entire being more and more.

Note: You say this to activate the Trigger. In theory, you only have to do this once (during your first visualization) and then after that, in future visualizations, you just have to use the name along with the visual, "film" part of the visualization to boost your DC identity. For some people, though, it can take a few times before they feel it really working. How easily we respond to this kind of input is very individual. I suggest that to be sure, you do it a few times in the beginning.

- Pause.
- Then continue:

I am XX.

And therefore, every time I say the word(s) XX, this identity—this natural part of my being, this image that I hold of myself, this symbol of my being the absolute best that I can be, living my full potential, serving myself and my purpose fully, being my ideal, ultimate self, the most natural me there is—is becoming stronger and stronger.

- Pause.
- Then say:

I am XX.

I am XXXXX. (Here, list important qualities and intended qualities from your lists.)

- Repeat regularly during the exercise (and after if you like to boost effects): *I am XX (Your DC Name/Trigger).*
- At the end of your visualization say "end of visualization" and slowly start making your way back to the surface, again counting steps, this time from one to ten. Take one step at a time, taking good time to adjust and reconnect to your fully conscious body and mind. At

ten, you are back in the room, fully present and aware, completely comfortable and revitalized, energized, inspired, and empowered. You are now infused with the wonderful energy of your DC. Well done!

• Now celebrate and congratulate yourself on your efforts and your results so far! I hope that you can really feel the difference and that you like being your DC so much that you will repeat the exercise and connect with your DC again and again as often as possible to experience really great results.

<u>Recap</u>

Connect your DC Name/Trigger to the visual images/symbols and the feelings from Exercise 10, Creating the Dream Character, so that every time you project those images in your mind's eye, your DC identity is being boosted even more every time you use the name.

Repeat your DC Name/Trigger many times during your visualization exercise. You can say the name quietly in your mind or out loud—it doesn't matter. You can also record it and listen back to it. Later, when you create your DC Vision Board, you are also going to write it and read it back. All these ways of reminding yourself of the DC and connecting it to the name are helping to strengthen and speed up your progress even more. Once the DC Name/Trigger is activated, you don't need to spend time doing a full visualization exercise every time you need to boost your DC. You just need to relax and concentrate, as you do when doing the Performance Prep as described in chapter 13, "Great Showmanship." Introduce the Name/Trigger, and your subconscious mind will recognize it and boost the conditions/inner images associated with the name. There will be an example of how to do that in chapter 21, "Meditation for Focus, Balance, and Relaxation."

When using words and statements to strengthen your images, make it a habit to use the kinds of words and phrasings described in Exercise 4, the Positive Affirmations List.

<u>How Long Should Visualization Take?</u>

For a booster or a Performance Prep in general, not long—perhaps 3–5 or even 10 minutes.

For a real visualization, like the one I just took you through where you are essentially doing the ground work and initial programming, I would say anything from 15 minutes (very short) to 60 minutes. More than 60 minutes and you'd probably fall asleep or get restless or impatient and lose your focus and concentration. My advice would be to just try it out. See how long you need and what feels natural to you. Don't force anything—do it for as long as you enjoy it, and when you start feeling restless or impatient, count yourself out. You may have to try it a few times before it works. That's natural—just have patience. Some people immediately take off on an exciting journey; others need a bit longer to find their space.

What Should This "Dreamy" Condition or State of Mind Feel Like?

You know that you are on the right track when you experience any of the following:

- Feelings of peace and calm
- A slight spinning sensation
- Goosebumps (but not from being cold)
- Heightened sense of awareness and sensitivity
- Heightened senses like hearing or smell
- Feeling of wonder and happiness
- Feeling of being immersed in or overflowing/bursting with love (similar to being in love or perhaps even holding your newborn baby in your arms for the first time)
- Intense feeling of joy and reassurance
- Feeling of inner knowing
- Feeling of complete sincerity and truthfulness
- Feeling high or ecstatic
- Suddenly feeling very positive and balanced
- Tears in your eyes
- Feeling of bright or sharp white light shining or passing over your (closed) eyelids
- Rapid eye movement
- Temperature changes, often feeling cold
- Warm ears
- Heaviness or slight numbness of body

- Shaky sensation in the body like when you are freezing without necessarily feeling cold
- Being "split in two"—like having two personalities at the same time, one observing the other
- Disrupted time reference—or completely losing sense of time
- Feeling like being in a glass bowl, with sounds and voices from the outside clearly audible but having a disassociated, "from afar" feel to them—like just before falling asleep, only you're not asleep

Experiencing any of the above may indicate that you are having what is sometimes referred to as a "peak experience." It is a slightly altered state of mind. In this state you are more receptive to your own new ideas and thoughts. When you communicate directly and purposefully with your subconscious mind in this way, you add potency and speed to the process of learning and progress. By adding a Trigger, you create a quick and easy way to make use of this advantage even at times or in situations where you do not have the time to do a full visualization. It is like switching on the light.

There is nothing strange or mysterious about this. It is completely natural and safe. In fact, you probably enter naturally into this state of mind several times every day without even noticing, such as when you find yourself drifting off deeply in your own thoughts or when deeply engaged in some activity, being so preoccupied that you forget the world around you. Reading a good book or watching a movie, being completely immersed in this other world or reality, are other examples of being in a slightly altered state of mind. When watching a movie, you can push the stop button at any time; you can decide to watch a different movie. The same is true here. You are in control. It is your experience.

When you have finished such an experience, you are going to notice that your perception of the world and the people around you has changed slightly—you are seeing both in a more positive, accepting, and loving light. You are also feeling calmer, more relaxed, confident, balanced, and at the same time bright, refreshed, energized, revitalized, and empowered. Basically, you feel great!

What's more, you begin to feel inspired, get ideas, find new opportunities, see new options, and seek out possibilities. In short, you find yourself laying out the foundation for your new, successful path forward. You recognize ways to take action leading toward your new expanded DC reality.

In part 5 we are going to use some of those ideas and inspirations to create the DC Action Plan. This plan is going to be in constant progress—constantly evolving as you are.

As you get into the habit of visualizing, you find that inspiration comes to you frequently and easily. When you feel inspired, act on it immediately, if at all possible. Inspiration is a gift from the Universe (or whichever name you prefer to use). It is given to you for a reason. Inspiration shows you opportunities and guides you toward new possibilities. Often, when you take action based upon inspiration rather than on rational planning according to what is considered to be sensible and "real," you will get the best results.

Learn not to dismiss inspiration. Instead, recognize the real creative power that it possesses and trust that it will work for you.

Use your imagination to get inspiration to produce results.

Guided DC Visualization and Script Samples

If you prefer a guided tour, you can make and record your own scripts or download an all-purpose audio script from my site: www.SuzannRye.com. There you will also find a Performance Prep audio and a DC Visualization audio.

Part 5
Simple Steps to Great Results

CHAPTER 18

The DC Action Plan Introduced: Believe It—Intend It— TRUST It—Create It!

Working with thoughts, affirmations, and visualizations on their own is very powerful. You can completely change the way you feel about something, the way you react to certain things and certain people, and the kinds of circumstances you attract into your life. You decide if you choose to see the glass half full or half empty—if you see opportunities and challenges on the one side or perils and obstacles on the other. It really is that simple. Believe that you can succeed, intend to succeed, trust that you will succeed—and you are going to succeed!

Your attitude toward life, yourself, other people, etc. absolutely creates your experience—in other words, your reality. So you see, you have a lot of power—especially if you add some inspired action to the equation! So this is the next step.

The second part of the Dream Character Program is about making plans and taking action. I suggest that you move forward with this part only if you feel ready. If the first part of the DC Program hasn't quite settled in yet, allow that to happen before you press on with more things. Also, if your goal is merely to improve your vocal and performance skills, deal with anxiety, and build confidence, then you might not need to complete this part for now. Keep it in mind for later when you need an extra boost to get things going.

If, however, you have some concrete goals that require you to take action beyond the kind of inner work you did in Part 4, then the DC Action Plan can help you with this. This could, for instance, be finally getting those keynote proposals done and sent out to clients or organizations. It could be getting in touch with agents or setting up a new seminar. It could be embarking on a new course or joining a group of like-minded people. Or it could simply be that you need to add some further structure to your everyday life that includes training and practicing the things that you have learned so far in this program.

Wherever we are headed, one thing is clear: if we feel stuck, the only solution is to start walking—somehow. It doesn't matter whether we take baby steps or big giant steps, as long as we start walking. The first step is often the hardest, but it is also the most important. Ideas and visions alone are not enough to create change and progress in our lives; we need to trust and believe in our visions and dare to act on them. We need to persistently move forward, following the path that our thoughts and visions have lit up for us and acting on the grand ideas and opportunities that appear.

We need to fine-tune our focus and hold it steady. Like I said, when we hold a steady focus on something and our intent to achieve it or to have it is clear and strong, then we *will* create it. We will attract the people, situations, and opportunities we need to help us move forward. We need to be alert and ready to take advantage of these opportunities when they appear. Last but not least, we need to trust that the Universe (or whichever name you prefer) is forever conspiring to assist us on our quest, and we need to acknowledge and be grateful for all the little miracles that constantly come our way.

It is when we dare to trust and believe in our ideas and visions and then take decisive action to carry them out that we can truly achieve great things. When we take the time and make the effort to first prepare ourselves thought- and energy-wise and then take what we genuinely feel to be the right (inspired) action—we simply cannot fail.

If you want to take your Dream Character even further—if you feel ready to take some inspired action beyond what you've already started in the first part of the DC Program—then the DC Action Plan can help you.

Again, I suggest that for now you focus solely on goals pertaining to speaking/performing. Then, as with the rest of the DC Program, you can always expand on it to include other areas of your life later.

Following are the eight DC Action Exercises.

EXERCISE 13: CLARIFY OUTSIDE GOALS

Examine your goals again.

- Did the Goals Review bring up any new thoughts and ideas?
- Do you need to add anything?
- Did you perhaps underestimate yourself and your potential at first?
- Have your new skills and improved confidence brought other goals closer to you?
- Do any of your goals require any outside action? Do they directly involve the outside world and other people?
- If so how?
- Why?
- Who?
- What?

EXERCISE 14: IT'S IN THE BOX!

Did you divide your goals into boxes as described in exercise 1 of the DC Program, the Goals List? If not, do it now. You should have two boxes, one with immediate goals and one with long-term goals. Now redefine and restructure your goals.

- Make two more boxes. In one put all the goals that require outside action by you, such as sending out proposals, joining a club, or embarking on a course. In the other put those that are dependent on direct involvement by other people, such as needing approval for something before you can move ahead (see illustration 20.)
- You now have four boxes. Draw a line between the boxes, connecting them.

- Imagine yourself in the middle and connect with a line to each box, like a cross or a star. This is to remind yourself of the connections among the different areas of your life and to emphasize that they are all equally valid. It is also to visualize yourself as the center point and creator of your goals.

Illustration 20 - Practical Clerk

Structure and definition help make goals clearer and simpler and thus easier to comprehend and to focus on. You cannot focus on something if you're not sure what it is. You cannot get something without a clear focus. In other words, you cannot get something if you're not sure what it is that you want to get.

EXERCISE 15: HOW CAN I . . . ?

Look at each box one at a time.

Ask yourself:

- *How can I* make this happen? What does it take?
- Do I really need something from somebody else to achieve this goal? If so, what do I need?
- How can I get what I need? What does it take? What can I do?
- *When* can I do it?
- What else can I do?
- *When* can I do it?

What can you do to bring yourself closer to your goals?

Write down everything that springs to mind—every single idea that pops up.

Continue doing this at your own pace. Some or many of your goals may be connected; that's OK—but do try to define them individually as much as possible so that they look simpler and become easier to chop into small steps.

Note: Now that you've learned visualizing, take advantage of it. Continue to use visualization exercises before you answer any big questions or make any big plans. When you are in a DC state of mind—a wonderful, secure, confident, and inspired state of mind—you're much better geared to come up with good ideas, answers, and solutions.

The state of mind that you are in when you make decisions is very important. It's often like this: good state—good, in-control decision; bad state—bad, panicky decision.

EXERCISE 16: CHIP CHOP

You wouldn't swallow a huge steak at one time, would you? You'd cut it up into bite-size chunks and eat one at a time. At some point, you will have eaten the whole steak.

A great outcome is the result of many small actions, as we discussed earlier. Make your goals manageable. Think big but be prepared to take smaller steps. If your goal is inconceivable in its full glory, chances are you might not dare to go for it.

Challenge is good, but choking can be fatal.

- Look at your previous answers to Exercise 15. Is there a natural sequence of events leading to the end result(s)?
- Define small individual steps that gradually lead to your goals. Chip chop your goals into smaller, more digestible pieces so they become easier to swallow.
- Write down those steps.

EXERCISE 17: GIVE YOURSELF A DEADLINE

By now you have listed your goals, both short-term and long-term. You have put them into boxes, reviewed them, clarified them, chopped them into manageable bite-size pieces, and asked yourself "How can I?" "What can I?" etc.

So let's start cooking!

- Think very carefully. Can you do anything *today?* If so, *what* can you do *today?*
- Which practical steps can you take *now* toward achieving any of those things on your lists? What can you do *immediately* that is going to bring you even closer to your goals and your Dream Character?

There is bound to be something! It might be just a small thing like making a phone call—it doesn't matter. Record the first things that spring to mind. These ideas are fueled by inspiration, and they carry the potent seeds of true miracles.

Remember that small steps are better than no steps at all. Every time you do something that in some way brings you closer to your dream, it makes you feel good and in turn encourages you to do even more.

To be really efficient, most of us need time frames. Without some sort of time frame, goals tend to disperse into thin air or at least take way too long to materialize. The best way to keep track of time is to create deadlines for yourself, just as if someone else gave you an important deadline to meet. Your own deadlines and your commitment to yourself are equally important.

- Look again at your goals. What timeline are we looking at here? What feels good to you?
- Ask yourself:

- Where am I in XX years from now?
- Where am I in XX months?
- Where am I in XX weeks?
- Where am I in XX days?

- Then work your way backwards. Ask yourself:
  ◊ How many small steps do I need to take every year to be where I want to be in XX years?
  ◊ Which steps can I take?
  ◊ When can I start?
  ◊ How many small steps do I need to take every month to be where I want to be in XX months?
  ◊ Which steps can I take?
  ◊ When can I start?
  ◊ How many small steps do I need to take every week to be where I want to be in XX weeks?
  ◊ Which steps can I take?
  ◊ When can I start?
  ◊ How many small steps do I need to take every day to be where I want to be in XX days?
  ◊ Which steps can I take?
  ◊ When can I start?

- Write the answers down.

You now have an action plan. Combined with the answers from Exercises 13-17, these should give you plenty of inspiration to give you a head start!

You've done a tremendous job by now. You've worked the program and you've made great plans. Now, let's make sure that you stick to those plans and make all your dreams and goals come true! Let's get you to where you want to be.

EXERCISE 18: COMMITMENT

Ask yourself:

- Am I willing to make the effort it takes to accomplish my goals?
- Am I going to?
- Am I willing to make a commitment to myself to do this?

Write a letter to yourself, sign it, and mail it to yourself. When it comes back, post it on your Vision Board (see next chapter).

If you dare, send a copy to a dear friend whom you trust as well. This makes your commitment more official, and you are then even more likely to stick with it.

EXERCISE 19: SUPPORT

We all know that sometimes it can be hard to walk the road alone. Support can make all the difference.

Create a supportive environment for yourself. Tell the people close to you what you are up to. Ask your partner, family, friends, work colleagues, etc. to respect and support your goals and your decision to pursue them. Tell them that this is important to you.

Consider joining a group of like-minded people (a mastermind group) or even creating your own group. Share with them what you've learned and help support them in reaching for their goals too. You are going to find that gradually you begin to attract your own kind—people with similar vibration, outlook, and perhaps even similar goals and interests.

Recently a friend of mine took a quantum leap. After years of being very overweight, insecure, unhappy and feeling generally powerless and victimized, she decided that this was it! She wanted something better for herself.

I told her about the Dream Character Program. At first she was very dismissive of the whole idea. But then, I guess, her frustration was so overwhelming that she knew she had to do *something*. I asked her what she had to lose by at least giving it a try. Wasn't it at least better than just sitting back and watching things go from bad to worse?

It made sense to her. She decided to give herself a complete makeover—body, mind, and Soul. She took small steps every day and gradually started to change. Soon everybody noticed, and this compelled her to continue on her way forward. She felt increasingly better about herself, and her entire demeanor was changing. She got very actively involved in all sorts of new, exciting things, including sports for the first time ever. Her overall lifestyle improved, she became much healthier, and as a result of all of this she lost loads of the weight that had been troubling her so. After a while, she met someone, fell in love, and got involved in a relationship for the first time in her life. (She's 28 and always thought that men wouldn't like her, because what was there to like, she wondered!) Now she looks great, she beams like a star—and she knows it. She is like a new person and has never been happier. In fact, she told me that she did not recall *ever being happy at all* before this!

Now she has truly transformed herself and her life beyond her wildest dreams. She has completely become her Dream Character as she didn't even dare to see it back when she first started her journey. Now, of course, her dreams are much wilder, but for her there's no question that whatever she sets her heart and mind to achieve—she can! The fact that she has come this far proves it.

So where am I going with this? My point is that sometimes there can be a backside to great transformations, and when there is, we need to be prepared to deal with it. You would think that her friends and family would be supportive and over-the-moon happy for her. Not so. One day she came to see me and seemed not her usual chirpy self. When I asked her what was wrong, she burst into tears. She told me that she was so disappointed. Both her sister and her best friend found it hard to cope with her newfound happiness. She felt that they were either jealous or just plain disapproving—as if suddenly they didn't like her anymore. So in a weird, roundabout way, she became sad that she was happy. I really felt for her. Here was this beautiful young lady, beaming with joy that she finally discovered in life—and now she felt sad and guilty about it because it somehow seemed to offend her sister and her best friend.

"You know, sometimes," I said to her, "when we move forward in our lives—especially if we take a quantum leap—it can be difficult for people around us to understand.

"If suddenly we change and lift our energy—our vibration or 'vibe,' if you like—and they stay in the old vibration, an imbalance or disharmony can occur. Our friends or family members may subconsciously try to hold us back because they resist change and would like things to remain the way they were. Human beings are creatures of habit—they naturally like to hold on to what they know. Change can disturb the balance in a relationship if only one party moves.

"However, in most cases our friends just need reassurance that this change is a good thing and that it will *not take anything away from them*—in fact, they may very well *benefit* from it. Most people just need some time to adjust, especially if the bond between you is strong. Of course, sometimes friendships outrun their course. I don't believe in coincidences. I believe that we meet people for a reason and that most relationships in our lives occur because a mutual exchange needs to take place. This exchange can consist of various things such as love, knowledge, and common interests. As we grow and evolve as human beings, we cannot always expect to grow in the same direction as the people around us. It sometimes happens that we simply *grow apart*. What this means to me is that the exchange or the 'job' is done, and the relationship is no longer serving any of us. In that case, we need to decide if it is time to move on, thanking our friends for everything that was but which can no longer be. This can be a difficult situation but one, I'm sure, that most people have found themselves in at one time or another in their lives."

My friend left here that day intent on having a long heart-to-heart talk with her sister and her friend. As far as I know, they sorted things out. In fact, the last I heard, her sister joined her on her DC quest. Way to go! At the end, not only did my friend turn her own life around, but she also managed to inspire her sister to do the same thing.

EXERCISE 20: THE NEW SUCCESSES LIST

- Keep a track record of your successes and achievements. Update it every day or at least once a week.
- Add your new track record to your Previous Successes List. You will soon realize that actually you are doing really well, and this is going to encourage you to continue your great work like it did my friend. Be proud of yourself!
- Congratulate yourself on your achievements, however small you think they are. Do this often—every time you take a small step. Make a point out of marking every accomplishment. Take time to relish your results. Set up rewards for yourself, celebrate, and make it fun! This will make the journey toward your goals even more enjoyable and give you perspective along the way. It will also remind you that little steps do make a huge difference. Finally, it will keep you in a flow of gratitude, which will help you attract even more of what you want.

Start right now by congratulating yourself for completing the entire DC Program!

You've now done all twenty DC Exercises and set yourself up for success and expansion.

Congratulations—well done my friend! Why not relax and enjoy yourself with a nice, inspiring, mega-success boosting DC Viz? Then take a well-deserved break.

A COUPLE OF EXTRA POINTERS

You can use visualization to strengthen your actions in advance. If, for instance, you are writing an application, be in a good space when you write it and infuse it with positive expectations before you send it off. Visualize that your application is well received.

If you are going for an interview, use visualization to strengthen the positive outcome of that interview. If you have an important meeting to attend, imagine the meeting running smoothly and producing fantastic results. If you are telling somebody about decisions or plans that you've made and you expect them to object, imagine the opposite—imagine that they are being understanding and respectful of your decision and pleased on your behalf, even if they would have chosen differently themselves.

When you feel positive and confident about the actions that you are going to take, positive results are bound to follow. Create a good feeling—then take action!

When you are steadily strengthening your actions in advance, it works to your advantage in more than one way. The fact that you are likely to get better results is going to increase your confidence and your positive expectations, which is in turn going to motivate you to take even more action—which is again going to produce even more results, and so on.

CHAPTER 19

The Personalized DC Training Program—Everything You Need in One Neat Package

You've been introduced to a lot of different exercises and completed a lot of tasks. Now it is time for you to create a personalized training program that works for you and your particular needs. The idea is to have a planned schedule so you don't have to think about what to do every time you want to practice. You simply go through your own customized program that exactly fits your needs.

You are the only person who knows exactly what you need and which areas you should work on. Therefore, only you can create your customized program with the tools I have given you. Once you've done it, it's going to save you heaps of time and frustration in the future. Often the biggest problem people have with practicing is that they don't know *what* to do and *how* to do it. You won't have that problem at all, so you're far ahead of the game already.

HOW TO BUILD YOUR PROGRAM
Build your program by picking out all of your favorite exercises from chapter 11, "Basic Voice Exercises," and gathering them in one place. This should be

a comprehensive list of exercises that work well for you and cover the things that you feel you need to work on. You can always upgrade the list or change it along the way as you develop or simply get bored of doing the same stuff over and over.

Now take your Positives Selection and do the same. Compile a list of your favorites or the most important ones, or simply take *all* of your positive affirmations, qualities, intended qualities, successes both previous and new (don't forget to make space for a lot more here), etc. Put this compilation next to the previous one. (If you can't find a surface big enough, make yourself comfortable on the floor where you can really spread out.)

Write your DC Name/Trigger on a separate piece of paper. Place it in front of you.

Place the Performance Prep from chapter 13 and the DC Visualization Exercise script with your DC Name/Trigger on the floor or table as well.

Do you have a particular speech that you are working on at the moment? If you do, place that speech—the entire written speech or just notes or outline if that's what you have—on the floor or table as well.

So far, so good. What you have in front of you now will be the main ingredients of your Personalized Training Program. You will use these ingredients to make your DC Vision Board, which will be your point of focus for your practice. In the next chapter, I will explain how to create your board.

DAILY PRACTICE

- Remind yourself of being your DC every day by at least reading through the DC Visualization script, which should include your chosen DC Name in writing.
- Go through your chosen relaxation, breathing, and support exercise and voice exercises (in that order), preferably the whole lot every day or at least as often as you can. Obviously, the more you do it, the better the results. If you are unsure about how to work with your Basic Exercises, reread chapter 10, "How to Practice." There will also be a short recap at the end of this chapter.
- *Between each exercise,* read out loud or inside your head *at least* one positive affirmation from your list and remind

yourself of *at least* one quality from your Qualities/
Intended Qualities List *and* one of your successes.

- When you're done with your exercises, do the
  Performance Prep. Remember to include your DC
  Name/Trigger. There is an example of how to do that
  in chapter 21.

- After that, conclude your daily practice by working on a
  speech of your choice. This is the best and most logical
  way to implement the techniques that you have been
  practicing and put them into real use. It is also the best
  way to track progress. It puts everything into perspective,
  speeds up the learning process, and strengthens your
  understanding of your voice.

You *can* run through all of it fairly quickly in, say, 15–25 minutes, or you
can choose to do the *Ultimate DC Workout for Ultimate Results.*

On busy days or weeks, spend less time; when you have more time to
spare, invest some of that time in your DC future. I'm sure I need not tell you
that for all of this to work its wonders—in order for you to reap the real long-
term results of all the work you've already invested in this program—you
need to continue working with it, at least till you reach a point where you
feel that you have gotten what you came for. But don't overcommit yourself.
Remember to take baby steps. Set goals that are realistic and only make
promises to yourself that you can keep. Otherwise it will backfire and you'll
end up doing nothing at all. We can't have that!

If you decide that you want to maintain a routine of the ultimate
workout, it requires a bit more commitment on your part—the same kind of
commitment that you have to make when, say, you start going to the gym on
a regular basis. If you want really dramatic results, you have to put in extra
work. However, just like going to the gym, once you get started and get into
it, chances are that you'll become so addicted to it and how good it makes you
feel that you wouldn't miss it for the world!

The same can be said for your daily program. Once you get into it, you
are really going to enjoy it and find it to be therapeutic, very inspiring, and
most of all efficient in producing the results that you want! It will not be
wasted time. On the contrary, it will save you time and effort in the end, as
you are gaining more power and energy. You are also gaining confidence, and

gradually the anxiety and perhaps crippling nerves and stage fright that once haunted you is going to disperse. If you have followed the program and you stick with the practice, this *is* going to happen—I promise you that.

THE ULTIMATE DC WORKOUT FOR ULTIMATE RESULTS

For the best results, I recommend that you do this Ultimate Workout at least once a week. Consider it part of your job.

- **Full Body and Mind Relaxation Combined with Visualization**

Find a good, comfortable spot to sit or lie down and relax completely.

Follow the preliminaries as described in the DC Visualization Exercise in chapter 17. Then continue following the script all the way through. As you become more used to this, you can extend your visualization to include different scenarios. You do not always have to use the script or words at all as long as you get the overall feeling right and remember to include your DC Name/Trigger.

You can also use positive affirmations or suggestions from your Positives List. Simply focus on the statements and repeat them either in your mind or out loud—whatever works for you. If you do, though, remember to use the exact same wording as you did when you first wrote them according to how I described it to you.

Other than that, play away! Do your thing—let your DC shine and enjoy how amazing it makes you feel.

Either have your room quiet or have some calm, soothing music playing—again, it is a matter of preference. Some people find that they cannot concentrate when they have music playing, while others feel that it actually helps them drift off more easily. Experiment and see what works best for you. You may find that on different days you have different preferences. That's fine. The important thing to always remember is that ultimately you are doing this for you! Try to spend *at least* 15 minutes or more on this exercise alone.

This is your investment into your dreams. Look at it as pure self-indulgence—your own little secret ritual that is giving you special powers to achieve your goals! And you know what? This *is* going to happen!

- **Relaxation and Preparation Exercises—Physical Warm-Up**

When you're done visualizing, it's time to give your body a little brisk wake-up call. Simply move around and do a few jumps, stretches, shakes, and neck rolls. If you are into yoga or prefer any additional relaxing methods, feel free to use those. Then use any of the relaxation and preparation exercises described in chapter 11.

- **Breathing and Support Exercises**

Use any of the breath control/support exercises described in chapter 11. These are important, so don't skip this part.

- **Voice Exercises**

Use any of the voice exercises described in chapter 11. For more tips and details on how to work with your basic exercises, go back and read chapter 10, "How to Practice."

- **Your Positives Selection List**

Your Positives Selection is as important as your other exercises, as it helps to keep you in the right frame of mind when practicing. When you practice and learn in the right frame of mind—an open, positive, comfortable, and confident frame of mind—you learn faster and enjoy better results.

Between *each* basic exercise, read out loud or inside your head *at least* one positive affirmation from your list and remind yourself of *at least* one quality from your Qualities/Intended Qualities List *and* of one of your successes. This way you are constantly and continuously building yourself up and reinforcing your progress. Look at the positive affirmations as little breaks or treats between each vocal exercise—praising you for your success on the last one and pacing or conditioning you for even more success with the next one.

- **Quick Performance Prep**

When you're done with your exercises, do a Quick Performance Prep. Include your DC Name to strengthen the effects of the prep and to associate the prep with the following speech (any speech of your choice) and with performing successfully in general. By doing this, you are basically teaching or conditioning yourself/your mind to naturally link the two and to know that when you do the Prep, great results follow.

- **Your Chosen Speech**

Conclude your practice/daily program by working on a speech of your choice.

SHORT RECAP ON HOW TO PRACTICE

Exercising just 10–20 minutes a day or a few times a week will do wonders. In any case, 10–20 minutes done properly and with enthusiasm is better than hours done half-heartedly. If you feel uninspired, do something else or simply relax and spoil yourself. Your inspiration will soon return.

Always use simple exercises that you understand and can do correctly. There is really no point in doing exercises that are too difficult because you won't do them correctly, and so they will do more damage than good. You don't necessarily need a selection of hundreds of different exercises to be able to practice efficiently. Choose a few that you like, that do the job, and that suit your particular needs. Remember that an exercise is a tool you can use to condition your body to work correctly by itself. The exercise in itself is not that important—*it is what it does for you that matters.*

If you encounter a voice problem, go back to the appropriate chapter or exercise, find the right way, adjust, and transfer to your speech. If trouble continues, maybe you haven't identified the real problem yet, or maybe the exercise is not the right one or is not being applied properly. Try again. Remember that you may need to adjust your settings and change modes as you work with increasing volume, etc.

Always respect your voice. Listen to it (metaphorically). Make sure to keep it healthy and allow it to get the proper rest it needs. If you wear it out, get hoarse, or lose it, you obviously can neither work nor practice, and it is a setback in time, not to mention the damage you can cause. Forcing yourself to work or practice when you are unwell is a waste of time. You won't do it properly, so you will condition your body to be slack too. When your body is slack and doesn't work properly, your technique suffers and you will try to compensate by using force or incorrect technique to achieve the same results as you would normally when doing it right. But you will not achieve the same results, and you will not gain time either. You will, however, damage your voice—so don't do it. Instead, rest.

Record yourself every now and again. That way you get used to the sound of your own voice, and you can better hear which sounds, colors, and inflections you want to work on. If you don't ever hear yourself played back, you have no realistic sense of how you sound. Remember the distinction between inner and outer hearing? What actually comes out is not exactly the same as what you hear inside.

Generally learn to rely on what you *feel* instead of what you hear. Learn to recognize the feeling of right versus wrong. Experiment till you achieve the results you want. When it feels right (comfortable), chances are that it *is* right.

KEEP UP THE GOOD WORK!

Sometimes it can be hard to get into a regular routine and even harder still to keep up the discipline when the initial excitement and resolve wear off—especially if we don't see the results we want fast enough. Again, it's a bit like when you first embark on a diet or start going to the gym. Hang in there! Find a rhythm that fits with your daily schedule and settle for goals that are realistic as opposed to idealistic. Create a realistic routine that you enjoy and look forward to—not one that you dread!

Allow your program to evolve over time and keep it interesting and inspiring. This is going to help you stay motivated and enable you to concentrate properly.

As you gradually expand your exercises and your vocal and performance achievements, your overall confidence and sense of success also grows. That in turn allows you to achieve even more. Remember that confidence creates success, and success creates more success. You will soon discover new ways of growing and evolving. You will soon find yourself paving the way for further expansion. Good for you—congratulations!

CHAPTER 20

The DC Vision Board

It's time to get really creative.

Your prospects of ultimate success with the DC Program are much greater if you are automatically reminded of the DC every day. The difference between having to dig out your notebook, folder, or binder whenever you can to look at it versus simply having all those wonderful goodies in plain view all the time is immense. It is also far more motivating—you don't forget about it easily, and it makes practice much simpler and easily approachable.

But that's not all. As by now you are very well aware, this program is not only about what you do—it is also about what goes on behind the scenes when you do absolutely nothing! Fortunately, this is really where this whole conditioning thing turns to your advantage. Because in all fairness, it works both ways. *You are as susceptible to positive influence as you are to negative.* This means that having your Dream Character in plain view all the time and having your Positives Selection and your DC Name/Trigger staring you in the face every single day is going to boost everything associated with your DC even more. It increases the effects of the program and *multiplies* your odds for success. It helps to bring all those things on your lists closer to you, brings them into your sphere, brings opportunities and people your way, keeps you motivated to take action, and inspires you to move forward. Expect to live an ever-expanding life!

I *know* that this works. I've done it myself over and over, and I've seen other people do it time and again as well. Now it's your turn—get into the creative spirit, enjoy yourself, and have some DC fun!

Illustration 21 - Visionary Clerk

When I say creative, I really do mean *creative*. Your DC Vision Board is an artistic venture. It is up to you to design your board in a way that inspires you and is pleasing to your eyes. Otherwise you'll just stick it in the back of your closet, where it won't be of much use. The more inventive you are and the more individual and personal you make your board, the better. It is a representation of *you* and *your life* right now and in the near future.

Next I will tell you exactly what needs to go on it and give you some general guidelines on how to make the most practical board. Other than that, you're the artist. Don't worry if you've never done anything like this before. Maybe you see yourself as a very pragmatic, no-nonsense person—not creative or artistic at all. It doesn't matter; you can structure your board in any way you like as long as it makes sense to you and as long as you follow a few simple guidelines.

WHAT GOES ON THE DC VISION BOARD?

Simple—your entire Personalized Training Program that you created in the previous chapter. That includes:

- Your DC Name/Trigger clearly visible from all angles
- Directions for DC Visualization, preferably a full DC Visualization Exercise script with your DC Name/Trigger included
- Your own given name and perhaps a picture of yourself that you like. This will strengthen the link between you and your DC.
- All of your favorite exercises—your "best of" compilation, which should include relaxation and preparation exercises (plus directions for physical warm-up), breathing and support exercises, and voice exercises
- Your Positives Selection List—your favorites, most important ones, or simply *all* of your positive affirmations, qualities, intended qualities, successes previous and new, and goals
- The Performance Prep from chapter 13, which again includes your DC Name/Trigger.
- Your chosen speech —any speech that you are working on at the moment, either an entire written speech or just notes or outlines
- Quotes by others, if you like. They must be quotes that really mean something to you, that ring true to you, or that sum up your truth. They must *serve* you, meaning that they must *relate* to the energy of your DC. They must be *positive*, and they must *inspire and encourage* you on your DC quest.

- Other things of your choosing that are important and mean something positive to you.
- Finally you *can* choose to put a list of things to do inspired by the Action Plan. In my experience, some people find that highly motivating, while others find it a bit stressful. See what works for you. I suggest that you try without it first.

HOW TO MAKE YOUR VISION BOARD

You can use a big bulletin board or a corkboard with pins as your background. Stick all the ingredients on the board like a collage.

If you choose to go all the way out and create your masterpiece from scratch, like a painting, you'll need a large canvas or a large piece of cardboard. You'd be surprised how many people choose this option although it requires some extra work. If you do decide to go for this option, attach plastic pockets to the board. This makes it easy to add or exchange speeches, exercises, goals, etc. Simply write or print out new content and replace what's in the pocket or on the board.

As the ingredients will change along the way, make space for new items like successes, new goals, etc.

Put your focus point for voice focus and projection in the middle of the board, perhaps on a piece of mirror or other reflective material so you can check your face for tension. One of my clients built the entire board around an old mirror.

Have fun! Send me a picture of your board if you would like me to feature it in an upcoming edition of the DC Program.

BONUS CHAPTER 21

Meditation for Focus, Balance, and Relaxation

When you meditate, you *generally* aim to quiet your mind as opposed to feeding it thoughts and images as you do when you visualize. I say *generally* because many people add verbal input (often recorded) to their practice and still call it meditation. For this reason, I have added my take on meditation with verbal input as well. It doesn't really matter so much what we call it—it's all part of the same way of working from the inside out.

I see it like this: While visualization is an *active* process, meditation tends to be more of a *passive* one. You try not to consciously think of anything as opposed to *very consciously* using your thoughts and imagination to create a certain picture, like a film in your head. When you meditate without verbal input, you simply open up your mind to allow for thoughts, images, and ideas *to flow <u>to</u> you.*

When meditating, you are engulfed in your own personal space where you can truly know yourself. Meditation makes it easier to stay in touch with yourself and to have a greater understanding and knowledge of what is right for you—and it can give you the strength and the courage to act upon it even when challenged.

Illustration 22 - Relaxed Clerk

The wisdom that you receive in this heightened state of awareness represents your own personal truth. You are more receptive to new ideas and thoughts.

You are consistently being guided; you are constantly being fed information. If you strengthen your ability to perceive this information more clearly, it will be easier for you to decide what you want in life and therefore easier to focus on it.

It is up to you to decide where you think this information is coming from. For now, let us simply refer to it as *intuition*.

Meditation can be used to determine what you want, and it can help you achieve it.

You probably enter into a meditative or slightly altered state of mind several times a day without even noticing. There are countless ordinary, everyday actions that could easily count as mild forms of meditation. Daydreaming or drifting off in your own thoughts or getting lost in something would be classed as mildly meditative. Concentrating very hard or focusing attention on something can be meditative. Walking in the woods, painting, reading, watching a movie, being creative, exercising, listening to music, jogging, horse riding, even cooking and cleaning can be meditative! When you're so preoccupied that you completely forget the world around you—when you are deeply engaged in some activity or task, totally immersed in your own world—you are essentially meditating. You are in your own reality. This is sometimes referred to as a "waking trance"—a concentration of attention.

Next time you're doing something enjoyable and time just flies by without you noticing it, pay attention to how you feel inside afterwards. I bet you feel great! Because you just allowed yourself to connect with the deepest (or you could say the highest) part of you—your subconscious mind.

It is important to allow time and space for you to just be. Don't feel that it is a waste of time and that you need to constantly run around and stress yourself out to do and achieve things. You will achieve much more if you put yourself in the right frame of mind first.

You need to take time for you. The time that you invest in yourself is going to bring you great rewards. Don't think that investing in you is selfish—if you are happy and content, other people benefit as well. Your responsibility is first and foremost to yourself—for in order to be understanding, compassionate, responsible, loving, truthful, and respectful to somebody else, you must first be that to yourself.

MEDITATION WITHOUT INPUT

- To prepare yourself for meditation, follow the instructions that you learned earlier in chapter 17, "The Dream Character: Exercise 12: The DC Visualization."
- When meditating, many people choose to sit comfortably instead of lying down. See what suits you best. In any case, your spine should be straight to allow a good energy flow through your body.
- Keep your arms and hands by your side. Some people prefer to rest their hands and wrists on their knees as they sit. It is also common to join the thumb and middle finger (long, third finger) and press them lightly together to aid deep breathing. Also, avoid crossing your arms and legs, as it can block your energy flow.

- Close your eyes.
- Completely relax.
- Breathe deeply, slowly, preferably through your nose. Feel how your lungs are filling up all the way down. Breathe out naturally through your mouth, pressing your lips ever so slightly together, not closing your mouth completely. Repeat.
- Focus on your breathing till you feel really relaxed and comfortable.
- Release your thoughts—allow them to slightly drift off and leave your conscious mind. If your head remains full of thoughts, just let them be. Observe that they are there, but do not *engage* in them. Relax your mind. Don't worry if at first you are finding it hard to concentrate on nothing. Just enjoy the relaxation and take your time. Gradually you are going to find it easier and easier.
- Some people find it helpful to focus on a single sound or a word to keep all other thoughts at bay by repeating it out loud or in their mind. Often they choose a word that is considered sacred or has a high spiritual value or vibration attached to it, like *love* or *light*.

Illustration 23 - Meditation Clerk

Maybe you've heard of the word (or intonation) *Om* (or *Aum*) before. *Om* (or *Aum*) is a sacred Hindu symbol that represents the source of all manifest and unmanifest existence (All That Is/God). *Om* is referred to as *pranava*, meaning that it pervades life and runs through our *prana* or *breath*. It is believed to be the basic sound of the world and to contain all other sounds. If repeated with the correct intonation, it can resonate throughout the body so that the sound penetrates to the center of one's being or soul, quiets the mind and the body, and leads to the highest state of statelessness.

This is comparable to the Buddhist mantra or prayer/chant *Nam Myoho Renge Kyo* (very simplified: "Devotion to the Mystic Law of [universal] Life") which is also a representation of or dedication to the ultimate Truth summed up in a few words to encompass everything there is.

But you don't have to be of any particular faith or of any faith at all to meditate or to use words or mantras like *Om*. Many non-Hindus have adapted *Om* to their practice and use it simply because they like the vibration and feel that they get a soothing or calming effect from the overtones that it produces, just like a chant does.

Anyway, if you find any of this helpful, use it. If not, find your own way. Do whatever helps you to switch off and quiet your mind of the daily chatter and noise.

- Create a space in your mind that is your special, sacred and safe space to which and from which you can travel and have your experiences. This space can be anything, anywhere— an empty room, a white room, a cloud, a mountain, a cave, the woods, a meadow, or by the sea—anywhere that you feel safe and free, at peace, and in touch with your Soul, your inner self, and the Universe (or whichever term you are comfortable with). This is a place where you can receive information, wisdom, and insights and communicate with your Higher Self, your guides, God, or whomever you wish to communicate with that can assist you in your growth. Know that this experience is yours and that you are completely safe and protected and in control. You are free to enter and exit this space at any time.

HOW LONG SHOULD A MEDITATION LAST?

A meditation can last anywhere from a few minutes to several hours—it really is up to personal preference. Don't overshoot, though. If you are completely new to meditating, you'd probably find it hard to do more than half an hour straight.

Take your time, step by step, and you'll begin to really enjoy and relish this special *you time.*

What should this experience feel like? To make sure that you are on the right track, go back to chapter 17 and read the section called "What Should This 'Dreamy' Condition or State of Mind Feel Like?"

MEDITATION WITH VERBAL INPUT (SUGGESTION)

When you add verbal input to your meditation, you communicate directly and purposefully with your subconscious mind. This is a very efficient way of adding potency to your chosen messages and speeding up progress and learning.

It comes very close to something normally referred to as self-hypnosis. Self-hypnosis is giving suggestions directly to your subconscious mind. When you follow the preliminaries and put yourself in a relaxed, slightly altered state of mind, you gain access to your subconscious; that is why you can communicate directly with it more easily.

Before you start thinking about jumping chickens and barking guests on a TV show, let me explain a few things about hypnosis. Unfortunately a lot of stigma has become attached to the word *hypnosis*, which is why I shy away from it—the word, that is, not the method itself. Nowadays most people simply refer to it as NLP (Neuro-Linguistic Programming). NLP is quite a wide field, so to simply equate it with hypnosis would be misleading. It would make more sense to say that the principles of hypnosis represent the cornerstones of NLP.

There is absolutely nothing mysterious, supernatural, or dangerous about hypnosis or self-hypnosis. It is simply a way of communicating with your own subconscious mind. The kind of hypnosis presented on TV shows does not represent the real thing in any way. It is making a mockery of and giving a very bad name to an essentially wonderful and empowering way to work on yourself.

There is, however, a difference between the kind of very deep hypnotic sleep or state induced by a professional hypnotherapist and the kind of mildly hypnotic state of mind that you are learning about here. This mild form of hypnosis is referred to as a "waking hypnosis," meaning that you are awake and aware and able to control the hypnosis yourself at any time. You are open only to your own intended suggestions.

As I'm sure you know, the word *subconscious* refers to the part of the mind that remains hidden "under" the conscious, meaning that we are not aware of everything that goes on "down there." However, when we are able to access this part of the mind and intentionally instruct or reinstruct, as the case may be, our mind and our emotions to adapt new ways of responding and reacting that serve us better, we are able to create seemingly miraculous changes both mentally and physically. Your subconscious mind is the seat of all your emotions and therefore directs nearly all your responses and behavioral patterns. When you access this part of your mind directly, it is like taking a shortcut. This is why when you use this kind of communication, you can achieve such great results fast.

Verbal inputs are simply called suggestions or intended (hypnotic) suggestions.

When given in the proper way, as described chapter 17, "The Dream Character: Exercise 4: The Positive Affirmations List," they are extremely powerful. They enable you to sharpen your focus and point it directly at something. They work best when you make them very specific and concentrate on one thing at a time. This is why I asked you to first concentrate on your DC as your Stage Persona and then perhaps extend it to cover other things as well. I also advised you that if, for instance, you specifically want to boost your confidence, you could do a visualization (and formulate a verbal input or suggestion) that deals with just that.

Intended hypnosis is nothing but focused relaxation. It is using the natural powers of your mind with awareness. You could say that hypnosis provides a doorway to your inner world. Physicians and doctors have worked with the power of hypnosis for centuries, and these days it is finally becoming more and more recognized even by the established medical society and conventional science.

One of the most famous hypnotic suggestions was in fact formulated by a French physician named Émile Coué, who found that to be more helpful to his patients, he had to somehow enable them to participate in curing themselves faster. He encouraged them to repeatedly, at least twenty to thirty times every day in a relaxed state, say this to themselves: "Every day in every way I'm getting better and better!"

He also made a point of deliberately delivering positive suggestions when prescribing medication (as opposed to *just* prescribing it or handing it out). He had astonishing results, and everybody was wondering how he did it! The fact is—*he* didn't! He opened the door for his patients to be able to do it for themselves.

This is the power of self-hypnotic suggestions. They are safe and can be used by anyone, even if you don't know a thing about NLP. It is not even necessary to be in a consciously induced hypnotic state for a suggestion to have effect. In fact, we experience "natural hypnosis" all the time, such as when we watch television, drive, walk, run in the park, daydream, etc.

A natural mild hypnotic state is basically the same as a natural meditative state or a state of active visualization. This state naturally has a calming, feel-good effect on its own. But when we apply suggestions while in this state, the results can be far more profound than simply calming.

When doing a meditation with verbal input, you should always give it a name or a label like you did with your Dream Character in order to associate the name/label with the images and/or the verbal input or suggestions you use in the visualization or meditation. That way it is easy to give yourself a quick boost—a mental reminder of the images/input. Every time you do this, you strengthen the effects of the input. If you are still not sure how this works, go back to Exercise 11 and read about the DC Name/Trigger.

You can visualize or meditate on anything you want. If you use verbal input, you can make as many new scripts with different names as you like.

Here's what your meditation with verbal input should look like:

- Prepare yourself for meditation in the same way as you prepared for visualization in chapter 17. Remember to count from ten to one. You can imagine taking ten steps if you like; this seems to work well for many people.
- When you feel ready, say the following, using *exactly* the kind of wording described in chapter 17, "The Dream Character: Exercise 4: The Positive Affirmations List." (Go back and read again before you start scripting your own suggestions.):
  ◊ "I'm going deeper and deeper."
  ◊ "I'm completely comfortable and relaxed."
  ◊ "I'm completely safe and protected."

◊ "All random thoughts and images simply pass through my mind—in fact they are helping me relax and go even deeper."

◊ "I am open only to my own *intended* suggestions."

- Now introduce your suggestions (verbal input).
- Repeat your input many times. Repetition takes your mind deeper and strengthens the effects of the input.
- Continue to use the kind of wording described earlier and stick with the rules, always using present and present continuous tenses (*am* be*ing*), focusing on the positive, what you *do* want, etc.
- Every now and again say, "With every breath this suggestion is growing even stronger."
- Introduce the name that you have chosen, saying, "I call this suggestion XX [your chosen name/label]."
- Finish your meditation by saying, "From this moment in time, whenever I say the word(s) XX, these images that I have put forth are drawing closer and closer into being, and this suggestion that I have given is working stronger and stronger every day more and more—and therefore, every day, every hour, every minute, and with every breath I am becoming more and more XX [whatever it is that you want to become or achieve]. End of suggestion."
- When you feel ready, slowly start making your way back to the surface, again counting steps, this time from one to ten. Take one step at a time, taking time to adjust and reconnect to your fully conscious body and mind. At ten you are back in the room, fully present and aware, completely comfortable, revitalized, energized, inspired, and empowered.

You are now infused with the wonderful energy of your recent (peak) experience. Congratulations—well done!

QUICK DC PERFORMANCE PREP

To make things easier for you, I have added the Quick Performance Prep here at the end as it should be done with the DC Name added for even greater effect.

- Close your eyes.
- Quietly, inside your head or out loud, say *I am XX* (your DC Name/Trigger).
- Breathe deeply a few times.
- Recall the overall, all-encompassing feeling that represents your Dream Character.
- Smile. Say *I am XX*.
- Shake your arms and roll your neck.
- Relax your body. Continue to breathe calmly.
- Ground yourself.
- Take a moment to clear your head. Rid yourself of any outside influences that may disturb you. Relax your mind.
- Say *I am XX*.
- Breathe deeply. Imagine that with every breath you are breathing in the very essence of your DC, becoming more one with it than ever before.
- Compose yourself. Calmly, in your mind, go through what you are about to do; completely immerse yourself in it. See your DC doing it.
- Stay grounded, keep your eyes closed, and keep breathing deeply. The increased oxygen flow to your brain will help calm you and help increase your focus.
- Remind yourself of previous feelings of success and accomplishment. Remind yourself that you have been invited to speak because you have a valuable contribution to offer. Be grateful for the opportunity to share; look forward to it. Imagine the joy it will bring.
- Send love to the audience. Thank them for welcoming you. Feel how they are already responding by sending love and gratitude back to you. Feel how you have already bonded.
- Now they are ready and waiting for you, looking forward to meeting you, looking forward to your sharing your love and your wisdom with them.
- Allow yourself to feel the same way. Expect great success. Expect your DC energy to serve you better than ever before.

- Breathe deeply. Shake your arms and roll your neck again to release any last bit of tension. Wiggle your face. Relax your jaw.
- Breathe deeply.
- Say *I am XX. Now I am ready.*
- Open your body.
- Walk in.
- Make eye contact.
- Acknowledge the audience with love, gratitude, and appreciation. There is already a bond between you, and now it is strengthening even more. Feel the positive, loving energy spreading in the room.
- Now, claim your space and naturally "demand" the attention just like you envisioned.
- Take in the room. Settle. Maintain eye contact.
- Breathe deeply.
- You are your DC.
- Begin.

CONCLUSION

So, my friend, that is it. We've journeyed a long way together and gone through a lot of information and exercises. Perhaps some of it was challenging for you. If so, great! In the greatest challenges we often find the greatest gifts.

I hope that you have enjoyed yourself. And I truly hope that you got what you came for. I trust that you've learned quite a few exciting new things and had some valuable new thoughts and ideas. I hope that you feel inspired to take what you've learned and go out and create something amazing. I am confident that you will continue on your journey just a little bit richer than before, a little bit wiser, and a whole lot stronger in your voice and in yourself. I hope you feel empowered.

If you do, it means that you and I have both done a good job.

It has been my absolute pleasure working with you.

I wish you joy and success and all the very best on your continuous journey in life—may it be a wonderful and exciting one!

May you continue to be bold and to dream—and may all your dreams come true!

Suzann

Glossary

accent. Distinctive manner of oral expression; the usage or vocabulary that is characteristic of a specific group of people.

alto. The lowest pitched female singing voice. Also called *contralto*.

amplitude. Greatness of magnitude.

articulation. Pronunciation of vowels and consonants; oral movements that shape the sounds of speech.

attack. Beginning of the vocal tone. Also called *onset* or *initiation*.

baritone. A male voice, lower in range than tenor and higher than bass.

Basics. Fundamental principles of voice technique.

bass. The lowest pitched male voice.

Belting. Vocal mode; style of singing that requires specific settings of the jaw, tongue, and epiglottis funnel; produces a very powerful sound.

blade of tongue. Front, flat part of tongue.

blend. Smooth transitions between the registers of the singing voice.

body language. Communication via the movements or attitudes of the body, including facial expressions.

breath control. Efficient and appropriate (correct) use of the breath and support mechanisms required for speaking or singing.

bright. Abundant in high harmonic partials.

chest register. Voice register that produces tones in the lower range of the voice. Also called *chest voice*.

constriction. A narrowing that reduces the flow through a channel; tight or tightening feeling in some part of the body; prevents normal functioning.

countertenor. The highest adult male singing voice, higher in range than tenor.

crooning. Style of singing popular during the Big Band Era, characterized by a smooth tone.

Curbing. Vocal mode; style of singing that has a complaining sound. Described as half-metallic, more powerful than Neutral, and less powerful than Belting and Overdrive.

dark. Rich in low harmonic partials, perhaps lacking high harmonic partials.

deep breathing. Breathing in which the muscles of the lower back and abdomen are consciously engaged, in conjunction with the lowering of the diaphragm. Also called *diaphragmatic breathing*.

diaphragm. The wall or floor of muscle between the chest and abdomen that helps to control breathing and to control the flow of air to the vocal cords when speaking or singing.

diphthong. A vowel sound that starts near the articulatory position for one vowel and moves toward the position for another.

dramatic. Theatrical, sensational, exciting, or thrilling. In singing, also used to designate a large operatic voice, especially suited to the performance of Verdi or Wagner ("dramatic soprano").

dynamic. Using dynamics to enhance or embellish a performance; also used to describe a forceful personality. The description "a dynamic speaker" would typically encompass both explanations.

dynamics. Variations in amplitude or loudness/softness (volume) in the production of sound, as when speaking.

dysphonia. See **hoarseness.**

edge. Distinct, metallic, slightly hard or sharp sound; also refers to the root of the tongue.

epiglottis. Flap of cartilage that covers the windpipe while swallowing.

epiglottis funnel. The area above the vocal cords forming a funnel. When twanging, the opening of the epiglottis funnel is made smaller by bringing the arytenoid cartilages closer to the lower part of epiglottis. As a result, the sound gets clearer and non-breathy, and you can increase your volume.

epithelium. Membranous tissue covering internal organs and other internal surfaces of the body.

epithelial cells. Closely packed cells forming the epithelium.

equalizer. Electronic equipment that creates a balanced sound by reducing frequency distortion. To equalize = to counterbalance.

falsetto. The highest, male voice register(s); same as head voice/register.

flageolet(s). The very high notes that a guitarist can produce by "cutting off" the strings, using only the top part of the guitar neck to produce very high-pitched, flute-like tones. Technically, the same effect happens to the vocal cords when singing in the whistle (or flute) voice/register, which is the voice equivalent to flageolet. Originally, a flageolet is a small flute.

focused. When referring to singing tone: acoustically efficient, condensed, non-breathy, without spread.

forced. Produced with muscular tension.

free. Produced without muscular tension.

frequency. In acoustics, the number of repetitions of compressions and rarefactions of a sound wave that occur at the same rate over a period of time, usually expressed in Hertz (Hz) or cycles per second.

full voice. Singing at maximum volume and capacity; condensed sound without breathiness.

glissade. Also called *glissando*. See **slide**.

glottis. Vocal apparatus of the larynx, vocal cords, and the space between them.

grounding position. Position of the body used when doing voice exercises; where the voice tone is generated.

hard palate. Forward, hard, bony part of the roof of the mouth.

head voice. Register that produces sounds in the higher end of the scale. Also called *head register*.

hoarseness. A disorder of sound production (unless produced correctly on purpose as a special effect). Also called *dysphonia*.

hum. Vocal sound made with closed lips.

infection. Pathological state resulting from the invasion of the body by pathogenic microorganisms.

inflammation. A response of body tissues or organs to injury, irritation, or infection; characterized by pain, swelling, redness, and heat.

initiation. See **attack.**

laryngitis. Inflammatory condition of the larynx.

larynx. The voice box; basically the little cage or "box" that contains the vocal cords; situated at the top of the windpipe and the base of the tongue.

legato. Smooth and connected.

lowered larynx. Positioning of the larynx used to expand the vocal tract for a richer, bigger, or darker resonance. Also called *depressed larynx.*

lower resonators. Throat and chest.

mask. Front, upper resonators; the resonating cavities above, behind, and around the nose, the forehead, and the cheekbones.

metallic. Distinct, edgy, slightly hard or sharp sound.

mezzo-soprano. A voice slightly lower than a soprano, with a darker tone quality.

middle resonators. Mainly the throat.

middle voice. Vocal register that produces tones in the middle area of the voice. Also called *middle register.*

mucous membranes. Mucus-secreting membrane lining body cavities and passages.

mucus. Protective secretion of the mucous membranes. In the gut it lubricates the passage of food and protects the epithelial cells; in the nose and throat and lungs it can make it difficult for bacteria to penetrate the body through the epithelium.

musical note. A notation representing the pitch and duration of a musical sound.

scale. Series of notes differing in pitch according to a specific scheme (usually within an octave).

nasal. Of or in or relating to the nose. A nasal tone is produced by lowering the soft palate (velum) and using the nose as a *resonator.*

nasal passageway. The passageway between the mouth cavities and the nasal cavities.

nodule. See **vocal nodule.**

Neutral. Vocal mode; style of singing, soft or light in intensity; also refers to casual singing like singing a lullaby.

nonverbal communication. Communication through the use of body language, gestures, and facial expressions. Some claim that nonverbal communication includes the use of emotional and subconscious signaling.

note. See **musical note.**

open throat. Condition necessary for healthy use of the voice and sound production.

opera. A large musical work in which drama and music are combined and performers sing and act. Term also refers to the classical singing style typical of this musical genre.

oral cavity. Mouth.

Overdrive. Vocal mode; style of singing; produces a very powerful sound.

overtone. Harmonic partial higher than the fundamental frequency, which contributes to the resonant quality or timbre of sound.

partials. Overtones; harmonics with a frequency that is a multiple of the fundamental frequency.

pathway. Journey or route of air.

permanent nodule(s). Vocal nodules that have hardened and become permanent, requiring surgical removal.

pharyngeal space. Back of mouth and throat.

pharynx. Cavity at the back of the mouth and nose, where the passages to the nose and the mouth connect with the throat.

phonation. Production of voiced sound by means of the vibration of the vocal cords.

pitch. Location on the musical scale where a tone sits.

pitch range. See **range.**

placement. The imagined positioning of tones and tone quality, guided by sensations of vibrations in the face, behind the teeth, in the nose, etc.

projection. Focusing the voice forward, creating strong sound.

pronunciation. Manner in which someone utters a word; the way a word or a language is customarily spoken.

psychogenic. Produced or caused by psychic or mental factors rather than organic factors.

pure tone. Full tone, without air or breathiness. Generally, the term is also used to describe a tone having no overtones. Also called *simple tone.*

range. The distance between a person's highest and lowest tones; usually determined by instructing the individual to sing the highest note possible and then the lowest note possible. Describing the area (frequency compass) of the individual voice which is most comfortable, efficient, and aesthetically pleasing.

rate. Speed.

register. See **voice register.**

resonance. The quality imparted to voiced speech sounds by the action of the resonating chambers of the chest, throat, and mouth and nasal cavities.

resonators. All the resonating cavities of the chest, throat, and head.

restriction. Act of limiting or restricting, keeping something within specified bounds (by force if necessary).

rich. Containing many harmonic partials.

root of the tongue. The back (rear) of the tongue. Also called *edge.*

shallow breathing. Inhaling by means of the muscles which normally move the shoulders and the upper chest; does not provide adequate power and control over exhalation (support). Also called *clavicular breathing.*

sinuses. Various air-filled cavities, especially in the bones of the skull.

slide. A series of consecutive ascending or descending notes (without individual definition) on the musical scale.

soft palate. The rear, soft part of the roof of the mouth. Also called *velum.*

soprano. The second highest-pitched female singing voice. (Many class the soprano voice as the highest. However, the lyrical soprano is really the highest but can be regarded as part of the soprano range).

sound color. Sound qualities; natural color or colors added to the voice by expanding or retracting the vocal tract.

special effects. Embellishments of vocal sound.

spread. Unfocused tone. A tone with too much excess air spreading or fizzling out.

staccato. Each note separate, detached by a brief silence.

Stage Persona. A professional performer's stage personality.

support. Controlled exhalation. Refers to how much air you can hold off and then gradually release, how slowly the diaphragm and the ribs return to their normal resting position after inhalation.

tenor. Highest-pitched male voice, except for the countertenor.

throaty. Characterized by pharyngeal tension; a strained and tight sound.

tone. A pitch or change in pitch of the voice that serves to distinguish words in tonal languages. Also, the quality of a person's voice.

tremor. Involuntary trembling or quivering.

upper resonators. See **mask.**

verbal inflections. Patterns or modifications of dynamics used when speaking, including volume, intonation, and pitch.

vibrato. Pulsating, rhythmical fluctuations in pitch and timbre of the voice; effect used by many singers.

vocal abuse. Mistreatment of the voice without regard for the consequences; includes incorrect implementation of the Basics and incorrect use of the vocal modes.

vocal break. A sudden shift in vocal register or mode; can feel like a crack in the voice; occurs by accident or is used on purpose for effect; often used in country music or in yodeling. Also called *voice break.*

vocal cords. The two elastic, vibrating bands situated in the larynx, responsible for creating sound. Also called *vocal folds, vocal bands, vocal lips.*

vocal fatigue. Deterioration of vocal quality due to prolonged use without rest; may be the result of vocal misuse or abuse, or may be indicative of a pathological condition.

vocal nodule. Small knot or cyst on a vocal cord; bilaterally occurring thickenings at the junction of the anterior and middle thirds of the vocal folds, resulting from vocal misuse or abuse. In the worst case, nodules require surgical removal. Also called *vocal cord cyst*.

vocal modes. Vocal gears, including Neutral, Curbing, Overdrive, and Belting. Different vocal functions or singing styles, requiring different jaw and tongue settings (and epiglottis funnel adjustment) to produce different sounds.

vocal tract. Space above the vocal cords extending to the lips and including the nasal passages.

voice box. See **larynx**.

voice category. Voice type, such as soprano, tenor, bass, etc.

voice maintenance. Keeping a healthy voice in good working order by using correct technique and leading a healthy lifestyle.

voice register. A certain tonal area within the vocal range (on the musical scale). The human voice range is divided into different registers. Each register represents a specific tonal area on the musical scale and features main resonance from the chest, throat, and head cavities respectively.

volume. The magnitude of sound (usually in a specified direction).

vowel modification. Adjustments in the usual pronunciation of vowels for the sake of a shift in vocal mode or a more favorable resonance throughout the singing range.

windpipe. Tube through which air passes in and out of the lungs.

whistle voice. The highest female register. Also called *whistle register* or *flute register*.

yodeling. Singing characterized by obvious shifts in registration or mode like vocal breaks; often used in country music.

yoga. System of exercises originally practiced as part of the Hindu discipline to promote control of the body and mind; now a common practice by people from all religious or spiritual backgrounds and walks of life; almost considered a sport.

About the Author

Suzann Rye grew up with her Danish grandma, who was a jazz singer, an actress, and a children's book writer. She was also an extraordinary, vivacious lady who instilled in the young Suzann a firm belief that you can do anything you want to do in this world. So she did. This took her to many remarkable places and led to an unusual order of events that doesn't read like your average biography.

Thirty-five years ago, Suzann's second-grade music teacher came knocking on her grandma's door. She wanted her to know that Suzann had a special gift that she felt needed nurturing—her voice. Since then, the voice has been a main focus in Suzann's life.

She has worked as a professional vocalist and performer all over the world.

She has toured as a solo artist, released several records, and had top twenty releases in the U.S., Brazil, Europe, Australia, the Middle East, and Japan.

She has been teaching for nearly twenty-five years in colleges and at seminars and workshops internationally. For five years, she was a voice coach and eventually the Head of the Voice Department at the prestigious London Music School, London, UK.

Today, Suzann is a best-selling author, speaker, and artist—and an internationally renowned expert on voice and performance training. Her many years of vast experience have helped her develop a strong set of tools that has become the trademark of her coaching style. She has helped thousands of people find their voice and transform their lives. Her work is rooted in a deep understanding of the human spirit, a trait that has always allowed her to appeal to a broad audience.

A Danish American, Suzann divides her time between Europe and the U.S.

Free Bonuses to Help You Jump Start Your Progress

I promised you a free bonus. In fact, if you act now, I'll give you two!

The first bonus will really help you get a jump start with your voice skills.

Sometimes training your voice on your own can be challenging. What exactly do you do, where do you start—and how can you be sure that you're doing the right thing?

In this book you've been given a very comprehensive voice training program. Still, even though the exercises are explained very thoroughly, sometimes it can be confusing and hard to recognize right from wrong. For the ultimate voice training experience, I invite you to go to www.SuzannRye.com/CallingCardBonuses and download the voice training audio that I created to go with the exercises in this book. Listening to the exercises will make it much easier for you to recognize the sounds and tell the difference between right and wrong. This audio is the perfect tool for fast and easy progress. Use it to become even more masterful at using your voice effectively and to become an even more exciting and dynamic communicator. To make learning a breeze, claim your FREE voice training audio straight away.

The second bonus is a relaxation audio. This guided exercise is designed to put you into an instant state of calm, control, and excellence, and it will help you prepare for any performance. Whether I am singing or speaking, I always use this exercise myself before going on stage. It is simply referred to in the book as Quick Performance Prep. Try it out for yourself—it is simple yet extremely powerful.

Please visit www.SuzannRye.com/CallingCardBonuses to download your free gifts now. No additional purchase is required.

To your success!

Suzann

P.S. If you enjoy the book, please recommend it to anyone who you think might benefit as well. I greatly appreciate your referral.

BUY A SHARE OF THE FUTURE IN YOUR COMMUNITY

These certificates make great holiday, graduation and birthday gifts that can be personalized with the recipient's name. The cost of one S.H.A.R.E. or one square foot is $54.17. The personalized certificate is suitable for framing and will state the number of shares purchased and the amount of each share, as well as the recipient's name. The home that you participate in "building" will last for many years and will continue to grow in value.

Here is a sample SHARE certificate:

HABITAT FOR HUMANITY

THIS CERTIFIES THAT
YOUR NAME HERE
HAS INVESTED IN A HOME FOR A DESERVING FAMILY

1985-2005
TWENTY YEARS OF BUILDING FUTURES IN OUR
COMMUNITY ONE HOME AT A TIME

1200 SQUARE FOOT HOUSE @ $65,000 = $54.17 PER SQUARE FOOT
This certificate represents a tax deductible donation. It has no cash value.

YES, I WOULD LIKE TO HELP!

*I support the work that Habitat for Humanity does and I want to be part of the excitement! As a donor, I will receive periodic updates on your construction activities but, more importantly, I know my gift will help a family in our community realize the dream of homeownership. **I would like to SHARE in your efforts against substandard housing in my community!** (Please print below)*

PLEASE SEND ME _____ SHARES at $54.17 EACH = $ $_____

In Honor Of: _____

Occasion: (Circle One)   HOLIDAY   BIRTHDAY   ANNIVERSARY

       OTHER: _____

Address of Recipient: _____

Gift From: _____ *Donor Address:* _____

Donor Email: _____

I AM ENCLOSING A CHECK FOR $ $_____ PAYABLE TO HABITAT FOR HUMANITY OR PLEASE CHARGE MY VISA OR MASTERCARD *(CIRCLE ONE)*

Card Number _____ Expiration Date: _____

Name as it appears on Credit Card _____ Charge Amount $ _____

Signature _____

Billing Address _____

Telephone # Day _____ Eve _____

PLEASE NOTE: Your contribution is tax-deductible to the fullest extent allowed by law.
Habitat for Humanity • P.O. Box 1443 • Newport News, VA 23601 • 757-596-5553
www.HelpHabitatforHumanity.org